M000316515

SCRIPT ANALYSIS

A comprehensive step-by-step guide to deconstructing screenplay fundamentals, this book will allow readers to understand the elements, functions, and anatomy of a screenplay. Not only will this book enable readers to accomplish a thorough analysis of a screenplay and understand the dramatic elements and their functions, but screenwriters will be able to apply these steps to their own writing as well.

The book explores theme and premise, provides an in-depth study of character development, and breaks down the dramatic elements needed to construct a solid screenplay. It provides examples of the three-act structure, the hero's journey, and the sequence method. Furthermore, it explores how the main plot and subplots are used in a storyline and discusses the importance of setting. Finally, it reveals screenwriting techniques and tools used by professional screenwriters, such as dramatic irony, reversal, and setup/payoff. To connect with a broad range of readers, the case studies used in this book are mainly from contemporary films, including *Get Out* (2017), *Lady Bird* (2017), *The Dark Knight* (2008), *Toy Story* (1995), *Parasite* (2019), and *Whiplash* (2014). Readers will understand how professional screenwriters use fundamental elements to construct, shape, develop, and tell a visual story. After reading this book, readers will comprehend the components critical to developing a screenplay.

This book is ideal for students of screenwriting and filmmaking who want to better understand how to comprehensively analyze a screenplay, as well as screenwriters who want to utilize this method to develop their own scripts.

James Bang teaches screenwriting and film production at The New School in New York City. He earned an M.F.A. in Film – Screenwriting/Directing from Columbia University, and he has worked on several film productions. His films have received several awards, including a nomination for the 35th Student Academy Awards®.

SCRIPT ANALYSIS

Deconstructing Screenplay Fundamentals

James Bang

Routledge
Taylor & Francis Group

LONDON AND NEW YORK

Cover image: © Warner Bros / Photofest

First published 2022
by Routledge
4 Park Square, Milton Park, Abingdon, Oxon OX14 4RN

and by Routledge
605 Third Avenue, New York, NY 10158

Routledge is an imprint of the Taylor & Francis Group, an informa business

© 2022 James Bang

The right of James Bang to be identified as author of this work has been
asserted in accordance with sections 77 and 78 of the Copyright, Designs
and Patents Act 1988.

All rights reserved. No part of this book may be reprinted or reproduced or
utilised in any form or by any electronic, mechanical, or other means, now
known or hereafter invented, including photocopying and recording, or in
any information storage or retrieval system, without permission in writing
from the publishers.

Trademark notice: Product or corporate names may be trademarks or
registered trademarks, and are used only for identification and explanation
without intent to infringe.

British Library Cataloguing-in-Publication Data
A catalogue record for this book is available from the British Library

Library of Congress Cataloging-in-Publication Data
Names: Bang, James, 1972– author.
Title: Script analysis : deconstructing screenplay fundamentals / James
  Bang.
Description: Abingdon, Oxon ; New York, NY : Routledge, 2022. |
  Includes bibliographical references and index.
Identifiers: LCCN 2021057896 (print) | LCCN 2021057897 (ebook) |
  ISBN 9780367687380 (hardback) | ISBN 9780367687397 (paperback) |
  ISBN 9781003138853 (ebook)
Subjects: LCSH: Motion picture plays—Technique. | Motion picture
  plays—History and criticism.
Classification: LCC PN1996 .B3817 2022 (print) | LCC PN1996 (ebook) |
  DDC 808.2/3—dc23/eng/20220406
LC record available at https://lccn.loc.gov/2021057896
LC ebook record available at https://lccn.loc.gov/2021057897

ISBN: 978-0-367-68738-0 (hbk)
ISBN: 978-0-367-68739-7 (pbk)
ISBN: 978-1-003-13885-3 (ebk)

DOI: 10.4324/9781003138853

Typeset in Bembo
by Apex CoVantage, LLC

CONTENTS

For my brother

ACKNOWLEDGMENTS

I started my career in the corporate world, but the aftermath of the 9/11 attack made me reevaluate my career path, and I chose to pursue storytelling instead. I fell in love with every aspect of screenwriting and filmmaking, and I've been living in a world of visual storytelling ever since. Along the way, I've met mentors, collaborators, and friends. I'd like to mention a few of their names with gratitude in my heart: Annette Insdorf, Malia Scotch-Marmo, Milena Jelinek, Tom Kalin, Eric Mendelsohn, Maureen A. Ryan, Dan Klein, and Richard Peña at Columbia University School of the Arts for their mentorship; Lana Lin and Marcus Turner at The New School for their continued support in letting me pursue teaching, my second passion; and Sheni Kruger, Claire Margerison, and Sarah Pickles at Focal Press, Routledge, for their ongoing support and guidance. I also want to thank my friend and editor, Tracy Majka, for helping all along the way, from the proposal to the final draft. Lastly, I would like to thank my wife, Stella Min, and my brother, Bang Jun-Seok, for exploring the world of storytelling with me.

Part I
INTRODUCTION

SCREENPLAY

Before we discuss script analysis, let's define the term "script" or "screenplay." Screenplays have been evolving since the beginning of film history. The evolution of screenwriting goes hand in hand with the development of film production. The screenplay for the silent film *A Trip to the Moon* (1902) by Georges Méliès was just a 30-line description with locations and action sequences. Méliès' document was one of the earliest recorded forms of a screenplay.

In the early twentieth century, as motion pictures became a more viable form of storytelling and more easily accessible to the masses, the film industry started to grow, and directors found the need to share the story and the production plan with actors and crew. The director wrote a basic description of each scene and shared them on set. This basic scene description evolved into the modern-day screenplay. Studios began to use screenplays to count the personnel needed for the production and tally the cost of making the film. What started as notes to help directors communicate on set became a screenplay, and it helps to plan film production. Today, screenplays are used throughout preproduction, production, and postproduction. And the screenwriting format has evolved so much that today if you write one page using the standard screenwriting format, it approximately represents one minute of screen time.

Before films, there was – and still is – the play. The history of theater goes back to the time of the ancient Greeks, and myths go back even further. There was an obvious similarity between plays and films. The storytelling in films derived from storytelling techniques used in the theater. In fact, most of the story elements, structure, and even terms used in film originated in the theater. Playwriting became the foundation for screenwriting, and screenwriters continue to apply its narrative structure and story elements, which have been evolving for centuries.

DOI: 10.4324/9781003138853-1

The film industry has changed significantly since the creation of the Hollywood studio system. During the Golden Age of Hollywood, the 1920s through 1960s, screenplays were developed within the studio system for internal use only, and this form of production continues to exist. Today, major studios have their own screenplays in development and films in production, but we now also have smaller production companies developing screenplays and producing films. As more people attempted to enter the film industry, the term "spec scripts" found a place in the industry. A spec script is also known as a speculative screenplay; it is a non-commissioned and unsolicited screenplay. Screenwriters write "spec scripts" in the hope that they will be either optioned or purchased by production companies or film studios.

Film is the medium for telling a visual story. On its own, the screenplay is an incomplete form of this story. For the screenplay to come alive, it must be produced and projected on a screen. Therefore, when you read an unproduced screenplay, your imagination visualizes the story. Everyone will project their own version of the story in their minds. This process is very subjective; every reader will have a different reaction. However, like a great novel, a well-written screenplay engages with the reader. A great screenplay has a great story, and a great story always stimulates our minds; it provokes emotions and thoughts. A screenplay can make you laugh or cry. It can enlighten you, and stay with you; it's a powerful means of communication.

Analysis

One afternoon, my 4-year-old niece, Maribel, saw a red origami bird sitting on my desk, and it sparked her curiosity. I told her that an origami bird was something we could make together, and I showed her stacks of colored paper. She spent a second or two going back and forth between the bird and the colored paper. Then she started to examine the red origami figure. Suddenly, she started to unfold it, one fold at a time.

I believe the desire to learn is innate. Without this inherent curiosity, or desire to know more, we wouldn't have evolved as humans. We made advances in every aspect of our lives because of it. I believe "analysis" is a word that describes the process of fulfilling one's curiosity. An analysis is a process of examining, breaking down, and studying a complex substance, topic, or system into smaller parts to better understand its nature, elements, processes, and structure.

The study of an existing form – an analysis – is an integral practice for everyone who is learning a new discipline. Medical students take surgery courses in which they dissect cadavers to understand human anatomy. Law students pay rigorous attention to court case studies, a necessary study aid that helps them to learn the practice of law. Major art museums across the world, such as the Metropolitan Museum of Art in New York City or the Louvre in Paris, have a "copyist program," where skillful artists set up easels in front of paintings to study works, so that they can learn by replicating masterpieces.

Just as the masters in every discipline have their corresponding knowledge on their subject matter, the professional screenwriters are storytelling masters. They are professional practitioners of screenwriting. So, by studying screenplays written by screenwriters like Billy Wilder, Aaron Sorkin, Charlie Kaufman, Bong Joon-ho, Greta Gerwig, Jordan Peele, or Damien Chazelle, we can see how they are applying the fundamentals of telling visual stories through screenplays. Their visions, their stories, and their screenplays have been green-lit, and they have successfully connected with audiences around the world.

To analyze screenplays, I suggest you find the latest draft of the screenplay you want to analyze and read it in one sitting, without interruption, if possible. If you read a well-developed screenplay, you will have an emotional reaction to the story. Based on how rewarding, refreshing, compelling, satisfying, and moving these emotions are to the readers, they will find value in the screenplay.

Now, in script analysis, we must look into what causes this emotion, and examine the characters and story elements contributing to the connection between the screenplay and the reader.

Script Analysis

Many people believe the term "script analysis" refers to actors who analyze screenplays to study a character's emotional trajectory throughout the story. The actor gets into the character's psychological state in a given situation, as well as throughout the story. Therefore, breaking down the script and understanding the emotional journey of the character is an imperative step for the actor to play a convincing role.

Before actors are attached to the project, a screenplay goes through a rigorous approval process. The screenwriter forwards the screenplay to an agent, a manager, or a friend in the industry, or submits it to a screenplay competition. If the reader likes the screenplay, it gets passed along and moves upward, until it reaches an executive, who has the power to green-light the project. If a screenplay is picked up by a producer, production company, or a film studio, they will use the screenplay to attract actors and crew to the project. The screenplay will be used during preproduction to plan the necessary logistics to create the world of the story. During production, the cast and crew will rely on the screenplay to visually tell the story. And in postproduction, the screenplay will be used to reconstruct the story with the images and sounds that were captured during production.

Everyone who reads the screenplay during preproduction will analyze it. The areas in which the screenplay gets analyzed may differ depending on the person's role for the project, but everyone will have analyzed the screenplay in one way or another. In addition to actors, department heads in film production perform a thorough script analysis. A film composer spends a good amount of time analyzing the screenplay and speaking to the director to fully grasp the emotional journey of the protagonist. A cinematographer must have a complete understanding of the story structure and the emotional arc of the characters to apply the necessary techniques and skills in visually telling the story. Everyone has a common goal: to tell the story. Therefore, everyone makes an effort to study the screenplay and know what the story is about.

Now, a different way to use "script analysis" is to learn about screenplay fundamentals. The analysis, as discussed earlier, is a great learning tool – reading and analyzing a screenplay gives us the opportunity to understand how a specific screenwriter used the characters, story elements, and structure to tell the story. Furthermore, studying a screenplay that has already been made into a film gives us an opportunity to see how the screenplay was produced. Knowing all the elements that form a screenplay is crucial, and understanding how each of the story elements interacts with one other is an imperative step in learning how a screenplay is developed.

Script Breakdown

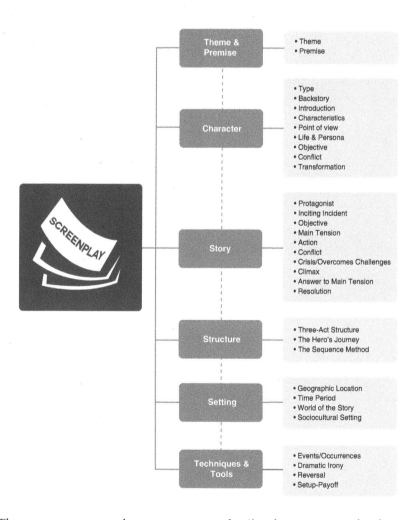

There are many ways to deconstruct a screenplay. I've chosen to group the elements of a screenplay in this figure to explain its components and their interactions with one another.

Part II
DECONSTRUCTING SCREENPLAY FUNDAMENTALS

1

THEME AND PREMISE

When studying a screenplay, we tend to look at the characters and story components first, overlooking the two most important elements of a screenplay: theme and premise. For screenwriters, the theme and premise become the foundation for all the creative work in crafting the story, developing characters, and defining a structure. After reading a screenplay or watching a film, one question needs to be asked: "What is the film about?" or "What is the story about?" The answer can either be the theme, the premise, the plot, or a combination of the three.

The screenwriters ask the same question time after time during the screenplay development phase: "What is my story about?" If a screenwriter is not content with the story, they don't waste their time writing it. In other words, screenwriters know what their story is about or generally have a clear direction by the time they start to draft the screenplay. There are exceptions: at times, screenwriters think they are telling one story, but end up discovering a different story during the writing process. One way or another, by the time they reach the final draft, screenwriters know precisely what their story is about, and it will be reflected in their screenplays.

When screenwriters search for stories to tell, they look for themes that contain a universal truth and premises that grab the audience's attention. If the audience feels a truthful theme resonating from the story, they will most likely empathize with the characters and their objectives and conflicts. In an online class, James Cameron spoke of the importance of staying true to the central governing idea of the story. He said, "Never forget your principles." When Cameron was in a meeting with studio executives trying to get financing for *Avatar* (2009), a top studio executive said, "We really like this script, but is there a way that you can take out some of the tree-hugging hippy stuff?" Cameron responded: "No, because the tree-hugging hippy stuff is the reason I want to make this movie. So if that's important to you, then we're kinda done here, and I'll have to take it somewhere else." The executive

DOI: 10.4324/9781003138853-3

wanted to remove the plot related to the theme – the central governing idea of the screenplay – and because of that, Cameron was willing to walk away from the meeting.

When screenwriters develop an idea into a screenplay, they believe in the story's theme. The theme must have a universal truth. Even in situations where the screenwriter works for someone else's project, they believe in the theme, for the most part. The screenwriter's universal truth can be a belief system, a point of view, or a law of nature.

Screenplays are fictional stories, but they have value beyond fictional boundaries. They have the power to influence reality. If you think about films that have had some type of impact on you, you can relate to the power of the stories and their influence on a personal level. Perhaps you saw a film that made you laugh hysterically, or made you cry, or made you think about things you rarely thought about. We have memories of stories from films that are precious to us, which perhaps have helped to shape some aspects of who we are today. Screenwriters know the power of this medium, and they devote weeks, months, or even years to complete the story they want to share with the audience. It all starts with a theme and a premise.

If someone asks, "What is *Groundhog Day* (1993) about?", you might say the film is about a weatherman living the same day over and over again, until he changes his outlook and finds the love of his life. This short answer contains a portion of the theme and premise, giving a general idea of what the story is about. Now when you break down the screenplay, you have the following:

- *Theme:* As director Harold Ramis put it, "You can live better and have a better life. People can change, and when you change you can get the rewards you wanted from life."
- *Premise:* The film is about a weatherman living the same day over and over again, until he changes his outlook and finds the love of his life.
- *Plot:* Phil Connors, a weatherman, who comes to report the annual Groundhog Day in Punxsutawney, Pennsylvania, a ceremony that predicts the arrival of spring, gets stuck reliving the same Groundhog Day over and over again, until he accepts himself for who he is. The daily reoccurrence forces him to go over the different emotional stages until he finds peace with himself, and gets the biggest reward in life: love.

The screenwriters, Danny Rubin and Harold Ramis, believe that "people can change, and when you change, you can get the rewards you wanted from life." This theme, this belief system, kept the screenwriters focused on developing characters and stories for the film. For screenwriters, the theme and premise are their guiding light through the development phase, writing, and rewriting process.

The screenplay's theme and premise should be studied first when you analyze a script. You must find the universal truth or the governing idea that the screenwriter conveys through the story, then see how the screenwriter has developed the characters, story elements, structure, and setting to best represent the theme and premise of the film.

Theme

The theme in a screenplay refers to the subject matter discussed in the story. Most screenplays have a central unifying theme, and the screenwriters might choose to consciously explore the main subject throughout the screenplay, or they might embed it underneath the surface. For example, *La La Land* (2016) is about two aspiring artists pursuing their careers, whose fates intertwine for a brief period of their lives, as they fall in and out of love. As he did with his previous film, *Whiplash* (2014), the governing theme of writer/director Damian Chazelle's two films is about artists pursuing their dreams. As the romance of these two characters helps move the story forward in *La La Land*, the film is more than a love story. It speaks to the challenges and difficulties artists through in pursuing their dreams.

The central theme gives depth to the story and permits the screenwriter to apply layers of complexity using the story elements. It all comes down to what type of story the screenwriter wants to tell, and how the screenwriter crafts the story's unifying central idea of the screenplay, the theme.

Most Hollywood films have central universal themes that address a mainstream audience. Generally speaking, these films have a high budget and a broad international distribution reach. For example, *Avatar* (2009), a sci-fi film whose premise deals with colonization of a planet, Pandora, touches upon imperialism, racism, corporate greed, spirituality, and religion. Now, *Avatar* has multiple themes, but the main theme deals with the conflict between humans and nature: how modern culture, society, politics, and economics are all geared to capitalism without taking into account the damage humans are causing to the environment. The central theme of *Avatar* has a serious undertone that affects everyone living on Earth. Cameron embedded a theme that is pressing and important to the human race as entertainment, and communicated this theme to a mass audience all around the globe.

Independent films are generally low-budget or micro-budget films, and stories tend to concentrate on characters. For example, in *Lady Bird* (2017), writer and director Greta Gerwig reveals the theme by showing us the contrast between Christine's senior year and her arrival at college as a freshman. Growing up and getting ready for adulthood is not easy, but her family helps her get through it, and Christine realizes their value after she leaves home. Family and home are a reminder of who we are and where we are from. The film's theme could be described as follows: "The value of the moment is realized after it's left behind." In an interview, Gerwig said, "I started to write the movie with the intention to make something about what home means and what family means and how it doesn't really come into focus until you're leaving them." The theme has authenticity and truth, and it resonates with teenagers and everyone in the audience, who were teenagers once.

Auteur films are films made by groundbreaking filmmakers such as Stanley Kubrick, Alfred Hitchcock, Akira Kurosawa, Federico Fellini, Robert Bresson, and Michael Haneke, just to name a few. They explore serious themes like humanity's fundamental aspects, such as redemption, death, perseverance, or existentialism. For example, the Coen brothers' adaptation of *No Country for Old Men* (2007) follows the story of three different characters, as each of them deals with their own moral and ethical choices. The central theme of this film explores the order of nature as a belief system. As one of the characters, Anton Chigurh, says, "The more we try to understand the nature of the universe, the less we are likely to understand it." The theme deals with the consequences of the actions deriving from the characters' moral and ethical choices, and at times, there is no explanation why the specific aspects of lives are the way they are, and it is just the way it is, and that is what the film is about.

There are no shortcuts to identifying the theme used in a screenplay. After reading a screenplay, one should think about what the story is about, the protagonist's journey, and the governing idea of the story. The main character's actions drive the main idea, so it's always helpful to look at the protagonist's objective to discover the theme. The protagonist's actions in pursuing the goal reveals their point of view, which correlates with the theme of the film.

Premise

The premise defines how the theme will be used in a story and lays the foundation for a story. The theme is the subject matter that holds the truth – the governing idea of the story – but the premise is more specific to the story than the theme.

Let's say a filmmaker, John, gets inspired to write a screenplay. He sees an elderly couple holding hands and walking in the park. This image of them holding hands makes an impression on him because it's rare to see elderly people being affectionate with their significant others. This couple is very much in love. Now all he has is an image on which he can base the story. So he asks: what is the story about, and whose story is it? The filmmaker decides on the protagonist, an elderly woman, and gives her a name, Helen. After giving it much thought, he decides on the theme: "The story is about elderly people needing affection; every person wants to be loved, regardless of their age." Next, John has to work on the premise of the screenplay. He has to set up the premise to effectively deliver the established theme to the audience. This is not an easy task, but here is where the writer's creativity and vision come into play. He has to build a solid premise to deliver what he wants to say with the story. After revising the premise several times, he decides: "An elderly woman is devoted to her dying husband, but her new and fulfilling relationship with another man awakens her moral dilemma." Now, John uses the theme and premise to develop the characters, story, structure, setting, and the actual screenplay.

For screenwriters, the premise becomes a story's road map for the writing process. Deciding on a premise draws boundaries and defines circumstances of what the story needs, and the screenwriter develops characters and story elements to meet the conditions set by the premise. Every screenplay's development is unique, and inspiration can come from anywhere, but deciding on the premise that supports the theme is important. Without it, the screenplay has no governing idea to hold the story steady on its subject matter.

For example, in *Lady Bird*, the premise is about Christine's growing pains, which come at a high price. Throughout her senior year in high school, Christine has an identity issue. She gives herself a new name, "Lady Bird." She is a misfit – a confused and spontaneous but honest teenage girl. *Lady Bird* is a coming-of-age story capturing a teen's experience throughout her senior year. The film addresses family issues, especially the relationship between a mother and daughter, the stressful college application process, feeling out of place, exploring new friendships, falling in and out of love, and experiencing social class dynamics. The premise of the screenplay gives life to the characters and their surroundings.

We have all seen films with similar themes, but they are told in completely different stories. Themes have universality, but the premise is very specific to a story. Let's continue with the earlier example, *Groundhog Day*. The film's theme is "people can change and get rewards from life." Now, there are films with a similar theme as *Groundhog Day*, like *Sabrina* (1954), *Good Will Hunting* (1997), *The Family Man* (2000), and *The 40-Year-Old Virgin* (2005). The themes are very similar between these films, but the premises of the films are completely different. In *The Family Man*, the protagonist, a Wall Street executive, sees what his life could have been if he had made a different choice at a crucial moment of his life. And when he returns from seeing this glimpse, he starts to appreciate a different aspect of life, one he didn't appreciate before. Films can have the same themes, but the premise should never be the same.

In his book *The Art of Dramatic Writing*, Lajos Egri discussed what makes a premise. His definition can help us to understand what a premise is and how to identify it: "Every good premise is composed of three parts. . . The first part of the premise suggests character. . . The second part suggests conflict, and the third part suggests the end of the play (resolution)." A premise is a statement of what the story is about, usually told in a sentence or two. It is about someone who gets into a conflict and finds a resolution. So when you seek to identify the premise of a film, think about the central conflict that the protagonist is dealing with throughout the screenplay and how it is resolved.

Let's look at an example. Here's the premise of the critically acclaimed film *Oldboy* (2003): A man is kidnapped and put into solitary confinement for 13 years. As he is set free, he wants to find out who did this to him and why. Within this premise, we have a character, a conflict, and a resolution. The character is "a man," the protagonist. The conflict is that the man doesn't know why someone incarcerated him in solitary confinement for 13 years. The resolution is that he finds out who did this to him and why. We get a general sense of what the story is about without further details by identifying the premise.

Let's look at another example from another critically acclaimed film, *Uncut Gems* (2019). The premise of the film concerns a New York City jeweler in the Diamond District who makes a high-stakes bet that could change his life. While he waits for the ultimate win, he must maintain a balancing act in all aspects of his life, including his business, family, and adversaries, or else he could lose everything. Again, we are looking for a character, a conflict, and a resolution. We know the story is about a jeweler in the Diamond District. The conflict is the high-stakes bet that could change his life. The resolution is the result of the high-stakes bet and how it impacts the character's life.

When you are looking for the premise of the film, first identify the protagonist, the central conflict, and how the conflict is solved (the resolution). A good premise helps to reveal the protagonist's objective and demonstrates an antagonistic force that keeps the protagonist from achieving their goal. A good premise does not only apply to the character's journey, but holds a broader truth for the audience, as they can see it reflected in their own lives.

The theme and premise explain why the characters and story elements are designed and developed the way they are. The story flows flawlessly when they are properly developed, giving the audience an emotional experience the screenwriter intended to write.

2

CHARACTER

Whenever I think of a great film, a memorable character comes to my mind. When I think of *The Godfather*, I think of Michael Corleone. In *Fight Club*, it's Tyler Durden. In *Moonlight*, it's Chiron. In *La La Land*, it's Mia. The list goes on and on. We all have favorite characters from our favorite films. Have you ever wondered why these characters stay memorable? Why do we remember them? As the audience, we identify with the characters, and their actions resonate within us – for example, when Joel tries to erase his memory of Clementine because it hurts too much in *Eternal Sunshine of the Spotless Mind*, or when Christine tries to attend the college of her choice against all odds in *Lady Bird*, we identify with their actions because we have experienced similar desires. Their actions throughout the film make us relate to their emotional journey in the story. By identifying with the protagonist, we relate to the character's objectives, conflicts, and transformation.

In life, memorable events, such as your first kiss or your graduation day, stay with you because they have emotional significance. As in a worthy life event, a film can have an emotional resonance with the audience, while providing a psychological experience. The more specific the screenwriter gets with a character's emotion, the more universal the story becomes. The more the audience empathizes with the characters, the more in-depth emotional experience they will have from the film.

Before we dive into studying characters, let me ask an important question: Are the characters in films human beings? This question helps us think about who the characters are in a screenplay. When I ask students this question, I get two different answers. The first: "The characters are not human beings. They are fictional on-screen characters." The second: "They are human because the stories are always about human beings."

Both statements have solid arguments. A film tells a story about us, so characters are human in the context of the story, but they are fictional beings created by the

DOI: 10.4324/9781003138853-4

screenwriters. Technically speaking, characters are not human beings, but for the duration of the film, the characters come alive and are as real as any of us.

The characters have two main functions in a screenplay: the first is to drive the story forward, and the second is to connect with the audience. The character's first function in a screenplay is to drive the narrative forward with story elements. When the protagonist is in their *ordinary world* in the first act, they encounter an *inciting incident* that evokes their desire for a want and a need – an *objective*. As the protagonist begins the journey of accomplishing the objective, the protagonist's want and need create the *main tension*, the story's spine, or the story's central conflict: "Can the protagonist achieve their objective?" As the protagonist navigates toward the *objective* in the second act, they are confronted by the antagonist, who opposes or hinders the protagonist's pursuit. The protagonist must overcome *conflicts*, obstacles, and challenges to achieve the *objective*. As the protagonist enters the third act, they get closer to attaining the *objective*. There is a final confrontation. The *climax* is where the protagonist defeats or is defeated by the antagonist, which provides the *answer to the main tension*: yes, the protagonist achieved their *objective*, fulfilling the want and need, or no, the protagonist didn't attain their goal. One way or another, in a traditional screenplay, the *main tension* is answered. The aftermath from the *climax* leads the protagonist to a *resolution*. As the protagonist returns to the *ordinary world* in the third act, there is a *character transformation*. In most screenplays, the *character's transformation* is one of the final stages of the character's journey. The experience from this journey helps the protagonist realize something different about themself. This realization has a psychological significance in transforming the character.

The character's second function is to connect with the audience. The connection comes from the audience understanding who the character is, understanding their situation, and empathizing with their goals. When people read screenplays, they suspend disbelief about the world and the characters they are about to encounter. The *suspension of disbelief* is the audience's willingness to accept, forgive, or forget the fictional aspects of the story, so they embark unconditionally on a journey with the characters.

The main character's appeal is pivotal in connecting the character with the audience. A character doesn't have to be beautiful, genuine, pleasant, or friendly to be appealing; the character can be unattractive, unethical, and immoral, and still be appealing to the audience. What is important to the audience is the character's resemblance to us as human beings. The characters must feel real to us – they must think like us and behave like us. They must have human *characteristics and traits* so that they can be easily understandable. The characters have work life, family life, and private life. Therefore, characters have *personas* when they interact with other characters. The characters have a *point of view of the world* when pursuing the objective. The characters have *external* and *internal conflicts*, and they go through a *transformation* during the journey. So what makes characters appeal to the audience are their human characteristics and traits, the circumstances they are in, how they react to the conflicts, and how they transform.

Characters and stories are inseparable. Stories can only be told with characters, and characters only exist within the story. Therefore, the characters act and react within the boundaries set by the story. For example, the protagonist is as brave as the story allows them to be.

Character studies can help us understand who the characters are in the story's context and how they were developed and molded to exist within the story. Compelling characters have dimensions, feelings, desires, belief systems, moral compasses, ethical value systems, and every other human trait. To understand who a character is, we must observe and comprehend the motives behind the pursuit of their objective. Their intention and motivation drive their actions, and actions define who they are.

CHARACTER TYPES

At the center of a screenplay, characters drive the story – for example, Woody and Buzz in *Toy Story*, or Chris and Rose in *Get Out*. The story consists of characters pursuing objectives. In a screenplay, characters have a specific role based on their character types. The *protagonist* is the main character – the hero or heroine. The story is always told from the main character's point of view, and the story follows the main character's journey. The antagonist is the villain in the story, the enemy of the main character. The *antagonist* is someone who always stands in the way of the protagonist, either because both are pursuing the same goals, or because both are on the opposite side of the fight. The *supporting characters* are the characters who walk the path with the protagonist or the antagonist to help them meet their objectives.

Protagonist

When a screenwriter gets an idea for a screenplay, the story can be conceived from a plot or a character. However, the idea was conceived, the story is told from a single person's point of view. There are screenplays with multiple protagonists, like Hitchcock's *Psycho* (1960), *Tarantino's Pulp Fiction* (1994), and *Iñárritu's Babel* (2006), but let's focus our attention on screenplays with a single protagonist, since they are most common. The screenwriter needs a character who will carry the story throughout the screenplay.

The protagonist may like or dislike conflicts, and they may or may not shy away from the opposition when it comes to achieving their objectives. The protagonist may be ruthless at times, aggressive if need be, or extremely loving, caring, and forgiving – it all depends on what the story arc calls upon them to be. At times, writers put the protagonist in the most difficult situation possible to test their true nature and reveal human characteristics.

The protagonist must provoke a strong emotional and psychological response from the audience, and to achieve that, the screenwriters expose every aspect of the protagonist's life pertaining to the story. *Interstellar* (2014), a sci-fi screenplay written by Jonathan and Christopher Nolan, is set in the near future. Cooper, the protagonist, must go on a space mission to find habitable planets for mankind because human survival is threatened on Earth. It is a dangerous mission, and Cooper has a very slim chance of returning to Earth. With much to lose, Cooper decides to go, leaving his family – including his daughter, Murph – behind. This mission is personal for Cooper; he wants to save his children's lives as well as save mankind. He confronts every possible life-threatening challenge during the journey, but his will to return to Earth remains strong. The audience relates to Cooper's objective of wanting to complete the mission and keep the promise he made to his little girl. Cooper has promised Murph that he will come back. What drives him to achieve the mission is the love he has for his children, a genuine emotion that is universal.

Let's look at this example from a different angle. If Cooper doesn't make it back, he has something significant to lose. In setting up the story, the screenwriters give the protagonist a mission to accomplish, and they raise the stakes by connecting the goals with the protagonist's personal interests. The future of mankind and the lives of his children depend on the success of this mission. Therefore, the protagonist has a lot to lose if the objectives are not met. The protagonist knows what is at stake – knowing the stakes add urgency and immediacy to the goals he sets out to achieve.

Another example linking the protagonist's objective to personal interests takes place in the film *1917* (2019), a screenplay written by Sam Mendes and Krysty Wilson-Cairns. The story is set during World War I. Schofield and Blake are given a mission to travel through hostile enemy terrain and deliver a message to Colonel Mackenzie on the front lines. If the message doesn't get delivered on time, 16,000 soldiers will walk into an ambush, including Blake's brother, Joseph. Schofield and Blake know what is at stake. They have a strong need to accomplish their mission.

More often than not, screenwriters set the story at the beginning of the screenplay to communicate the protagonist's strong desire to accomplish the objectives and expose what is at stake if the objectives are not met.

Antagonist

The antagonist always has a justification for their actions. Just like the protagonist, most antagonists are strongly motivated to achieve their goals. The antagonist tries to prevent the protagonist from achieving his or her goals to fulfill their own goals. This character is best equipped to confront, challenge, attack, or fight the protagonist. Often, the antagonist is stronger, wiser, and smarter than the protagonist. In many traditional screenplays, the antagonist tends to be in a superior position, and the protagonist tends to be fighting an uphill battle. A great antagonist is a master at identifying the protagonist's weakness and going after where it hurts the most. The antagonist knows when to attack, putting the protagonist in a disadvantaged and vulnerable position.

The confrontation between the protagonist and the antagonist creates a conflict. The stronger the opposition, the stronger the conflict. The stronger the conflict, the harder the protagonist must fight. The harder the protagonist fights, the more the protagonist will expose their *characteristics and traits*. Therefore, one of the antagonist's functions is to reveal the true nature of the protagonist.

The main conflict with the antagonist results in the protagonist's realization of the self. There is a self-reflective moment as the protagonist returns to the *ordinary world* at the end of the screenplay. Depending on the intensity of the fight or the struggle, the protagonist will have a specific realization. So, in shaping the protagonist's character transformation, the antagonist plays an important role. The antagonist takes the protagonist to the lowest emotional point in the story; by doing so, the antagonist helps the protagonist to realize the value of reaching the highest emotional point in the story.

In *The Matrix* (1999), written and directed by Lana and Lilly Wachowski, the antagonist, Agent Smith, is programmed with artificial intelligence (AI) to keep order inside the simulated reality. The main objective of Agent Smith, an AI-programmed leader, is to track down and terminate awakened humans who are threatening the system. He has supernatural powers, with the speed and strength to dodge bullets and jump from rooftop to rooftop, and if he is killed, he is resurrected. Their physical characteristics make it impossible for the human rebels to have a fair fight. As Neo, the protagonist, fights for human existence, he is constantly tested and challenged by Agent Smith. During Neo's last stand against the agent, he fights back, knowing that he is no match for the agent. As the fight continues, he starts to believe something different about himself, foreshadowing what he will become. Before he has a chance to reach his realization, Neo is gunned down. However, he is resurrected from the dead, and realizes he is the "One." Now, Neo instinctively understands the rules and algorithms of this simulated reality and can free himself from those boundaries and limitations. Neo can stop bullets by controlling time and space, and he infiltrates Agent Smith in order to destroy him. Agent Smith has pushed Neo to realize his full potential. The antagonist not only hinders the protagonist's goals but also sends the protagonist to his lowest emotional state, causing a character transformation in the third act.

Supporting Characters

The supporting characters have stories of their own; they have reasons for their actions in the story. They may share the same interests, goals, and objectives as the main character, but the story is never about them.

The supporting characters always surround the protagonist or the antagonist. They either support the protagonist on the journey, or they help the antagonist with their objectives. One of the primary roles of the supporting characters is to continuously interact with the main character, so the protagonist constantly reveals their thoughts, intentions, motivation, dilemmas, and action plans.

In *The Social Network* (2010), a screenplay by Aaron Sorkin, one of the major supporting characters is Eduardo Saverin, Mark Zuckerberg's best friend. In the story, when Mark first gets the idea to create a social network site, he goes to see

Eduardo, and they decide to go into business together. Mark is in charge of developing the social network, and Eduardo is responsible for the business side of their operation. Eduardo is an important character in the story: he invests funds to keep the company afloat. He helps not only to move the story forward, but also to reveal Mark's characteristics and traits. Through Eduardo, we have access to Mark's inner thoughts. As they discuss the future of the company, we comprehend Mark's drive to make the social network site work. As a real-life person, Eduardo Saverin was the co-founder of Facebook, an important figure starting up the company. As a supporting character, Eduardo helps to tell the story of Mark Zuckerberg.

Identifying characters according to their types is an essential step to studying each character's functions and roles. One of the first steps in a character study is to identify the characters and their types.

CHARACTER BACKSTORY

To portray characters as human in the context of a story, the screenwriter must show them as having lived a life leading up to the beginning of the screenplay. Screenwriters understand the importance of knowing their characters thoroughly, including their backstories. The screenwriters have all the freedom to create and mold the characters as they wish, and they strive to develop them to help serve the story.

The protagonists in *Eternal Sunshine of the Spotless Mind, Sideways, Inception*, and *Her* have something in common. They are haunted by memories of their past lovers – and their memories play as an important backstory. A character's backstory is something that never gets revealed to us, unless the screenwriter wants us to see certain aspects of their past. The backstory is revealed via a flashback or character exposition. A flashback is a technique in which the screenwriter shows an essential segment from the character's past life that is relevant to the story. Character exposition is when a character reveals valuable character information through dialogue and action.

The characters must have existed before the screenplay began. The screenwriters don't have much time to establish who the character is. Rather than explaining, screenwriters put the characters in a situation where their actions reveal who they are. Therefore, character introduction plays an important function in exposing who our main character is to the audience.

How did the characters get to their positions at the beginning of the screenplay? In *Toy Story* (1995), why is Sheriff Woody, the protagonist, worried about Buzz Lightyear becoming Andy's favorite toy? It's because Woody has been Andy's favorite for some time, even before the start of the screenplay. Thus, jealousy takes over Woody's emotions at the beginning of the screenplay.

In the opening-credit montage of *The Wrestler* (2008), written by Robert Siegel, the audience learns that Randy "The Ram" Robinson was a wrestling icon in the 1980s. The news article clips, magazine covers, photos of sold-out arenas, and voice-overs from match commentators explain that Randy was at the top of his game. Now, 20 years later, Randy is introduced to us in a different world. Instead of Madison Square Garden in NYC, he is sitting in an elementary school class-room, beat up after a wrestling match, in a corner and alone. The dramatic contrast between the opening montage and the character's introduction creates an immediate interest in this story. Siegel allows the audience to draw their own conclusions after seeing Randy two decades later.

Backstories are revealed when the screenwriters feel it is appropriate to share the information with the audience throughout the screenplay. A character's back-story is important in defining and understanding who the character is in the main story. Therefore, as you perform a character study, you must pay attention to the character's situation, dialogue, and actions to pick up on the backstory, since the screenwriter may not present it in an obvious manner. Obvious exposition tends to bore the audience.

CHARACTER INTRODUCTION

The screenwriters have one chance to create a memorable first impression for their characters. So, screenwriters carefully construct the best scenario possible to intro-duce them. The screenwriters serve four purposes with the character introduction:

1. to reveal and establish the protagonist's characteristics and traits
2. to introduce the protagonist's ordinary world
3. to establish the protagonist's emotional state
4. to mark the starting point of the protagonist's character transformation

The character's introduction is their starting point in the story, and the starting point of their transformation. The ending reveals the trajectory of their character transformation. Therefore, the character's introduction is not a random day in the character's life; it is constructed carefully to reflect the character's transformation.

In *Whiplash* (2014), the protagonist, Andrew Neiman, is introduced playing the drums alone late at night at the rehearsal studio. Andrew is sweating and appears to have been there for quite some time. He rehearses, trying to perfect the strokes, maintaining a constant beat. His practice is interrupted by Fletcher, who enters the room. Andrew, noticing Fletcher, stops playing. Andrew is intimidated by the man standing in front of him. Fletcher seems to have an interest in Andrew's talent and asks for his name. Andrew knows Fletcher looks for talented players to join his jazz studio ensemble, one of the best in the nation.

During this character introduction, they establish their power dynamics. Fletcher is the teacher and Andrew is the student. Fletcher humiliates Andrew for his indecisive behaviors, then asks him to play. Andrew starts to play drum rudi-ments, one after another. Fletcher demands more, a "double-time swing." Andrew tries his best, but he is out of his comfort zone. He closes his eyes to concentrate. Suddenly, the door slams shut. Andrew looks up. Fletcher is gone. Andrew is not sure if Fletcher liked or disliked his rudiments. From the opening scene, we know each character's dramatic needs. Andrew's *wants* is to be in Fletcher's jazz ensemble, and Fletcher's *wants* is to find the best performers for his band.

Why did the story begin that evening, when Andrew was rehearsing alone at night? The scene introduces Andrew's *ordinary world*. It shows the audience who he is, what he does, and what he wants from the start. The writer/director of *Whiplash*, Damien Chazelle, talked about the opening scene in an interview:

> The movie was going to be about a drummer, so [we] literally open with a guy drumming and the story itself is really about the drummer's relationship with the teacher. So what the first scene had to introduce was the drummer, the teacher and tell you exactly what that relationship was going to be, and then the rest of the movie could basically vary [and] riff on that, but I like the idea of basically having the entire movie within the opening scene.

In *Drive* (2011), an adapted screenplay written by Hossein Amini, we are introduced to the Driver's *ordinary world* as the film begins. The protagonist, the Driver, doesn't have a name and is only referred to as Driver in the screenplay. He is a loner, and works as a mechanic and a stunt driver by day. At night, he moonlights, running routes for criminals. He knows the streets of Los Angeles, and he knows how to outsmart the cops. Within the first five pages of the screenplay, we get a complete sense of who he is and how good he is at what he does. Furthermore, he is a character who only cares for himself. He has nobody in his life. But at the end of the screenplay, he is ready to give up his life to protect the people he's learned to love. There is a complete character transformation. Therefore, showing who the protagonist is at the beginning of the film is as important as showing who he becomes at the end of the film.

The screenwriter knows the importance of a great character introduction and will think of ways to make the introduction count. In a screenplay, find and read the scene(s) where the protagonist is introduced, and then think about why the screenwriter chose this moment of the protagonist's life to introduce them in the screenplay. Do not rely only on the protagonist's dialogue, but read into their actions, intentions, and motivation in the introduction scene(s).

A CHARACTER'S TRAITS

What makes a character unique are their *characteristics and traits*. To identify them, you must recognize the character's physical, social, and psychological attributes. Lajos Egri's *The Art of Dramatic Writing*, a book first published in 1942, is widely known as a classic playwriting guide and has influenced multiple narrative forms, including screenplays. Egri shares the idea of characters having dimensions: "Every object has three dimensions: depth, height, width. Human beings have an additional three dimensions: physiology, sociology, psychology. Without a knowledge of the three dimensions we cannot praise a human being."

The character's *psychological attributes* include the character's personality traits, ethical and moral values, political and social views, and traditional and religious beliefs. For example: Are they optimistic, realistic, or pessimistic? Are they emotionally stable? Are they open-minded or close-minded? Are they extroverted or introverted? Are they self-disciplined? Are they easygoing, diplomatic, or confrontational? Do they have an attitude? Are they liberal or conservative? These are just a few of the character's inner characteristics and traits. The best way to perceive these is to understand the motive behind the action, because the characters' actions define who they are. For example, in *Star Wars: A New Hope* (1977), Luke Skywalker wants to help save Princess Leia and become a Jedi to fight the Galactic Empire. Luke's psychological attributes are influenced by his motivation to fight the Dark Side of the Force, based on his strong moral values and his want for peace and justice in the universe. His beliefs are shown by joining Obi-wan Kenobi to save Princess Leia and helping the Rebel Alliance destroy the Death Star.

At times, during the script development phase, screenwriters assign an *archetype* to their characters. A character's archetype is a set of predefined physical, psychological, and/or social attributes that affect a pattern of behavior. Some screenwriters opt to apply human archetypes to the characters in order to display familiar traits to the audience, and mold characters' psychological attributes from predetermined conditions set by the archetype. The director of *Drive*, Nicolas Winding Refn, said of his film, "It has these archetypes that come from noir – the silent hero. There's also the samurai, who is a classic mythological hero. Here, he is more of a cowboy." Winding Refn is applying the silent hero *archetype*, providing him with the characteristics and traits of a cowboy. In a western genre film, a typical cowboy protagonist is someone who lacks social skills, and trouble comes knocking on their door. Cowboys tend to alienate themselves from communities, but learn to accept the needs of others. Their ethics overrule their moral values, and they take justice into their own hands. They are not afraid to hurt or kill someone for a greater cause. When screenwriters assign an archetype to a character, they give specific psychological characteristics and traits to make them unique to the story.

The character's *physical attributes* include age, sex, race, appearance, health, posture, hairstyle, and any other physical limitation, abnormality, or even physical skill sets. The screenwriters tend only to describe the essential physical attributes in the story, like age and physical appearance, unless there is a specific need to expose their unique physical attributes.

One film where physical attributes govern the central theme of the screenplay is *Get Out* (2017), written and directed by Jordan Peele. The protagonist, Chris, is an urban photographer with the sensibility of a great artist. He is a young and healthy African-American man. All of his physical attributes are important, as the story's central theme deals with systemic racism.

Another film where the physical attributes govern the theme of the story is *The Theory of Everything* (2014), an adapted screenplay written by Anthony McCarten. The story shows how physical limitations can cause difficulties in a character's life. The protagonist, Stephen Hawking, has a neurological disease that paralyzes him as he is about to start his career. Stephen's physical challenges could have easily broken his spirits, but he chooses to accept it and live an inconvenient yet fruitful life, marrying his girlfriend, having children, writing books, and even giving public speeches. The protagonist's physical conditions test his willpower, but his psychological traits help him overcome his limitations.

The physical and psychological attributes of the character are interconnected. The physical attributes influence the psychological attributes and vice versa. The character's physical attributes can be as important as psychological attributes for the types of stories the screenwriters want to tell. The screenwriters know that compelling characters have a body and a soul.

The character's *social attributes* define the character's relationship to the world in the story. Social attributes include the age group the character belongs to, social class, occupation, marital status, and any of exterior attributes that help define the character in the community or society. The characters' social attributes help the audiences identify who they are in the world of the story. In *Schindler's List* (1993), an adapted screenplay written by Steven Zaillian, the protagonist, Oskar Schindler, is a businessman who wants to make his fortune during World War II. He joins the Nazi Party, not because he agrees with their political views, but because of the convenience and practicality in running a business. Oskar Schindler employs Jewish workers in the factory for pragmatic reasons. During the Holocaust, Schindler makes arrangements to protect his workers and keep the factory in operation. At first, he acts to fulfill his business goals, but soon he realizes that he is saving innocent lives. His social attributes make it possible to affiliate with the Nazi Party, and his status as a businessman means he can protect his workers from going to the concentration camp. Without his social attributes, he wouldn't be able to save innocent lives.

Every character imitates life, and stories mimic different aspects of our lives and existence. Thus, the character must have a physical body – including physical attributes, and a world and setting they interact with – as well as social attributes, and thoughts that drive their everyday life, also known as psychological attributes.

When analyzing a character's characteristics and traits, one must pay close attention to the character's psychological, physical, and social attributes. There are no shortcuts in identifying these attributes. You will have to pay close attention to the character's actions, dialogue, intentions, and demeanor.

A CHARACTER'S POINT OF VIEW

One psychological attribute that we must examine further is the character's *point of view* of the world. The character's worldview mainly encompasses ethical and moral values, political and social views, and cultural, traditional, and religious beliefs, or they may not be bound to any social norm or preset conditions. Now, by analyzing how the protagonist reacts to conflicts, we see where they stand on an issue, and we get to study their point of view of the world. Regardless of the types of conflicts the protagonist faces, they always reveal their value system through actions. The character's point of view of the world is more than just choosing between good or evil, right or wrong, or ethical or unethical, but having the freedom to see life however they want to see it. The protagonist's actions are always motivated by the need to accomplish the objective, and their actions are justified in their mind because of the way they see the world. The character's point of view can be determined by identifying the reason for pursuing the objective. Therefore, the audience must clearly understand the character's objectives in order to comprehend their point of view of the world. If you look closely at the protagonist's objectives and the actions in pursuing the goals, the character always reveals their point of view.

The Danish Girl (2015), an adapted screenplay by Lucinda Coxon, is based on a true story that took place in Denmark in the 1920s. Einar Wegener, the protagonist, is confronted with his sexuality as a married man. A small favor to his wife, Gerda, triggers his curiosity and changes the course of their marriage and his life. Gerda, a painter, wants to continue painting a piece, but the model cannot attend the session, so she asks her husband, Einar, to dress like a woman and pose for her. This *inciting incident* triggers Einar's want and need to explore his sexuality. His obsession with women's undergarments and clothing reveals his desire to wear them. Now, with encouragement from Gerda, Einar starts exploring how to dress like a woman. For Gerda, the wife, this is a game they play, but for Einar, the husband, this is the beginning of a new life and persona. Einar begins cross-dressing and meets men behind his wife's back, living a double identity as Lili. Gerda gives in, and with her support, Einar undergoes a sex-change operation and becomes one of the first known recipients of sex-reassignment surgery.

Einar's point of view on sexuality changes during the course of the story, affecting and contradicting his beliefs, values, and ethics, but that's okay, because his desire to be a woman is stronger than his desire to stay as a man. Einar overlooks the cultural and traditional social settings and sees the world as he wanted to see it by becoming Lili Elbe.

There is a strong correlation between the character's dramatic needs and the character's point of view of the world. The character's *want* and *need* drive the story forward, but the character's point of view provides a direction to the story.

Knowing the protagonist's point of view, the world can help us understand the theme of the story. Knowing the antagonist's worldview can help us to understand what the protagonist is fighting against. In order to discover the character's point of view on the world, you must look at the motive behind the character's main objective.

A CHARACTER'S LIFE AND PERSONAS

Screenplays tell the story of human experience, condition, and existence. In Oscar Wilde's essay, *The Decay of Lying*, he says, "Life imitates Art far more than Art imitates Life." This is the opposite of what Aristotle said in *Poetics*: "Art imitates life." We could discuss this further, but for now, one solid conclusion that can be derived from this disagreement is that art and life are inseparable. But, even without the artists and scholars proving the point, we can all agree that most stories are about us as humans.

If art imitates life or life imitates art, and if the screenplay tells our story, then the characters in a story have to feel real to the audience. There are exceptions, but for the most part, the characters have to resemble us. Screenwriters know the importance of building complete characters that must feel multidimensional. When developing a character, the screenwriter gives them life by assigning an occupation, setting up a social circle, establishing relationships, and giving the character a private life.

However, it is impossible to reveal every aspect of the character's life in a screenplay, and the writer shouldn't. Screenwriters know they are up against time; they only have 120 pages to tell a story. On the other hand, if the audience has questions or doubts about certain areas of the character's life, it will break their suspension of disbelief, causing them to lose interest in the story. Thus, the screenwriter portrays every aspect of the character's life that pertains to the story. Depending on the screenplay, one aspect of the character's life might be developed further than the others. However, generally speaking, the screenwriter reveals all three aspects of the character's life. The character's *work/professional life* includes their occupation, or how they make a living. The character's *family/personal life* is the life outside of work. It can be the life they spend with their family, friends, coworkers, or neighbors. The character's *private/secret life* includes the time they spend alone.

For the audience to identify with and relate to a character, they must know and understand all areas of the character's life. The readers will draw conclusions by seeing the contrast between different aspects of the character's life. Let's say a father is looking forward to seeing his daughter's school play. Every night for the past week, he has been practicing lines with her. He has been waiting to see his daughter onstage, but he ends up missing the play. Now, seeing what caused him to miss the school play can tell us a lot about the character. If he leaves work 30 minutes early but is caught in a terrible traffic jam, that says one thing about him. If he misses the play because he couldn't decline an extra shift to pay for her daughter's acting lessons, that says a different thing about him. Seeing different aspects of a character's life helps the audience see who the character is in the story.

Persona

A *persona* is a particular aspect of someone's nature that is presented and perceived by others. For example, we often say someone has a "public persona." According to psychiatrist and psychoanalyst Carl Jung, the persona is a social face that the individual presents to the world. In his book, *Two Essays on Analytical Psychology*, Jung says a persona is "a kind of mask, designed on the one hand to make a definite impression upon others, and the other to cancel the true nature of the individual." Jung says the first persona an individual develops is through interactions with one's parents. As children grow up, they develop different personas when they are with their grandparents, when they go to daycare, and so on. They develop a new persona in each new social setting they encounter.

Characters in the screenplays are no different. The protagonist has a different persona for each group they interact with throughout the screenplay. The nature of the story will determine the type of personas the character has, but usually the protagonist will have a separate persona for each person or group of people they interact with throughout the screenplay.

Every persona has a different set of character traits representing the character; therefore, to know who the character is, the audience must put the puzzle together and figure out who the real character is in the story.

In *Lady Bird* (2017), written and directed by Greta Gerwig, the protagonist, Christine, writes "Lady Bird" next to her name on a school bulletin board. This action says a lot about her character: she wants to create a new persona by changing her identity from Christine to Lady Bird. Her persona at her Catholic private school is rebellious, indifferent, impulsive, and spontaneous. She interrupts a school assembly during a discussion about a sensitive topic, abortion, and insults the presenter. Lady Bird plays a prank on her high school principal, taping a "Just Married to Jesus" sign on the back of her car. Lady Bird steals and throws away the math grade book when no one is around. As the math teacher uses the honor system to re-create the grade book, she lies about her grades. She tells him she got a "B."

Lady Bird's persona at home is different – confrontational, and selfish. Lady Bird constantly fights with her brother and his girlfriend, whether at the breakfast table or the supermarket; they don't seem to get along. With Marion, her mother, the fighting is even worse. Beyond their disagreement on where Lady Bird should go to college, the two of them are continually butting heads about everything. Marion argues that Christine is selfish in wanting to attend college on the East Coast, as the family is facing financial difficulties.

Lady Bird has a different persona when she is with her best friend Julie. She is honest, friendly, and full of camaraderie. Lady Bird can be herself with Julie. She opens up about her family and boy problems. Her persona with the cool kids from school, Jenna and Kyle, is awkward, superficial, and dishonest. Lady Bird lies about her social status to Jenna in order to get to her new love interest, Kyle. She tries to belong, but she is not happy with herself, and she learns that they are not her real friends.

When she arrives at college in New York, her persona is of someone who has matured. She presents herself differently, as she is more calm and down to earth. She has a moment of realization when she walks alone one Sunday morning and voluntarily attends Catholic mass. As the choir sings, she reflects on where she came from. After the service, she calls home, leaving a message for her mom and saying, "I love you." Her persona changes again as she goes from being Lady Bird to Christine.

In order to thoroughly understand the dimensions of a character, all aspects of the character's life must be examined, including all personas. A character's personas can be perceived through behavior and dialogue. Look at the way the main character interacts with different characters in the screenplay: What's the tone of voice? How sarcastic are they? How honest? How seductive? All nuances the screenwriter provides the character with – the way they behave and speak – are clues letting us into their persona.

A CHARACTER'S OBJECTIVES

One evening in New York City, I was walking to the subway station when I heard the sound of a tenor saxophone traveling through Union Square near 14th Street. It had been a rainy afternoon, so the ground was still wet, and the air was cold. As I got closer, I saw an old man playing the melody to *My Funny Valentine*. As I was enjoying the music, I caught myself thinking about the street performer. His saxophone case was open with loose coins and dollar bills, his feet were tapping to the beat of the music, and his facial expression changed as he hit the high notes. Whatever his circumstances may have been, as an artist, a part of him needed to express himself, and he wanted to perform in front of people.

If you think about it, our *wants* and *needs* drive us to do things or go places in life. "I need to go to culinary school because I want to be a chef." "I need to endure, because I want to succeed." "I need you, so I want to be with you." This pattern of identifying a need or a want and pursuing the objective is what we do in life. And because the story in a screenplay mimics life, it's not surprising that the character's *want* and *need* are one of the most important story elements in a screenplay. They are the heart of the story. Without them, there is no life in the story.

An *objective*, a task, a challenge, or a mission, can be a *want* and *need* of a character in the story. The *want* is a personal goal, and the *need* is an inner desire. The *want* drives the story, and the *need* drives the premise of the story. The *want* provides a character transformation, and the *need* provides a character's emotional transformation. The *want* can be unique to each story, but the *need* is something universal to the audience. A protagonist's *objective*, therefore, affects their external transformation as well as the inner change of a protagonist at the end of the screenplay.

Protagonist's Objectives

The protagonist's *wants* and *needs* are what drives them to move forward in a screenplay. In the first act, the protagonist's *wants* and *needs* are revealed through an *inciting incident*. At the end of the first act, the protagonist decides to embark on a journey to achieve the *objective*. The question that is raised at the end of the first act is "Can the protagonist achieve their objectives?" For example, can Lady Bird go to school on the East Coast? Can Neo find out if he is the One? Can Batman catch the Joker? This question becomes the *spine of the story*, the *main tension* that keeps the audience captive and engaged. The second act is the protagonist's journey to achieve their *objective*. All the *conflicts*, challenges, and obstacles test the character's willpower. Whether the protagonist successfully attains the *objective* or fails miserably, the *answer to the main tension* is revealed at the end. The third act is the *resolution*, mostly reflecting on how the character transformed through the journey of pursuing the *want* and *need*.

In *The Apartment* (1960), written by Billy Wilder and I.A.L. Diamond, the protagonist, C.C. "Bud" Baxter, wants to climb the corporate ladder by getting on the executives' good sides. Baxter lends his bachelor pad to corporate executives for their secret sexual affairs. In his personal life, Baxter wants privacy and time to himself, as he is forced to spend a lot of time outside of his apartment. In his private life, Baxter is in love with the elevator girl, Fran Kubelik. He wants to win her over. As the story enters the second act, the main tension is "Can he climb the corporate ladder and become an executive?" Baxter works very hard to please the executives to get the promotion, but tension arises when he discovers that one of the executives, Mr. Sheldrake, is having an affair with Ms. Kubelik, the woman Baxter is in love with. In the third act, the main tension is answered: Baxter gets the promotion from Mr. Sheldrake, but soon after, he quits the job in order to become a "mensch," a person of integrity and honor. Baxter goes through a clear character transformation. At the beginning of the screenplay, he is miserable, but at the end, he is happy with himself – a change in his emotional arc.

Antagonist's Objectives

The antagonist's objective is as important as the protagonist's objective. The antagonist must have a want and need of their own, and they are in direct conflict with the protagonist's objectives. An antagonist with strong objectives raises the stakes for the protagonist. The stronger the antagonist, the harder the protagonist must fight. The harder the protagonist fights, the more they reveal about their characteristics and traits. The same goes for the antagonist: the harder the antagonist fights for their objective, the more we get to see their true nature, exposing what the protagonist is fighting against.

The antagonist is someone who tests the protagonist by pursuing their own wants and needs, like the Winklevoss twins in *The Social Network*, or Agent Smith in *The Matrix*. They all have their own objectives and goals. *Mad Max: Fury Road* (2015) is a post-apocalyptic action film co-written and directed by George Miller – the same filmmaker who made the original film, *Mad Max* (1979). In this fourth installment of the Mad Max franchise, the antagonist is Immortan Joe, a tyrannical ruler. He is introduced as a brutal leader who is using the water supply as a commodity to govern the tens of thousands of people living under his oppression. When he discovers that his young wives have escaped with the help of the protagonist, Furiosa, his objective is clear: he aims to retrieve the young wives at all costs. He gathers up his army and calls the Gas Town boys and the Bullet Farmers, his neighbor allies, for aid. Immortan Joe's *want* and *need* are strong, and his fight is personal. He has a lot to lose if he doesn't bring back his wives: he will lose face in the community and be humiliated. His ego can't allow him to go back empty-handed, so he goes after Furiosa with conviction. The story has a strong conflict because Immortan Joe and Furiosa have the strong motivation and drive to achieve each of their goals.

On the other hand, understanding the antagonist's objective makes the audience realize what the protagonist is fighting against. Furiosa is fighting to free the young women who were forced to serve and become the wives of Immortan Joe.

Supporting Character's Objectives

The screenwriters create a world to tell the story, and in this world, everyone has a drive; everyone has a *want* and a *need*, whether it is the protagonist, antagonist, or any of the supporting characters – for example, Morpheus and Trinity in *The Matrix* (1999), or the Kim family members in *Parasite* (2019).

It's important to identify and break down the want and need of the supporting characters to see how they contribute to the main tension of the screenplay. In *Interstellar* (2014), Earth is becoming inhabitable. A supporting character, Professor Brand, a NASA physicist, aims to save mankind by finding a habitable planet and transporting the population to a new home via a wormhole. He has been planning his mission for years. As Cooper, the protagonist, finds his way to NASA, he is asked to go on a mission to fulfill Professor Brand's first objective: finding a habitable planet for mankind. The supporting character's objective plays an integral part of the story elements, supporting the main tension of the screenplay.

In order to identify the drama of the story, we need to define the protagonist's objectives. Furthermore, it's also important to identify the antagonist's objectives to determine what the protagonist is fighting against. A protagonist's *objective* is the heart of the story, and their *objectives* can be identified by looking into the *inciting incident* and following their *actions* through the second act.

CHARACTER CONFLICT

Screenwriters know the value of *conflict* in a screenplay. *Conflict* always creates tension, and tension is what keeps the audience engaged. The *conflict's* first function in a screenplay is to reveal a character's psychological attributes. The *conflict* always exposes the character's motivation and desire to accomplish the goal. At times, when plotting a screenplay, screenwriters think of ways to put the character in the worst possible situation within the context of the story, then they will think of a way to get them out of the situation convincingly, and thus expose the character's willingness, drives, and any other inner characteristics that define them.

The *conflict's* second function is to drive the story forward. If the character doesn't have opposition, challenges, or obstacles to overcome, the story becomes lifeless, and the audience becomes disengaged from the film. If the protagonist gets what they *want* and *need* without conflict, it's not a story.

Conflicts are anything that get in the way of the protagonist achieving the *objective*. In addition to the main conflict, there are smaller conflicts – the everyday conflicts. Whether they are forced to take a detour around a roadblock when they are late for work, spill coffee on their shirt before an important presentation, or run out of bullets in the middle of a fight, these are all conflicts. There are conflicts the protagonist has control over, relies on others to help with, or are simply beyond their control. Normally, the protagonist confronts two types of conflicts: *external conflict* and *internal conflict*.

External Conflict

External conflicts are the types of conflict the character has no control over. They are divided into two major categories: *character vs. character* and *character vs. environment*.

Character vs. character is the most common type of external conflict in a screenplay: the conflict that arises between characters. As the protagonist embarks on a journey, the antagonist is always in the way of achieving their goals. As discussed earlier, an antagonist is someone who desires the same goal as the protagonist, or is on the opposite side of the fight because they have a different set of values from the protagonist.

A strong antagonist provides a strong challenge to the protagonist. At times, the villains are stronger than the hero or heroine, and the circumstances always seem to favor the antagonist. For the protagonist, it can always feel that the odds are against them. The reason for setting the drama within this paradigm is to test the protagonist's will, integrity, dignity, or any other inner traits pertaining to the story.

In *Whiplash*, the antagonist, Fletcher, abuses his power and creates a hostile environment to push the students around. He demands perfection. Fletcher humiliates, intimidates, and insults the students to motivate them to perform at their best. Andrew, the protagonist, must push himself to the limit each time, or else he will be replaced. He lives in constant fear and stress, and it takes a toll on him. To Andrew, there is nothing more important than getting into Fletcher's band. Once he is in the band, nothing is more important than practicing hard, so that when the time comes, he can take the lead drummer's seat. Once he's the lead drummer, there is nothing more important than keeping the seat. Andrew is pushed around and constantly tested by Fletcher throughout this process. Finally, Andrew breaks down. He gets into a car accident on the way to a performance, and instead of going to the hospital, he resists the pain and goes onstage. As the band starts to play, he slowly falls apart and can't keep up with the rest of the band. Andrew endures physical and psychological humiliation from Fletcher because his desire is greater than Fletcher's abuse, and Andrew knows Fletcher holds the keys to his future. Andrew vs. Fletcher is a great example of character vs. character.

A *character vs. environment* type of conflict comes from the challenging conditions in which the character must operate within the story. "Environment" could mean Mother Nature, opposing points of view within society, a supernatural force, cultural differences, or a language barrier. The character's conflict with their surroundings hinders them from achieving their objectives.

The *character vs. environment* conflict can be the central conflict of the screenplay. Films like *The Martian*, *Gravity*, *Interstellar*, and *Apollo 13* deal with the challenges of traveling into outer space. Films like *Alive, Twister*, and *The Perfect Storm* deal with challenges presented by Mother Nature. Films like *Erin Brockovich, Gandhi*, and *Milk* deal with challenges from opposing belief systems. Films like *Paranormal Activity, The Conjuring*, and *The Exorcist* deal with supernatural conflicts.

Internal Conflict

An *internal conflict* is called the *character vs. self* conflict. An internal conflict occurs when two opposing wants, needs, or beliefs coexist within the self. The opposing motivations pull the character in two different directions, affecting the character's psychology and creating the character's inner dilemma.

More often than not, the protagonist's *inner conflict* is revealed to the audience during the first act, between the *inciting incident* and the protagonist pursuing their goals. It may be a split-second decision, or it may take several scenes, but the inner conflict is there before they embark on the journey to achieve their goals in the second act. The same *inner conflict* may return and cause the protagonist to question their "character" during the second act. When the protagonist's willpower is tested, when the fight becomes tougher, when there is nowhere to run or hide, the protagonist falls into self-doubt. This usually takes place at the midpoint of the screenplay. As the protagonist presents their resilience or cowardliness, the inner conflict helps to define the character transformation and emotional arc at the end of the screenplay.

The protagonist's *inner conflict* is another psychological attribute that can make the character appeal to the audience. The protagonist's *inner conflicts* help to reveal the character's psychological traits. If the audience can identify with the character's *inner conflict*, they can easily empathize with the protagonist's objective and become psychologically invested in the character and their journey.

In *Toy Story*, Woody's *inner conflict* is whether to do something about Buzz Lightyear, the new toy who's becoming extremely popular with Andy. Woody's intent is to just push Buzz behind the desk to hide him from Andy, but it goes terribly wrong. He accidentally pushes Buzz out the window. This action leads to an unforeseeable event, which takes the story into the second act, where Woody and Buzz must navigate through the human world to make it back to Andy's room. Woody's *inner conflict* in the first act occurs because of his insecurity and jealousy. The *inner conflicts* help to define the character's worldview, characteristics, and traits that are important to the story and the character's transformation.

The protagonist's *external* and *internal conflicts* force them to reveal a great deal of who they are. As the character acts and reacts to the *conflicts*, we are allowed insight into the reasoning behind their actions. When studying a character, we must define all of their *external* and *internal conflicts*.

CHARACTER TRANSFORMATION

Once in a while, I come across different versions of this quote: "Life is about the journey and not the destination." I couldn't agree more. Every time I hear this quote, I think: What if we applied this to characters in a screenplay? How does this quote affect the way we think about the characters' journeys and destinations?

The screenwriters are the gods of the worlds they are creating. For the characters, is it the journey or the destination that counts more? If we look back to the first act, when the protagonist is in their ordinary world, who were they back then? What is their emotional state at the beginning of the screenplay? As the story is about to end, who have they become, and what is their emotional state? How did the journey transform them? Did they go from being trapped to liberated, or from being suppressed to free? Did they go from being dependent to independent? Cowardly to courageous? Insecure to secure? Stubborn to open-minded? Pessimistic to optimistic?

What does the audience get by empathizing with a character's transformation? Why is character transformation in a protagonist so important? Character transformation fulfills the story paradigm that the audience is accustomed to. The character's transformation gives the audience a fulfilling ending to the story by concluding the audience's psychological journey.

One of the four functions of myth, according to mythologist Joseph Campbell, is the psychological function. In *Occidental Mythology* (1964), Campbell wrote:

> It is this pedagogical function of mythology that carries the individual through the various stages and crises of life, from childhood dependency to the responsibilities of maturity, to the reflection of old age, and finally, to death. It helps individuals understand the unfolding of life with integrity. It initiates individuals into the order of realities in their minds, guiding them toward awareness and realization.

There is a strong correlation between character transformations and the audience's psychological experience and enrichment. The character transformation is a pivotal story element that determines how much the audiences take away from the story. In a good story, a profound character realization resonates with the audience. It helps us to shape our moral and ethical compass, and broadens our understanding of the human condition and its limitations.

For characters in a screenplay, the destination is equally as important as the journey.

Emotional Arc and Character Transformation

There are two types of changes a protagonist undergoes at the end of a screenplay. The first type is the character's emotional change – the emotional arc – and the second is a character's transformation as a human being.

The term *emotional arc* refers to a protagonist's emotional stages throughout the screenplay. Each dramatic shift in a story influences the protagonist's emotional state, sending them from one emotional state to the next. The emotional arc has a starting and an ending point, and these are the two points connecting the arc – for example, from trapped to liberated, from selfish to selfless, or from empty to ful-filled. The arc has a trajectory; it is not a linear path. The emotional arc must have the highest and lowest emotional points. So the character's emotional arc has a beginning and an end, but in between these two points, the character's emotions fluctuate with the twists and turns in the story. At the end of *Schindler's List* (1993), the protagonist, Oskar Schindler, laments that he has not saved more lives. After seeing how he helped to save so many people, he wholeheartedly regrets not doing more when he could have. He experiences an emotional change from the realiza-tion. By the end of the film, he has begun to see the effects of his earlier actions, and his emotional state is different from when he started the film.

The *character transformation*, which is different from the emotional arc, occurs when the character changes. At the beginning of *Blade Runner* (1982), a sci-fi screenplay written by Hampton Fancher and David Webb Peoples, Deckard, the protagonist, is a Blade Runner, an insensitive detective working for the police unit which tracks down and kills the Replicants – human clones. In the process of chasing down the recent escapees, Deckard falls in love with Rachael, a Replicant working for their creator, Eldon Tyrell. Because of love, Deckard's emotional state changes, affecting his point of view of the world, and transforms him into someone else. Deckard goes from being a detective to a fugitive in order to be with Rachael. Now, in seeing the change, the audience can draw their own conclusions as to whom the protagonist has become and why he has transformed.

The *character transformation* is the final dramatic shift in most screenplays, provok-ing the final emotional reaction in the audience. We must identify the protagonist's transformation and emotional arc in the screenplay to understand how the charac-ter has been shaped to tell the story.

3

STORY

How can we define the story in a film? We can look at the story from two different perspectives: from the creator's point of view and from the audience's point of view. For the screenwriters, story is everything. Screenwriters are constantly searching for great stories to write. Film studios and productions around the world are always searching for great stories to produce. And the audience is always waiting for the next great film.

For the screenwriters, the story has to meet certain criteria to be worth developing. The audience has to find some sort of value in the story. Whether the story is dramatic, about an emotional journey, or thrilling, as in an action film, the story has to provide something meaningful in an entertaining format to the audience. In addition, the story has to provide a psychological experience for the audience. The journey through the protagonist's pursuit of their goal has to provide an emotional experience. Finally, the story must engage with the audience, and arouse their curiosity and interest.

For the audience, the story serves multiple purposes. We, as the audience, have certain expectations. The theme and premise of the story resonate in every one of us, but what each of us takes away from the film is subjective. At the beginning of each semester, I give students an assignment to think about what story is to each of them. I ask, "Why do you crave stories, and why do you watch films?" Each student gives personal reasons for craving stories and watching films. While they give a wide range of reasons, I can categorize them into three different groups: to escape, to be entertained, or to have an experience. Do you concur with their answers? Do you crave stories and watch films to escape reality, put the worries or stress aside, and transport yourself into the world of the characters? Do you watch films to be entertained for two hours, or do you watch films to have an experience and learn or feel something new? Maybe it's a combination of the three reasons,

DOI: 10.4324/9781003138853-5

depending on the type of films you are watching – or you may have your own specific reasons.

Each of us has reasons for loving films, and each reason is a personal and subjective one. Now, before analyzing a screenplay, each of us should clearly understand what stories are.

Great films always have great stories. Stories have the ability to affect an individual, the means to influence a group of people, and the power to change the world. Some stories help us to get to know one another better, sometimes exploring what is apparent and sometimes exploring deeply hidden human emotions. Great stories influence and affect us. In his book, *Story*, Robert McKee writes:

> To retreat behind the notion that the audience simply wants to dump its troubles at the door and escape reality is a cowardly abandonment of the artist's responsibility. Story isn't a flight from reality but a vehicle that carries us on our search for reality, our best effort to make sense out of the anarchy of existence.

When someone says they saw a movie, we often ask: "How was the film? Did you like it? Was it good?" The answer will depend on how entertained they were watching the film. In this case, the entertainment comes from visual, audio, and psychological stimulation. What triggers the psychological stimulation in the audience's mind is the protagonist's journey in the story. The screenwriter plans the fate of a character according to what the story demands from them.

After watching a "feel-good movie," the audience feels good, generally speaking. The story is designed to create an emotional effect on people. Using the story and characters, the screenwriter creates an emotional experience. Young children are fascinated by animated films like *Toy Story*, *Shrek*, *Finding Nemo*, *Cars*, *Kung-Fu Panda*, *Moana*, *Trolls*, *Frozen,* and *Encanto*. Each new generation of children never gets tired of watching their favorite films over and over again. They pretend to be the characters in the film, they recite lines, and sing along to the soundtracks from the films. Why?

Joseph Campbell, a scholar, mythology professor, and author, studied the distinctions and similarities among the mythologies of various regions and cultures and explained the four functions of myth. These four functions can help us to relate to the functions of the stories in a film. As more and more films become modern myths in our time, I believe it is a natural progression to look at certain films as derivations of myths. More and more screenwriters are being influenced by the mythological concept and approach; therefore, the screenplay's functionality reciprocates the functions of myths. Myths are stories and images that have metaphors and meanings, and a good story well told in a film also contains metaphors and meanings, touching the hearts and minds of the audience.

In this chapter, I'll discuss the four functions of myth as outlined by Joseph Campbell: metaphysical/mystical, cosmological, sociological, and psychological/

pedagogical. I briefly spoke about the fourth and final function of myth in Chapter 2, "Character," to support how character transformation serves as a pedagogical function.

Campbell describes the four functions as follows.

Metaphysical/Mystical Function

> First is the metaphysical function. Myth awakens and supports a sense of awe before the mystery of being. It reconciles consciousness to the preconditions of its own existence. Myth induces a realization that behind the surface phenomenology of the world, there is a transcendent mystery source. Through this vitalizing mystical function, the universe becomes a holy picture.

Campbell speaks about metaphysical function, also known as the mystical function, as an experience that helps us make sense of what is theoretical and conceptual. Basically, stories have allowed us to see the beauty and ugliness of our existence. They help us to realize the order of things, see what makes the world go around, and allow us to understand what's beneath the surface of our existence. The line, "It [the mystical function] reconciles consciousness to the preconditions of its own existence," explains how the mystical function of the myth helps us become aware of who we are and the conditions of life. A film whose theme is "love can transcend time" speaks about a precondition existing in love, by showing how love is not conditioned by time. For example, in the sci-fi film *Interstellar*, a father's love for his daughter helps him to complete his space mission. When Cooper and his daughter, Murph, meet for the first time after several decades, they rejoice; this is the moment they both were waiting for. For all those years they were apart, they were connected through love and not time. The mystical function helps us realize and validate the preconditions of our existence.

Cosmological Function

> The second is a cosmological dimension that deals with the image of the world that is the focus of science. This function shows the shape of the universe, but in such a way that the mystery still comes through. The cosmology should correspond to the actual experience, knowledge, and mentality of the culture. This interpretive function changes radically over time. It presents a map or picture of the order of the cosmos and our relationship to it.

The cosmological function of the myth helps us experience the different images of the world, including its cultures and traditions, and how everything fits together. The cosmological function shows how the universe is interconnected and interdependent. It helps us experience inclusiveness and exclusiveness as we identify with the world. Each of our lives is an integral part of this world, and each of us matters as much as everything else that makes up this universe. Thus, the cosmological function explains how everything comes together. For example, *The Trial of the Chicago* 7 (2020), written and directed by Aaron Sorkin, is a film about antiwar movements in the late 1960s. It clearly displays a world in which the story is taking place. In the 1960s, the U.S. government sends troops to Vietnam. The story focuses on antiwar demonstrators.

Sociological Function

> Third is the sociological function. Myth supports and validates the specific moral order of the society out of which it arose. Particular life-customs of this social dimension, such as ethical laws and social roles, evolve dramatically. This function, and the rites by which it is rendered, establishes in members of the group concerned a system of sentiments that can be depended upon to link that person spontaneously to its ends.

The sociological function helps us experience a specific social dimension and social order. The sociological function helps us establish social norms, moral codes, ethical guidelines, rules and laws, including political and cultural settings, and social guidelines. To continue with the same example, *The Trial of the Chicago* 7, the story concerns the social disorder that occurs when a particular group is against the government's political agenda.

Psychological/Pedagogical Function

> The fourth function of myth is psychological. The myths show how to live a human lifetime under any circumstances. It is this pedagogical function of mythology that carries the individual through the various stages and crises of life, from childhood dependency, to the responsibilities of maturity, to the reflection of old age, and finally, to death. It helps people grasp the unfolding of life with integrity. It initiates individuals into the order of realities in their own psyches, guiding them toward enrichment and realization.

A myth's psychological/pedagogical function is designed to relay wisdom and offer guidelines that lead to wisdom. Myths teach us how to live well, and they help us through the different stages of life. Campbell has said that the psychological function is the most important function of a myth.

In summary, the first function, the *metaphysical/mystical function*, helps the audience connect with the film's theme and premise. The second, the *cosmological function*, helps the audience experience the world of the story and how a character fits in with this world. The third, the *sociological function*, helps the audience experience the rules of engagement, the sociopolitical–sociocultural settings and norms. The fourth, the *psychological/pedagogical function*, helps the audience experience a psychological enrichment or helps them to gain a specific type of wisdom.

A film is essentially a story, and a screenplay is a story description composed of scenes, descriptions, and dialogues. A film is the final visualization of the story, produced from a screenplay. Now, whatever our reasons are for craving stories and watching films, the stories in films have significant value to each of us. We demand visual stories; therefore, films exist. There is something at large that we are getting in return from the films.

Screenplays cover a wide range of subjects, topics, themes, and premise, and they are categorized into genres. A well-developed screenplay will provide a *cathartic* experience for the audience. *Catharsis* refers to the cleansing and purification of emotions, a relief from repressed emotions, or accepting a new set of emotions. When the audience is deciding what film to watch, essentially, they are choosing the type of experiences they want to have for the next two hours. If someone has had a long day and wants something low-key and humorous, they might watch a comedy instead of a heavy drama. If they are on a date, perhaps they'll choose a romantic comedy instead of a war film. Regardless of the genre, stories in the screenplay have *story elements*. Each of the story elements has a specific function in a screenplay.

Now, without any one of the story elements, the screenplay will feel incomplete. The audience may or may not pinpoint the missing or underdeveloped elements, but they will know something is not working in the film. We've all watched films where the story feels flat. It constantly breaks the suspension of disbelief, we can't engage with the character, or it doesn't have a cohesive ending – that's because the story elements are not working properly. Story elements on their own are just components of stories; they need to work together to create the whole story. What makes a story great is the creative use of the story elements.

STORY ELEMENTS

The definition of *story elements* will vary depending on where you are hearing it. Certain books have their own definition of what these elements are, and different methods of screenwriting teaching may call for different elements. The story elements listed in this chapter are commonly used dramatic elements discussed in the screenwriting community, and they are the common phases the protagonists go through in screenplays.

These elements can help us break down the story in a screenplay: a *Protagonist* encounters an *Inciting Incident*, which evokes an *Objective*, a want and a need. The protagonist's objective raises the *Main Tension* for the story (film). The protagonist takes *Action*, fights *Conflict*, and confronts a *Crisis*, overcomes challenges to attain their objective and the journey leads to a story *Climax*. The final confrontation between the protagonist and antagonist provides an *Answer to the Main Tension*, and the journey concludes with a *Resolution*.

STORY ELEMENTS

1. Protagonist
2. Inciting Incident

 3. Objective
 4. Main Tension
 5. Action
 6. Conflict
 7. Crisis
 8. Climax
 9. Answer to the Main Tension
10. Resolution

Protagonist

Characters and story are inseparable. Stories can only be told with characters, and characters only exist within the story. A character acts and reacts within the boundaries set by the story. As discussed earlier, the story elements are phases the protagonist goes through in a given story, so it would be in our interest to get to know the protagonist. When you are about to read a screenplay with the intent of analyzing it, make sure to pay extra attention to the protagonist, and to get to know their characteristics and traits (physical, psychological, and social), their professional, personal, and private lives and personas, their objective in the story, the actions they take, their *internal* and *external conflicts*, who helps and who is in the way, and how the protagonist transforms at the end of the screenplay.

As discussed in the last chapter, the protagonist has two functions in a screenplay. The first is to drive the story forward and the second is to connect with the audience. The character's first function in a screenplay is to drive the narrative forward with story elements. When the protagonist is in their *ordinary world* in the first act, they encounter an *inciting incident* that evokes their desire for a want and a need – an *objective*. As the protagonist begins the journey of accomplishing the objective, the protagonist's *want* and *need* create the *main tension*, the story's spine, or the story's through-line: "Can the protagonist achieve their objective?" As the protagonist navigates toward the goal in the second act, they take *action*, but they are confronted by the antagonist, who opposes or hinders the protagonist's pursuit. The protagonist must overcome *conflicts* and *crisis* to achieve the *objective*. As the protagonist enters the third act, they get closer to attaining the *objective*. There is a final confrontation. The *climax* is where the protagonist defeats or is defeated by the antagonist, which provides the *answer to the main tension*: yes, the protagonist achieved their *objective*, fulfilling the *want* and *need*, or no, the protagonist didn't attain their goal. One way or another, in a traditional screenplay, the main tension is answered. The aftermath from the *climax* leads the protagonist to a *resolution*. As the protagonist returns to the *ordinary world* in the third act, there is a *character transformation*. In most screenplays, the character's transformation is one of the final stages of the character's journey. The experience from this journey helps the protagonist realize something different about themself. This realization has a psychological significance, transforming the character.

The character's second function is to connect with the audience. The connection comes from the audience understanding who the character is, realizing the situation they are in, and empathizing with their goals. The protagonist must provoke a strong emotional and psychological response from the audience, and to achieve that, the screenwriters must reveal every aspect of the protagonist's life pertaining to the story. In setting up the story, the screenwriters give the protagonist an *objective* to accomplish, and they raise the stakes by connecting the *objective* with the protagonist's personal interests. Therefore, the protagonist has a lot to lose if the *objectives* are not met. The protagonist knows what is at stake — knowing the stakes adds urgency and immediacy to the goals they set out to achieve.

Inciting Incident

The name of this story element, "*inciting incident*," gives away what needs to happen during this phase of the story. It is an incident that fuels the story — an incident in which the protagonist gets ideas to attain a goal or an objective. During this incident, something happens that provokes and awakens the main character's desire to achieve something. Through the inciting incident, the protagonist's *objectives* are established.

The *inciting incident* sets the story in motion and hooks the audience. In *Interstellar*, the *inciting incident* starts during a sandstorm. When Cooper, the protagonist, and Murph, his daughter, return from a baseball game, they discover sand lines forming on Murph's bedroom floor. The sand lines happen to be map coordinates. This supernatural phenomenon raises more questions in the audience's mind. It makes them curious: Who is sending the sign? Why? How? There is a hook and a reason to follow Cooper on his journey through the first act. When Cooper arrives at the coordinates, we discover that he has arrived at a secret NASA base, and he reunites with Professor Brand, a former mentor. Cooper doesn't know who sent the map coordinates, but he refers to whoever sent the map coordinates as "they," and the mystery is explained later in the film. Professor Brand is surprised to see Cooper as well, and explains that NASA is about to launch a mission to save mankind, and he wants Cooper to lead it. Now, as Cooper learns the Earth is becoming uninhabitable, his wants and needs are to find a habitable planet for his children, as well as for mankind.

There is a difference between only knowing what the protagonist wants in a story and knowing why they want it. It is very important for the audience to witness the inception of the protagonist's desire for the objective. If they know how the want and need were conceived, they are that much more invested in the protagonist's journey. The audience knows why they are after the objective they desire. It helps to justify the protagonist's *actions*. Let's say our protagonist, Joe, wants to learn how to ride a motorcycle — this is his new objective. It's a dangerous hobby, and his immediate family members are against the idea. But perhaps that's because they don't know why Joe wants to learn. The idea of wanting to ride a motorcycle must have come from somewhere, right? So, how did Joe conceive the idea? The answer to this question is the *inciting incident*. Joe's father was a motorcycle racer. Before he passed away, he left Joe his favorite ride: a 1972 Ducati Cafe Racer. When Joe discovers that his father has left him the motorcycle, he wants to share the feelings his father experienced while riding it. Joe wants to learn and wants to take it out for a spin for this specific reason. Now, Joe's immediate family members might come along on his journey, regardless of the risk, because they are emotionally invested in Joe's objective. The same goes for the audience: if they know why the protagonist wants something, they might be more understanding of their needs and emotionally engaged with their objective. The protagonist's *objectives* can be simple, and the reason for wanting the *objective* can be personal, as long as the *inciting incident* clearly presents a reason for wanting to attain the *objective*. The *objective* alone cannot justify the protagonist's *actions*. The audience needs to see the reasons behind the pursuit of the goal.

One of the best ways to find the *inciting incident* in a story is to define the *protagonist's objective* – also known as the *want* and *need*. Consider when the protagonist conceived the idea for the objective. In *Interstellar*, Cooper's objective is to save mankind and his children's lives. Now, what made Cooper desire this goal, and when did he begin to want it? It all started when he saw the sand lines on Murph's bedroom floor. This *inciting incident* led him to travel to NASA and meet Professor Brand.

Another important reason to identify the *inciting incident* is to learn about the protagonist's *characteristics and traits*. Knowing what the *inciting incident* helps the audience to justify the character's *actions* in the screenplay. The *inciting incident* evokes the character's *objective*, and the occurrence itself tells us who the character is. In *Interstellar*, the *inciting incident* shows us that Cooper was an astronaut in the past, and it also reveals his love for his family.

The *inciting incident* takes place at the beginning stages of a screenplay, normally within the first part of the first act. If you submit a screenplay to competitions, normally, the organizers require you to send in the first 10–15 pages and not the entire screenplay. If the readers or the judges like the first 10–15 pages, you'll pass on to the next round, where they'll ask you for the entire screenplay. They want to know if the story grabs their attention within the first sequence. Also, have you ever turned off a movie after watching the beginning? If the answer is yes, then the film you were watching didn't grab your attention.

Through the *inciting incident*, the screenwriter makes the first emotional connection with the audience. Before this incident is revealed in a screenplay, everything is about exposition, character introduction, introducing the setting, and establishing relationships, as there is no emotional connection to the character. The screenwriter knows the importance of presenting the *inciting incident* as soon as possible and in an interesting manner.

The *inciting incident* can occur within a scene or a series of scenes. For example, the *inciting incident* in *The Matrix* takes place when Neo, the protagonist, meets Trinity for the first time. To make this encounter seem natural, the screenwriters set up a scene where Neo wakes up in front of a computer in the middle of the night. The monitor turns itself on, and a message tells Neo to follow the white rabbit. Moments later, Neo opens the front door to some partygoers who have stopped by to buy a hacked program from Neo. They invite Neo to a party. Neo sees a white rabbit tattoo on one of the women, and Neo accepts their invitation. At the party, Neo meets Trinity for the first time. Trinity warns Neo that he's being watched, and she fuels his desire to know what the Matrix is, which leads him to meet Morpheus. The first encounter between Neo and Trinity provides a lot of information, but there are more questions than answers. This *inciting incident* awakens the *protagonist's objective*: Neo's *want* and *need* is to learn more about the Matrix, a simulated reality.

Objectives

The *objectives* in the story element overlap with the *objectives* from the character studies from the last chapter. The only difference is that we mainly speak of the protagonist's objectives when we refer to story elements. Let's revisit some of the attributes of the protagonist's *objectives*.

The protagonist's *want* and *need* is what drives the story forward in a screenplay. In the first act, the protagonist's wants and needs are revealed through an *inciting incident*. For example, Neo wants to learn more about the Matrix. At the beginning of the second act, the protagonist embarks on a journey to achieve the goal. The question that is raised at the end of the first act is the *main tension*: Can the main character achieve their objectives? This question creates a dramatic tension for the audience and is the spine of the story, the main tension that keeps the audience captive and engaged.

The story in a screenplay mimics life. A goal, an objective, a task, a challenge, or a mission can be described as the *want* and *need* of a character in the story. It's not surprising that the character's *want* and *need* are one of the most important story elements in a screenplay. In the protagonist's pursuit of their *objective*, they will face their greatest fear or weakness, and they will have to overcome it to confront the antagonist in the climax.

The *objective* in the story is important because the *want* provides a personal goal and the *need* provides an inner desire. The *want* drives the story, and the *need* drives the theme of the story. The *want* provides a character transformation, and the *need* provides a character's emotional transformation. The *want* can be unique to each story, but the *need* has universal truth.

The protagonist's main *objective* can come from their work/professional life, family/personal life, or secret/private life. It all depends on the story they are telling, but the screenwriter knows how to intertwine the main *objective* with different aspects of the protagonist's life. When studying the protagonist's *objective*, analyze the main *objective* first, and then see how the secondary *objectives* are intertwined with the main *objective*. In *The Dark Knight*, Batman's main objective of protecting

Gotham City is intertwined with the *objectives* in his personal and private lives. Bruce's main *objective* is to catch the Joker, but he also *wants* to retire Batman (a personal life objective), and he *wants* to be with Rachel (a private life objective). As the audience starts to care about all aspects of the character's life, they connect that much more with the protagonist and their goals.

Main Tension

Often referred to as "dramatic tension," the *main tension* is the central question that is raised based on the protagonist's *want* and *need*. The *main tension* will carry the audience's curiosity through the second act as the protagonist pursues their goal. Can Batman catch the Joker to bring peace and harmony back to Gotham City? Can Shrek save Princess Fiona? Can Lady Bird go to college on the East Coast? Can Woody become Andy's favorite toy again? As the protagonist embarks on their journey to attain the objective in the second act, the *main tension* rises.

The *main tension*, the through-line, or the spine of the story, all refer to the same question: Can the protagonist achieve their goal? This question becomes subconsciously or consciously embedded in the audience's mind as the protagonist enters the second act. If the *inciting incident* provided the first emotional connection with the character, the question that is raised from the *main tension* is the second emotional connection the audience makes with the protagonist. If the screenwriter doesn't have your attention by this point, you will lose interest in the story for good. The great storytellers make us care for the protagonist's *objective*, and the screenwriters make us empathize with them and cheer for them on their journey. We want them to succeed, to win that championship fight, to cross the finish line, or to destroy the opponent.

We often hear the term "setup" – for example, a story setup, or the first-act setup. The term "setup" refers to the protagonist's introduction, and the *inciting incident* that provokes the protagonist's *objective*, which leads to the *main tension* as the protagonist enters the second act. Often, when screenwriters find problems with the third act (the *resolution*), they revisit the first act. When the ending is weak or vague, a seasoned screenwriter knows the problems with the third act come from the first act. If the character's *objective* is vague, the *main tension* becomes unclear, the third act will feel flat and underdeveloped.

The *main tension* has to grab the audience's interest. The *objectives* can be as grandiose as Cooper's efforts to save mankind or as personal as Lady Bird wanting to go to college on the East Coast. As long as the audience is in a position to identify with the protagonist's *objective*, they will go along the journey with the protagonist.

Now, how do we identify the *main tension* in a story? Usually, the *main tension* is introduced to the audience at the end of the first act. There is an occurrence or event where there is a moment of departure: the start of a road trip, an airplane taking off, the beginning of a semester, a boat sailing, an arrival at a girlfriend's parents' house. Or the moment of departure can be more psychological, such as starting a new job or a new relationship. As the story moves the protagonist from the first act to the second act, the audience asks the question, "Can the protagonist achieve the goal?" The *main tension* is not something the protagonist says, but it is a question the audience raises in their minds.

Actions

The *main tension* has been established based on the protagonist's *objective*. Now, the natural story progression is for the character to go after the objective by taking *action*. To act based on one's belief takes willpower. It takes conviction and requires motivation and justification. Every action the protagonist takes has a reason, and it leads to the pursuit of their goal, whether it's the act of preparing for a final exam, or the act of climbing to reach Mount Everest's summit. The *actions* are motivated by *objectives*, and the action itself is a proclamation and a manifestation to attain the *objective*. For example, climbing to the summit of the tallest mountain is an item on the protagonist's bucket list. Action derives from a desire to attain something one has set out to achieve.

We need to study the protagonist's main *action* to understand the degree to which the protagonist desires the *objective*. During the first act, the protagonist has realized their *want* and *need*. The second act follows the protagonist as they pursue their *objective* through a series of *actions*. The audience is still getting to know the characters throughout the second act. As the screenwriter reveals their *actions* in attaining their *objectives*, many of their *characteristics* and *traits* will be exposed throughout the second act. In *Whiplash*, Andrew's action is to learn as much as possible and practice until his fingers bleed to impress Fletcher and stay in his band. Andrew wants to become a great jazz drummer, and even breaks up with his girlfriend to dedicate more time to his music.

The protagonist always takes a noticeable *action*. As their life is altered, their *objectives* cause them to take *action* outside of their comfort zone. In the second act, the protagonist's *actions* take them into an extraordinary world. In *Mad Max: Fury Road*, Furiosa takes action to save the young wives from the tyrant ruler Immortan Joe by taking her War Rig, a powerful truck, on a 90-degree turn aborting the mission of delivering aqua-cola to Gas Town and going off-road into hostile territory – an *action* that indicates her will to escape from the clan. It is a clear and decisive action.

In *The Matrix*, when Neo first meets Morpheus, Neo is presented with a choice: take the red pill or the blue pill. The red pill will lead to a life-changing truth, and the blue pill will keep him in his blissful ignorant state. Neo takes a clear *action*, choosing the red pill. He enters the real world and gives up the simulated world. Neo's *action* of taking the red pill takes him to his journey of exploring the Matrix in the beginning of the second act.

In *Get Out*, the first meeting between Chris and Rose's parents takes place as the second act begins. Because Chris's initial *objective* in the story is to make a good impression and spend quality time with Rose and her family, Chris takes *action* to get to know Rose's family. Chris goes on a house tour with Rose's father, Dean Armitage. He attends the family dinner. Chris willingly meets and greets the guests who have come to the party in honor of Rose's grandfather. The protagonist takes action to attain his *objective*.

Actions are louder than words. Great characters rarely say what they will do; instead, they take *action*. A character's intentions are better perceived when the audience witnesses their desire to achieve the *objective* through *actions*.

Conflicts

Conflicts keep the audience engaged with the story. As the *main tension* of the screenplay becomes apparent in the audience's minds, screenwriters keep fueling the *main tension* with *conflicts* in the second act. As the protagonist takes *action* to attain the goal, the antagonist presents difficulties and challenges to keep the protagonist from achieving their *objective*. The stronger the main *conflict* between the two main characters, the stronger the *main tension*. And the stronger the *main tension* is in the story, the more the audience will empathize with the protagonist. The more the audience connects with the protagonist, the stronger the psychological experience they will have.

One of the functions of *conflict* in a screenplay is to reveal a character's psychological attributes. The *conflict* always exposes the character's motivation and desire to accomplish the goal. At times, when plotting a screenplay, screenwriters think of ways to put the character in the worst possible situation within the context of the story. The writers themselves may not know how to get the character out of the situation at first. The writers will think of a way to get them out of the situation convincingly, and thus present the character's willingness, drive, and other inner characteristics that define them. Another function of *conflict* in a screenplay is to help drive the story forward. If the character doesn't have opposition, challenges, or obstacles to overcome, the story becomes lifeless, and the audience becomes disengaged from the film. If the protagonist gets what they *want* and *need* without *conflict*, it wouldn't be a story.

As discussed in the last chapter, *conflicts* are anything that get in the way of the protagonist achieving the *objective*. In addition to the main *conflict* with the antagonist, there are smaller conflicts – the everyday conflicts hindering the pursuit of their goal. There are *conflicts* the protagonist has control over, relies on others to help with, or are simply beyond their control. Usually, the protagonist confronts two types of *conflicts*: *external conflict* and *internal conflict*.

External conflicts are the types of conflict the character has no control over. They are divided into two major categories: *character vs. character* and *character vs. environment*.

Character vs. character is the most common type of *external conflict* in a screenplay: the conflict that arises between characters. As the protagonist embarks on a journey, the antagonist is always in the way of achieving their goals. An antagonist is someone who desires the same goal as the protagonist, or is on the opposite side of the fight. At times, the villains are stronger than the hero or heroine, and the circumstances always seem to favor the antagonist. For the protagonist, it can always feel that the odds are against him. The reason for setting the drama within this paradigm is to test the protagonist's will, integrity, dignity, or any other inner traits pertaining to the story.

A *character vs. environment* type of conflict arises from the challenging conditions in which the character must operate within the story. Depending on the conditions, "environment" can mean Mother Nature, opposing points of view within society, a supernatural force, cultural differences, or a language barrier. *Character vs. environment* describes the protagonist's conflict with their surroundings, which hinders them from achieving their *objectives*.

An *internal conflict* is also known as a *character vs. self* conflict. An internal conflict occurs when two opposing wants, needs, or beliefs coexist within the self. The opposing motivations pull the character in two different directions, affecting the character's psychology and creating the character's inner dilemma. More often than not, the protagonist's *inner conflict* is revealed to the audience during the first act, between the *inciting incident* and the protagonist's pursuit of their goals. It may be a split-second decision, or it may take several scenes, but the *inner conflict* is there before they embark on the journey to achieve their goals in the second act. The same *inner conflict* may return and cause the protagonist to question their "character" during the second act. Generally, with some exception, when the protagonist's willpower is tested, when the fight becomes tougher, when there is nowhere to run or hide, the protagonist falls into self-doubt. This usually takes place at the midpoint of the screenplay or during the *crisis*. As the protagonist presents their resilience or cowardice, the *inner conflict* helps to define the *character transformation* and *emotional arc* at the end of the screenplay.

The protagonist's *inner conflict* is another psychological attribute that can make them appeal to the audience. The protagonist's *inner conflicts* help to reveal the character's psychological traits. If the audience can identify with the character's *inner conflict*, they can easily empathize with the protagonist's *objective* and become psychologically invested in the character and their journey. The *inner conflicts* help define the character's *worldview*, *characteristics*, and *traits*, which are important to the story and the *character's transformation*.

When analyzing the conflicts in a screenplay, we first need to identify the actual conflicts, then study how they are presented to the protagonist, how they affect the protagonist, and how the protagonist solves the conflict.

The term *unity of opposites* means that there is no compromise between the two main characters' objectives. In *The Dark Knight*, the main *conflict* is the fight between the Joker and Batman. They each want different things – a perfect example of the *unity of opposites*. The Joker wants chaos, and Batman wants order. The *conflicts* reveal information about the characters and story. Without conflict, we wouldn't have known how much Bruce Wayne loves Rachel. And without Rachel's death,

Harvey Dent would never convert into a villain. Without conflict, we wouldn't know how much Bruce cares for Gotham City.

The *unity of opposites* between the Joker and Batman is so strong that it can only be broken when one of the characters is emotionally and/or physically transformed at the end. The Joker goes from a villain to a prisoner. Comprehending the *unity of opposites* in a screenplay can help reveal the points of view of the world of both the protagonist and the antagonist and help you understand what the *conflict* is really about in the story.

Crisis

The *crisis* is sometimes referred to as *the midpoint crisis*. As the protagonist takes action to achieve the goal, they are confronted by *conflicts* and tough circumstances. Things will start to get worse before they get better. As the *conflicts* mount, the story moves the protagonist into a *crisis*. A *crisis* can come in many forms, but it usually makes the protagonist confront their worst fear or weakness. During the *crisis*, it feels as though the antagonist is gaining control of the situation, and the protagonist is pushed into a corner. They may also lose an important companion, or experience something drastic, which causes them to question the completion of the journey. The *crisis* tests the protagonist's willpower to complete their *objective* and their desire to attain the goal. Therefore, their *internal conflict* is revealed once again, and the way they act during the *crisis* helps to define their *characteristics* and *traits*.

The *crisis* results in the protagonist's realization of the self. There is a self-reflective moment at the end of the screenplay as the protagonist returns to the ordinary world. The protagonist will have an epiphany, depending on the intensity of the fight or the struggle. So, in shaping the protagonist's character arc, the *conflicts* and the *crisis* play an important function.

During the *crisis*, the presence of the antagonist is strong, because the antagonist is strongly motivated to achieve their own goals and imposes a strong challenge to the protagonist. A great antagonist is a master at spotting the protagonist's weaknesses and attacking where it hurts the most. The antagonist knows when to attack, putting the protagonist in a disadvantaged and vulnerable position.

Because the audience is going on an emotional journey with the protagonist, reaching the lowest emotional point is an important stage of the protagonist's storyline, and we must study how the *crisis* psychologically affects the protagonist. In *The Dark Knight*, the *crisis* occurs when the Joker's men kidnap Rachel and Harvey, and Batman has time to save only one of them. He chooses to save Rachel, but when he gets there, he finds Harvey. The Joker has switched addresses on purpose. You never get straight answers from the Joker. This is a *crisis* for Bruce Wayne, because Rachel dies and Harvey transforms into a villain, ruining his personal and private *objectives*. Bruce not only loses the woman he loves, but loses the future he could have had with her.

In *Whiplash*, the *crisis* occurs when Andrew arrives late to a jazz band competition, has an argument with Fletcher, and doesn't have his drum sticks to go onstage. Andrew is determined to keep the lead drummer seat and rushes to get the drumsticks he left behind at a car rental place. On the way back, Andrew gets into a car accident. Andrew, hurt from the car crash, still has his heart set on keeping the lead drummer's seat, leaving the accident scene to make it to the stage on time. Andrew's willpower to get to the concert hall is so strong that he is willing to endure the shock and pain from the accident. Andrew's abnormal behavior clearly shows how psychologically unstable he is. Bleeding and in pain, Andrew sits on the drummer's seat. As the band starts to play, Andrew seems to keep up with the song, but soon enough, he falls apart. His body can't take it, he can barely hold the drumsticks, and finally, he gives up. He stops playing. To make matters worse, Fletcher comes over and tells Andrew that he is "done." Andrew kicks the drum in front of him and goes after Fletcher, tackling and punching him.

The *crisis* puts the protagonist in a position to make a choice, and they have to make an important decision: to continue with their journey or give up. Usually, in a screenplay, the protagonist decides to continue, and they take action to overcome the *crisis*. During this stage of the screenplay, the protagonist gathers their strength. They reflect on the past and learn something about themself. During the *crisis*, they must confront their greatest fear or weakness and grow, mature, or realize something about themself. Now, overcoming the *crisis* helps define their new self. During this stage of the screenplay, the protagonist regroups for the final push toward their goal.

In *The Dark Knight*, after Rachel's death, Bruce grieves. In this scene, there is a voice-over of Rachel reading the letter she left for Bruce. At the last minute, Alfred decides to hide the letter from Bruce. Alfred makes this decision in order to protect Bruce's memories of Rachel, as the letter speaks about Rachel rejecting Bruce's offer and her plans to marry Harvey Dent. To overcome the *crisis* of losing Rachel and continue with his main objective, Batman must find the Joker and stop him from harming the people of Gotham. The death of Rachel pushes him to take action that goes against his moral and ethical code. In an attempt to capture the Joker, Batman decides to use the latest sonar technology as a last resort to locate the Joker. He accesses every mobile phone in Gotham City and invades the privacy of millions of civilians to track down the Joker's whereabouts. His *actions* are clear: Batman's main *objective* is stronger than his moral and ethical codes. Batman overcomes the *crisis* and confronts the antagonist one last time.

In *Whiplash*, the *crisis* is Andrew getting into a car accident, going onstage but being unable to perform, and tackling Fletcher when he loses control of the situation. What happens next in the screenplay? Andrew chooses to undermine Fletcher and make him accountable for his abusive behavior. Furthermore, Andrew is dismissed from school and puts his drum in a closet. He overcomes the *crisis* by trying to find normalcy in his life. Then Andrew sees Fletcher performing in a jazz bar. Andrew overcomes challenges from the *crisis* by reconciling with Fletcher. Andrew agrees to play with Fletcher at the JVC Jazz Festival at Carnegie Hall.

Overcoming challenges from the *crisis* helps the protagonist to regroup and prepare for the final confrontation with the antagonist: the *climax*. Seeing the protagonist go through the *crisis* and overcome it makes us think about the protagonist's *objective* one more time. The antagonist takes the protagonist to the lowest emotional point in the story; by doing so, they help the protagonist to realize the value of reaching the highest emotional point in the story. Alternatively, the antagonist takes the protagonist to the highest emotional point in the story; in doing so, they help the protagonist reach the lowest emotional point in the story at the end. It all depends on the shape of the story arc.

Climax

As we enter the third act, you'll see the story move with a faster tempo. The screenwriter has set up the story for us in the first act and developed the story in the second act, so we follow the protagonist's *actions* without much explanation. The *climax* is the final confrontation between the protagonist and the antagonist – the inevitable encounter that determines the outcome of the protagonist's pursuit.

The *climax* in *The Dark Knight* begins when Batman locates the Joker and goes to capture him. The final encounter determines the fate of the *main tension*: Can Batman catch the Joker and restore order for the citizens of Gotham City? In *Whiplash*, the *climax* takes place at the JVC Jazz Festival at Carnegie Hall. Andrew goes onstage to find out that Fletcher has switched the song. Instead of "Caravan," they play "Upswingin." Fletcher wants to take revenge on Andrew and ruin his life, and Andrew tries to improvise, but he can't. Humiliated, Andrew walks backstage. After seeing his father, Andrew goes back onstage. The final confrontation isn't over. Andrew plays the beats to "Caravan," surprising everyone. Taking the lead, he asks the band to join in. He is no longer the shy freshman who wants to be in Fletcher's band, and he won't take the humiliation and abuse from Fletcher anymore. By taking control of the situation, Fletcher is forced to follow Andrew's lead and conduct the band.

Usually, there is an event or an occurrence associated with the *climax*. In *Get Out*, it is the brain transplant between Chris and Jim Hudson, the man who won the auction. Another great example of an event during the *climax* is displayed in *Parasite* (2019). As the dramatic tension reaches its peak in the story, during the birthday party for Da-song, the wealthy family's son, all hell breaks loose on the house's front lawn. The *climax* typically takes place through an event or an occurrence that can help change the course of the protagonist's life.

The protagonist will give it all during the final confrontation. It's a do-or-die situation. The *climax* reveals the protagonist's true characteristics by showing how they deal with the antagonist. The question that arises from the *main tension*, "Can the protagonist accomplish the objective?", is answered during the *climax*. Therefore, the *answer to the main tension* generally comes from the aftermath of the climax.

Answer to the Main Tension

All the *actions* taken by the protagonist up to this point have been to achieve their *objectives*, and it all comes down to the *climax*. Most of the time, the *climax* reveals the *answer to the main tension*. The questions that get raised at the end of the first act must be answered. "Did the protagonist achieve the objective?" The *answer to the main tension* reveals the outcome of the *objective*: yes, the protagonist did achieve it, or no, the protagonist did not. For example: yes, Shrek saves Princess Fiona, and yes, Woody and Buzz are reunited with their toy friends and Andy. But no, Chris did not get to know Rose's family – he has to fight for this life.

In most instances, the outcome of the *climax* provides the audience the *answer to the main tension*. The *answer to the main tension* might be a yes or no answer, but the answer carries the protagonist's desire for the *objective*. In *The Dark Knight*, the main tension is: Can Batman catch the members of the mob, as well as the Joker, and restore order? The answer to the main tension is: Yes, Batman catches the members of the mob and the Joker. But Bruce pays a high price to attain his goal. In *Whiplash*, the answer to the main tension is: Yes, Andrew becomes a great jazz drummer.

Finding the *answer to the main tension* is relatively simple if you have correctly identified the protagonist's main *objective*. The *objective* raises the *main tension* for the screenplay, and the *climax* provides the *answer to the main tension*. Thus, knowing the main *objective* is the key to understanding the spine of the story and how the *main tension* is answered.

Resolution

The *resolution* is the final stage of the screenplay and the ending of the story. It lays out the aftermath of the *climax* and the entire journey. Regardless of the outcome, the protagonist is affected by the experience, causing them to have realized something different about themself, about life, and/or about the world they are living in.

In the *resolution*, screenwriters focus on three things. First, they show us how the character has transformed during the journey. Second, they give us a glimpse of what the future might hold for the protagonist from this point on – a new beginning for the protagonist. Third, all good stories tie up loose ends. This means that screenwriters conclude all the minor *objectives* or conclude subplots during the *resolution*.

In *The Dark Knight*, even after Batman attains the main objective of catching the Joker, he still has to clean up Harvey Dent's mess. Bruce's other objective of wanting to turn Harvey into a white knight needs to have a conclusion. Batman decides to take the blame for Dent's actions of killing the police officers, and project a false image of who Harvey Dent has become in order to keep him as a symbol for the citizens of Gotham City. Now, as a consequence of this action, Batman becomes an outlaw. He has to live in hiding.

Furthermore, if there are significant supporting characters with whom the audience has made a connection, they usually have an "exit" from the story. The word "exit" derives from theater – it was used to give a character a final "exit" from the stage, basically giving the character an ending in the story. Subplots have an arc of their own in relation to the main story arc, and providing closure to them will support the film's main story arc.

For example, let's look at the character Vito Corleone in *The Godfather*. He is an important character in the story. At the end, he has a final meeting with his son, Michael, where he tells him, "I never wanted this for you," indicating he regrets his son's involvement in the family business. Vito wanted Michael to be a congressman or a politician. In the next scene, he spends his last moments playing with his grandson in the tomato garden. It's a grand exit for Vito, an important character.

Another example is Dr. Brand in *Interstellar*. On the journey, she is Cooper's companion, an important supporting character. At the end, she is left behind to colonize the planet, and the screenwriter ties up this loose end by showing how she is living in isolation. The film ends with Cooper going to find her.

In the course of the story, the ending, or the *resolution*, is where the protagonist's transformation is clearly shown. In Chapter 2, "Character," we looked at the importance of the character transformation in a screenplay. During the *resolution*, the screenwriters display the final action to contrast who the protagonist was at the beginning and who the protagonist is at the end. Witnessing the protagonist's transformation, the audience makes the final emotional connection with the protagonist.

The *resolution* shows the protagonist's "new normal," a new way of life. The protagonist has been transformed, and now they have a different perception of the world. They are different from how we first saw them at the beginning of the screenplay. Psychologically, the protagonist is in a different place. The protagonist learns something about themselves, the world, or something particular about human characteristics or behavior. We, as the audience, get to indirectly experience it through their realization.

The *resolution* is the aftermath of conceiving the idea for the objective. It concludes the journey as the protagonist enters back to their ordinary life from the extraordinary world. Often, the ending is a new beginning. In some instances, it might feel like a new *inciting incident* to the protagonist.

PLOT AND SUBPLOT

More often than not, we hear the word "plot" when talking about stories, films, and screenplays. The plot consists of the situations the character faces in the story, from the opening image to the closing image. The choices and the actions the character takes have consequences and set up the next situation the character must face, and this process continues until the story comes to an end.

As the screenwriter conceives an idea for a screenplay, he or she develops a theme and premise, and then moves to the characters and story. What happens to the protagonist from the beginning to the end of the film? The screenwriter plans the protagonist's journey with a sequence of events that they must go through to reach the resolution. The plot is the series of events and situations that affect the protagonist's journey throughout the story.

One crucial fact to remember: A plot is not a story. A story in a screenplay has characters, story elements, structure, theme, premise, plot, and more. The plot is the sequence of events and situations that move the character from point A to point B.

For example, *Romeo + Juliet* (1996), a film based on William Shakespeare's romantic tragedy, was adapted by Baz Luhrmann, who co-wrote and directed the film. The film adaptation stayed true to the play's original theme, premise, and dialogue. However, what was different were the world, setting, and plot. In Shakespeare's play, the story is set in Verona, Italy, in the sixteenth century, but in Baz Luhrmann's film, it is set in Verona Beach in the present day. So the adaptation's world and setting are set in a modern city, with cars, tall buildings, roads, police, and guns. The film uses the original dialogue; the characters in this adaptation keep referring to the guns as swords. And rather than two families being at war as the backstory, in the modern-day setting, the Montagues and Capulets are two rival businesses. One other significant difference between the play and the film is in the plot. At various times, there are subtle and drastic differences. For example, in the original play, as the story reaches the climax and resolution, Romeo arrives from exile to see Juliet lying cold. Paris tries to apprehend Romeo, they fight, and Romeo kills Paris. Then Romeo finds Juliet, and believes she is dead. He takes the poison and lies next to her. Friar Laurence arrives, and Juliet awakens. She learns about Paris's and Romeo's deaths, and then stabs herself, dying next to Romeo. Now, in the 1996 film adaptation, the same sequence is plotted differently. Romeo arrives at the church, the police are after him, and they exchange gunshots before he enters and locks the church. Romeo walks down the aisle toward Juliet. He lies down next to her and gets ready to take the poison. Juliet wakes up, sees Romeo, and smiles. Without noticing Juliet, Romeo takes the poison, and during his last breath, he sees Juliet awaken. They have their final kiss. Juliet witnesses her lover's death. In the end, she takes his gun and shoots herself to be with him.

Both the play and the film arrive at the same resolution, but the way they get there is different. The ending is plotted differently. In the play, the ending has two more characters, Paris and Friar Laurence, participating in the *climax*. But in the film, they are not in the plot. Romeo doesn't kill Paris, and Friar Laurence does not come back.

Baz Luhrmann plotted an ending of *Romeo + Juliet* that was different from the original play. Why? Perhaps the filmmaker wanted to give a little twist and switch the ending to keep the modern audience captive and engaged. Or perhaps having the other two characters, Paris and Friar Laurence, in the third act could have slowed down this phase of the story. Or perhaps Luhrmann wanted the ending to be just about Romeo and Juliet. But one thing is clear: while the plots differ, they arrive at the same resolution.

Main Plot

The main plot is the main storyline of the screenplay. The main storyline is the protagonist's journey through the story. Throughout the story, the protagonist conceives the idea for their want and need, pursues their objective, and either succeeds or fails to accomplish their goal. The main plot consists of all the choices the screenwriter makes for the protagonist's journey.

Let's look at the main plot of *Parasite* (2019), co-written and directed by Bong Joon-ho. At the beginning of the story, Ki-woo is an unemployed high-school graduate living in a semi-basement apartment with his parents. By the end, he is still unemployed, living in the same apartment, but he has transformed as a character. The main plot removes any hope he had of moving up the social class ladder. The screenwriter shaped the story so that the protagonist grew and transformed. The protagonist is required to confront events and situations, and plotting does precisely that. First, the screenwriters display Ki-woo's ambition and determination to improve his financial and social status. Ki-woo lies about attending a prestigious university, and lands a tutoring job. Ki-woo's ambitions don't stop there: he helps his unemployed family members lie about their identities, and they too become employed by the Park family. His sister becomes an art therapist for the son, Ki-woo's father becomes the driver for Mr. Park, and the mother becomes the housekeeper. Ki-woo secretly develops a relationship with the high-school teenager he is tutoring and dreams of becoming the son-in-law someday. But when the old housekeeper finds out about the scam, Ki-woo and his family are pulling off, his hope is jeopardized. To take control of the situation, Ki-woo and his family use force to apprehend the old housekeeper and her husband, but everything goes wrong, and their identities are revealed during the *climax* of the film. It's an inevitable collision waiting to happen. During the *climax*, Ki-woo gets hurt, his sister is murdered, and his father kills the boss and hides from the law. At the end, Ki-woo and his mother are back in the same apartment. Ki-woo tried to move up the social ladder, but he fails. As you can see in this example, the main plot is always the protagonist's storyline.

The following exercise will help you to define the main plot. First, identify the main character and their objective, and then observe how the supporting characters help the protagonist or keep them from achieving his goals. Then define the major *conflicts* with the antagonists. Be sure to include the character's emotional arc from the beginning to the end of the story. This is a method I used when writing script coverage as an intern for the Likely Story production company. As an intern, I read screenplays sent to the production company and wrote coverage of them. Here is a sample script coverage form:

> The story is about _____ (the protagonist). He/she wants to _____ (objective) and he/she _____ (takes action) to attain the goal. The main tension of the film is: Can he/she _____ (attain the objective)? In the course of the story, _____ and _____ (supporting characters) help the protagonist by _____ (subplot). _____ (Antagonist) tries to prevent from attaining his/her goal by _____ (conflict). The protagonist and the antagonist meet for their final confrontation when _____ (climax). The final encounter results in _____ (answer to the main tension – did the protagonist attain the goal?/resolution). At the beginning of the story, he/she is _____ and by the end he/she is _____ (emotional arc).

Subplots

The subplots are all the other minor plots besides the main plot in a screenplay. Now, how do you identify the subplots in a screenplay? Subplots are sub-storylines supporting the main plot. Often subplots can be found by looking at the relationship between characters; a protagonist and the supporting characters, an antagonist and the supporting characters, or between supporting characters.

A story in a film follows a protagonist's journey, but because no man is on an island, they must interact with other characters. The subplots always either support or hinder the film's main plot. One of the subplots in *The Matrix* (1999) is Morpheus's search for the "One" who can help fight for human existence against agents with artificial intelligence. Morpheus is not the protagonist or the antagonist, but his objective becomes a subplot in the story and supports Neo's main plot of realizing he is the "One." Another subplot in this story is Cypher's betrayal. Cypher is contacted by Agent Smith and negotiates a deal to give away Neo, Morpheus, and the team. The Cypher subplot jeopardizes the protagonist's main objective. The third subplot worth mentioning is the love between Neo and Trinity. When Neo dies fighting the agents during the climax, Trinity's love for Neo helps to resurrect him. These subplots all support the cause of Neo realizing he is the "One" who helps humanity's fight against the machine – the main plot.

4

STRUCTURE

The narrative structure comprises a beginning, a middle, and an end. As rudimentary as the three parts may seem, numerous screenwriting publications define screenplay structure. There are many different interpretations of how the structure ought to be set up in a screenplay. Each variation takes a unique approach, but there are commonalities when the authors discuss narrative structure. Generally, it is understood that the basic underlying principle of screenplay structure is the three-act structure.

To create the story they want to tell, screenwriters need structure. To be more specific, screenwriters need a narrative structure to lay out their premises in a story-based format. A premise is a high-level idea of what the story is about. The premise becomes the foundation of the screenplay structure, and the story is developed from this foundation. But a premise is a premise, and not a story. The storyteller uses imagination to develop a story that resonates with the theme and the premise. If a hundred writers take this same theme and premise and write a story, we will get a hundred different stories.

When writers develop screenplays, they know the structure is an important narrative element. They know the importance of a solid beginning: the first act has to grab the audience's attention and make them curious about the protagonist and their objective. The middle – the second act – must engage the audience with dramatic tension as the protagonist encounters conflicts and crisis in pursuing their goal. By engaging with the dramatic tension, the audience empathizes with the ups and downs of the character's journey. The end – the third act – takes the audience to the climax and the resolution of the story. The screenwriter applies narrative structure to make the audience feel something for the protagonist and their journey, and transmits an emotional experience via the protagonist's realization of the self at the end of the screenplay.

DOI: 10.4324/9781003138853-6

THREE-ACT STRUCTURE

Good storytellers know how the audience will perceive the story in every moment of the screenplay. They know the information the audience has at every moment of the story. Screenwriters know how to guide the audience's expectations; they know when to withhold and when to release character and plot information to generate an emotional reaction. Some screenwriters rely heavily on the structure to convey ideas in a screenplay, and others allow the structure to fall into place as they develop an idea for a story. In the film *Eternal Sunshine of the Spotless Mind* (2004), written by Charlie Kaufman, the screenplay's structure is noticeable in the film, as the story jumps back and forth between timelines, the structure plays a major role in engaging the audience. However, in a film like *Amour* (2012), written and directed by Michael Haneke, the screenplay's structure is not as obvious and hides behind the story, as the drama of the story drives the screenplay.

Ancient Greek playwrights used this same narrative form to structure their plays; it might have been a five- or seven-act structure, but the principles are very similar to our modern three-act structure. The three-act structure is the most basic narrative structure used in films. When someone reads, hears, or watches a story, they know what to expect, because they are accustomed to this conventional way of comprehending a story.

Every story is unique. Therefore, every story's structure is uniquely shaped. However, the commonality among all screenplays is the protagonist's action pattern, which helps us differentiate the three-act structure in every screenplay. The character's action pattern consists of three parts. One, the protagonist conceives the idea for an objective in the first act. Two, the protagonist pursues the objective in the second act. Three, the protagonist transforms in the aftermath of pursuing the objective in the third act.

The first act shows the protagonist's ordinary world. Here is where they are most comfortable. In an inciting incident, the protagonist finds an objective, a desire to pursue a goal, and gets ready to embark on their journey. Most often, there is an event or occurrence at the end of the first act, and the story is set in motion. The first act introduces all the major characters and establishes their relationships. Furthermore, it establishes the world and the specific sociocultural setting of the story.

The first act sets up the drama that will unfold in the second act. It must establish a through-line, which will have to carry the story all the way to the resolution in the third act. The first act is important because it has to have all the dramatic elements in place. Therefore, when writers are having difficulties concluding a story, they often revisit the first act to align the dramatic elements and set them up to reshape the story for the desired ending.

The second act normally begins with the protagonist taking the first steps toward the goal. Therefore, in the transition between the first act and the second act, there is always a bus leaving, a plane taking off, a door opening, the beginning of a new semester, an arrival at a new place, or the start of a mission. The start of the protagonist's pursuit of their objective is always shown through actions. For example, in *Little Miss Sunshine* (2006), the entire Hoover family hops on the Volkswagen minibus to drive Olive to the beauty pageant. The protagonist is pushed out of their comfort zone and enters the extraordinary world in the second act. This extraordinary world is a world the protagonist is not familiar with. In *Whiplash*, Andrew enters Fletcher's rehearsal room for the first time. In *Get Out*, Chris meets Rose's parents and enters the Armitage house.

As the protagonist enters the extraordinary world in the second act, the main tension is raised in the audience's mind: "Can the protagonist achieve the goal?" Can Andrew become a great jazz drummer in *Whiplash*? Can Chris make a good impression and spend quality time with Rose and her family in *Get Out*? The story evolves in the second act until it reaches the climax. In this extraordinary world, the protagonist confronts external and internal conflict and a crisis. Here is where their will is tested and challenged, and in most stories, the protagonist has to have overcome their greatest fear or weakness to confront the antagonist one last time during the climax.

The third act is where the protagonist confronts the antagonist a final time. In the climax, the protagonist wins or loses, the verdict is out, and the answer to the main tension is revealed. Yes, Cooper helps to solve the gravity equation, extending human existence. Yes, Andrew becomes a great jazz drummer. The third act ends with a resolution. The protagonist is back in their ordinary world, but they are no longer same person. The journey has transformed them. Lastly, during the third act, screenwriters tie up all the loose ends. Subplots may need to be resolved, or if some of the supporting characters' through-line needs a conclusion, it will take place in the third act. A subplot must have a beginning, a middle, and an end, just like the main plot.

Three-Act Structure and Story Elements

Now, how do we analyze the three-act structure? How do we know when the first act ends? How do you know when the second act begins? In plays, changes between acts are clearly defined and shown to the audience; as the stage lights fade to black, the audience is informed of the act change. Some screenwriters use "Fade to Black" and "Fade In" as transitions to differentiate between acts. The film *King Kong* (2005), directed by Peter Jackson, uses "Fade to Black" to end the first act and "Fade In" at the beginning of the second act, and, again, "Fade to Black" at the end of the second act and "Fade In" at the beginning of the third act. Now, seeing act transitions in a screenplay are rare. Most screenwriters don't mark the transition when they go from one act to the next. Therefore, we have to look for clues, and the clues are in the protagonist's action pattern. As most films follow the protagonist's journey through the three different acts, we can differentiate the acts by first finding the protagonist's dramatic need, the objective. Second, we can break down the protagonist's action of going after the objective, while confronting and overcoming their greatest fear or weakness. Third, we see the protagonist's transformation from the pursuit of the objective. Now, for the purposes of script analysis, let's divide the 10 story elements we went over in Chapter 3, "Story," into acts.

The First Act

The PROTAGONIST
Via/because of an INCITING INCIDENT
Finds/evokes an OBJECTIVE, a want, and a need
The MAIN TENSION for the film is introduced

The Second Act

The protagonist takes ACTION
Fights CONFLICT
Confronts CRISIS (and overcomes challenges)

The Third Act

Arrives at a CLIMAX, a final confrontation
The ANSWER TO THE MAIN TENSION
Leads to a RESOLUTION

The order in which the screenwriters are using the story elements is not set in stone. Screenwriters construct the story elements based on the need of the story. Some films start with a character introduction, as in *Whiplash*, when Andrew is introduced practicing the drums alone in an empty rehearsal room. In films like *Star Wars: A New Hope*, the film opens with an inciting incident – in this case, Princess Leia is captured and taken away by Darth Vader, and the protagonist is introduced much later in the first act. In films like *The Apartment*, the answer to the main tension occurs before the climax. Baxter gets the promotion he wants before the climax, and he quits his job during the climax. When analyzing a screenplay, we have to be flexible with the order in which specific story elements are being placed, because it will vary from screenplay to screenplay.

CASE STUDY I

The Three-Act Structure: *Whiplash* (2014)

Screenwriter/Director: Damien Chazelle

The First Act:

PROTAGONIST: Andrew Neiman, a young, ambitious jazz drummer, attends an elite music conservatory in New York City. Andrew is introduced late at night practicing the drums alone in an empty rehearsal room.

INCITING INCIDENT: Andrew meets Terence Fletcher. Fletcher is a music instructor known for conducting the best jazz ensemble in the conservatory – one of the top ensembles in the nation – but he is also known for the terrifying teaching methods he uses to motivate the students. Later, in the first act, Fletcher sees Andrew's potential and recruits Andrew for his band.

OBJECTIVE: Andrew wants to be in Fletcher's jazz ensemble, as his objective is to rise to the top and become a great musician.

MAIN TENSION: Can Andrew rise to the top in Fletcher's studio band and become a great professional drummer?

The Second Act:

ACTIONS: Andrew joins Fletcher's jazz ensemble as a second drummer and flips the pages to the music sheet for the lead drummer. When Andrew is given a chance to play, he shines, revealing his potential. Andrew's goal and passion for achieving perfection drive him to practice hard, and he becomes obsessed with the pursuit of becoming a professional jazz drummer.

CONFLICTS: Andrew's main conflict is with Fletcher, a ruthless instructor who pushes his students to become the best they can be by using insults, humiliation, and fear as his teaching methods. Andrew endures the abuse and thrives in this hostile environment. Andrew's inner conflict is to overcome his limitation as a drummer. He even breaks up with his girlfriend to devote more time and energy to his practice. His obsession grows stronger as time goes by.

CRISIS: On the way to a jazz-band competition, Andrew gets into a car accident. He leaves the crash scene in a hurry to make it to the competition. Bleeding and in pain, Andrew sits at the drummer's seat onstage. His abnormal behavior clearly illustrates his unstable psychological state. Andrew keeps up with the song, but soon falls apart. His body can't take the stress, and he gives up playing. When Fletcher comes to tell him that he is "done," Andrew attacks Fletcher, tackling him to the ground. Andrew has reached a breaking point. After the incident, Andrew stops playing the drums. He overcomes the crisis by trying to find normalcy in his life. However, he later runs into Fletcher, who invites Andrew to play with him at the JVC Jazz Festival at Carnegie Hall.

The Third Act:

CLIMAX: The climax takes place at the JVC Jazz Festival. Andrew goes on stage and discovers that Fletcher has switched the song. Instead of playing "Caravan," the band plays "Upswingin." Fletcher takes revenge on Andrew for getting him fired from the school and ruining his life. He knows it was Andrew who snitched on him. Andrew tries to improvise, but he can't.

Humiliated, Andrew walks backstage. After seeing his dad, Andrew returns to the stage. The final confrontation isn't over. Determined, Andrew plays the beats to "Caravan," surprising everyone.

RESOLUTION: The resolution takes place during the final performance in the film. The protagonist's transformation is revealed through his attitude and performance. As Andrew starts to play "Caravan," he asks the bassist and the band to join in. Fletcher is forced to follow Andrew's lead and conduct the band. Andrew is no longer the shy freshman wanting to be in Fletcher's jazz ensemble, and he won't take the humiliation and abuse anymore. Andrew takes control of the situation with his skill and talent as a great jazz drummer.

ANSWER TO THE MAIN TENSION: If we recall the end of the first act, the main tension was: "Can Andrew rise to the top and become a great jazz drummer?" The answer to the main tension is: Yes, Andrew becomes a great jazz drummer.

Story Timeline and Story Structure

One important aspect of structuring a screenplay is the use of the story timeline. The screenwriters might opt to tell the story using different timeline structures, depending on the story they're writing. Creative minds will think of a way to best tell the story, and not think about how to follow the story elements. However, the screenwriter chooses to use the story timeline, the story will have a beginning, a middle, and an end – a three-act structure.

Linear structure: This is the most conventional use of a story timeline in a screen-play. The story moves forward in a linear fashion. The story timeline may move slowly, in a fragmented manner, or rapidly through the screenplay, but it will keep moving forward in a linear format. For example, films like *Sicario* (2015), *Star Wars* (1976), and *Toy Story* (1995) have this structure.

Nonlinear structure: In this structure, the story is not told in chronological order. In a nonlinear structure, the story jumps backward and forward. Examples include *Tenet* (2020), where the story timeline moves backward and forward, *Memento* (2000), which is in reverse chronological order, and *Arrival* (2016), which uses the use of flash-forward.

Real-time structure: In real-time structure, the story is told in real time; every minute of the film is the same timeline the audience experiences in real life. In other words, the character experiences the same time frame as the audience. For example, films like *1917* (2019), *Before Sunset* (2004), *Nick of Time* (1995), *12 Angry Men* (1957), and *Rope* (1948) use real-time structure.

Multiple-timeline structure: Some screenplays have multiple timelines following the stories of multiple characters or the same character. The connection between the stories comes from the shared theme and premise of the film. For example, *The Godfather II* (1974), *Cloud Atlas* (2012), *Sliding Doors* (1998), *Groundhog Day* (1993), *The Others* (2001), and *Babel* (2006) use a multiple-timeline structure.

MYTHOLOGY AND FILM – THE HERO'S JOURNEY

In Chapter 3, "Story," we discussed the functions of myth in films. This chapter will dive deeper into the 12 stages of Joseph Campbell's *The Hero's Journey*. But before we jump into that, let's briefly look at how myths have been told through cinema.

It didn't take long for filmmakers to start telling ancient myths through film. The first film production, *Helena* (1924), was silent. This German film told the story of beautiful Helen and the fall of Troy. Myths have metaphors and meanings that resonate in stories. The classical myths are stories we are familiar with, and now, thanks to the visual storytelling medium, film, the audience has a new experience with the stories they already know. Film studios are continuously producing films based on myths, such as *Troy* (2004), *300* (2007), *Clash of the Titans* (2010), and *Hercules* (2014).

Now, in addition to classical myths, the modern myth has been popularized in the film industry with the release of the original *Star Wars* trilogy (1977, 1980, and 1983). George Lucas, the creator of the *Star Wars* franchise, said about the films:

> With Star Wars I consciously set about to re-create myths and the classic mythological motifs. I wanted to use those motifs to deal with issues that exist today. The more research I did, the more I realized that the issues are the same ones that existed 3,000 years ago. That we haven't come very far emotionally.

George Lucas took the old stories from the classical myths and put them in a new sci-fi setting. He used the modern storytelling form, film, to tell a modern myth. Lucas researched and studied Joseph Campbell's *The Hero with a Thousand Faces*. Lucas met Campbell and they discussed the modern myth. Lucas applied Campbell's teachings to the *Star Wars* trilogy screenplays.

In *The Hero with a Thousand Faces*, Joseph Campbell discussed the commonality of the hero's adventure based on mythologies gathered from Eastern and Western worlds, also known as the hero's journey. The hero's journey found its place in the film industry as screenwriters turned to Joseph Campbell and *The Hero with a Thousand Faces*. The mythic structure of the hero's journey identified by Campbell was used in a screenplay for the very first time by George Lucas in 1977. As *Star Wars* films became mega-hits, studios, producers, filmmakers, and screenwriters took this approach seriously. Now, several decades later, the hero's journey is being widely used among the screenwriters in developing their mythic stories around the world. Countless filmmakers have come to see images as symbolic, characters as archetypal, and mythic stories as narrative forms. Lucas helped storytellers to render major psychological experiences by applying mythic structure to visual stories.

In 1992, Christopher Vogler published a book called *A Writer's Journey*, where he explored the use of the hero's journey, introduced by Joseph Campbell in *The*

Hero with a Thousand Faces. The adventure of the hero initially consisted of 17 stages, but in this book, it was streamlined to 12 stages. The book became popular among screenwriting students and professionals.

The Hero's Journey

1. The Ordinary World
2. The Call to Adventure
3. Refusal of the Call
4. Meeting the Mentor
5. Crossing the Threshold
6. Tests, Allies, Enemies
7. Approach to the Inmost Cave
8. The Ordeal
9. Reward
10. The Road Back
11. The Resurrection
12. Return with the Elixir

The Ordinary World: We see the hero's normal life at the start of the story before the adventure begins. The ordinary world gives us the opportunity to get to know the protagonist – his drive, urges, and problems.

The Call to Adventure: A challenge or quest is presented that must be undertaken by the hero. The hero is faced with an event, a conflict, a problem, or a challenge that makes him begin his adventure.

Refusal of the Call: The hero initially refuses the journey because of fear and insecurities that have surfaced from the call to adventure. The hero is not willing to make changes, preferring the safe haven of the ordinary world.

Meeting the Mentor: The hero meets the mentor to gain confidence, insight, advice, wisdom, training, or magical gifts to overcome the initial fear or items that ready them for the journey ahead.

Crossing the Threshold: The hero leaves his ordinary world and crosses the threshold into adventure. Crossing the threshold signifies that the hero has finally committed to the journey. The hero goes from the ordinary world to the extraordinary world.

Tests, Allies, Enemies: The hero faces trials, encounters allies, confronts enemies, and learns the rules of this extraordinary world. The hero needs to find out who can be trusted, a sidekick may join up, or an entire hero's team forged, and comes face to face with enemies.

Approach to the Inmost Cave: The hero faces his greatest fear or the supreme danger lurking in the special world. The hero must prepare to enter "the cave." The initial plan to take on the central conflict begins, but setbacks occur that cause the hero to try a new approach or adopt new ideas.

The Ordeal: The hero engages in the ordeal, the life-or-death crisis. He faces his greatest fear and confronts his most difficult challenge and experience. The hero may directly taste death, or witness the death of an ally or a mentor or a friend. Things go wrong and new conflicts are introduced. The hero experiences more difficult hurdles and obstacles, some of which may lead to a life crisis.

Reward: The hero has survived death or overcomes his greatest fear. The hero's reward comes in many forms: a magical sword, greater knowledge, or insight. The hero has earned the right to celebrate. After surviving the ordeal, he earns a reward that allows him to take on the largest conflict. It may be a physical item or piece of knowledge or wisdom that will help him to persevere.

The Road Back: The hero must finally recommit to completing the journey and accept the road back to the ordinary world. The road back needs an event that will push the hero through the threshold. The hero sees the light at the end of the tunnel, but he is about to face even more tests and challenges.

The Resurrection: During the resurrection stage or the climax, the hero faces a final test, using everything he has learned to take on the conflict once and for all. The hero faces resurrection, his most dangerous meeting with death. It may be a physical ordeal, or a final showdown between the hero and his "shadow" (antagonist).

Return with the Elixir: This is the final stage of the hero's journey. The final reward is earned. The hero has been resurrected and purified, and has earned the right to be accepted back into the ordinary world and he returns with the elixir as a reward from the journey.

CASE STUDY II

The Hero's Journey: *Star Wars* (1977) and *Toy Story* (1995)

Star Wars screenwriter: George Lucas

Toy Story screenwriters: John Lasseter, Pete Docter, Joe Ranft, Joss Whedon, Andrew Stanton, Joel Cohen, and Alec Sokolow

1. **The Ordinary World**

   - *Star Wars*: Luke Skywalker lives a humble life as a farm boy on his home planet of Tatooine with his uncle and aunt.
   - *Toy Story*: Sheriff Woody, an old-fashioned pull-string cowboy doll, lives in Andy's bedroom. Woody and his toy friends come alive when humans are not around.

2. **The Call to Adventure**

   - *Star Wars:* Luke is called to his adventure by R2-D2 and Ben Kenobi. Luke accidentally triggers Princess Leia's message in R2-D2, and is intrigued by her and the message. Ben Kenobi asks Luke to come with him to save Princess Leia.

- *Toy Story*: Woody brings all the toys together, and plans a mission to spy on Andy's birthday party. They want to find out if Andy is getting a new toy. At the party, Andy receives Buzz Lightyear, an astronaut action figure, as a present. Woody now has to compete for Andy's affection.

3. Refusal of the Call

- *Star Wars:* Luke refuses Ben Kenobi's request to travel with him to save Princess Leia. Luke can't leave his aunt and uncle behind for a space adventure.
- *Toy Story:* As Buzz gets more attention from Andy, Woody refuses to believe that he can be replaced as Andy's favorite toy.

4. Meeting the Mentor

- *Star Wars:* Luke meets Ben Kenobi.
- *Toy Story:* Woody meets Buzz Lightyear. Buzz is a character with multiple character functions. At first, he appears to be an antagonist, but Buzz and Woody become comrades in their effort to return home. Buzz is a mentor because without him, Woody would have never learned valuable lessons from the journey.

  The stages of the hero's journey can be reordered to fit the story the screenwriters are telling. In *Toy Story* and *Star Wars*, meeting the mentor takes place before the refusal of the call.

5. Crossing the Threshold

- *Star Wars:* When Luke discovers that the Stormtroopers searching for R2-D2 and C-3PO are tracking them to his farm, he rushes home and discovers that his aunt and uncle have been killed. Luke returns to Ben Kenobi and pledges to go with him to Alderaan and learn the ways of the Force, like his father before him, and help save Princess Leia.
- *Toy Story:* In an effort to hide Buzz from Andy, Woody tries to push him behind the desk, but it all goes wrong, and Buzz is accidentally pushed out the window. Andy can't find Buzz, so instead, he decides to take Woody to Pizza Planet. After falling from the window, Buzz sees Andy and Woody getting into the car, and Buzz hops into the car as well. Woody and Buzz cross over to the extraordinary world together.

6. Tests, Allies, Enemies

- *Star Wars:* Luke meets Han Solo and Chewbacca as Ben Kenobi hires pilots to transport them off of Tatooine and onto Alderaan. Ben Kenobi begins to train Luke in the ways of the Force and teaches him to trust his feelings.
- *Toy Story:* Woody and Buzz get into a fight at the gas station on their way to Pizza Planet. They fall out of the car. Woody and Buzz realize they

only have each other to rely on in the human world. They begin to work together.

7. Approach to the Inmost Cave

- *Star Wars:* When Luke and Ben Kenobi arrive at Alderaan, the planet has been destroyed, and they come across the Death Star. A tractor beam pulls in the Millennium Falcon, and now Luke must confront the Galactic Empire.
- *Toy Story:* Sid brings Woody and Buzz into his room from Pizza Planet. Sid likes to torture toys. Woody and Buzz fear for their lives.

8. The Ordeal

- *Star Wars:* Once trapped in the Death Star, Ben Kenobi tries to find the tractor beam so that they can deactivate it and escape. Luke, Han, and Chewbacca discover that Princess Leia is being held on the Death Star with them. They rescue her, but Ben Kenobi sacrifices himself. Luke watches Darth Vader strike him down.
- *Toy Story:* Woody and Buzz face torture and death. First, Sid tortures Woody, burning him with a magnifying glass. Sid plans to tie up Buzz to a rocket and launch it into the sky. Woody must bring Buzz back to Andy's room in order to clear up all misunderstandings with the other toys, because they believe Woody pushed Buzz out the window on purpose.

9. Reward

- *Star Wars:* Luke has helped save Princess Leia and retrieved the Death Star plans. They now have the knowledge to destroy the Galactic Empire's greatest weapon, the Death Star, once and for all.
- *Toy Story:* With the help of Sid's mutant toys, Woody saves Buzz from being launched on the rocket. Woody earns safe passage to Andy's house.

10. The Road Back

- *Star Wars:* Luke, Leia, Han Solo, Chewbacca, and the droids are headed to the hidden Rebel base. They realize that the Galactic Empire must be tracking them, but they must race against time to take the plans to the Rebellion and prepare for battle.
- *Toy Story:* Woody and Buzz are confronted with a new challenge as they make their way back to Andy's room. It's moving day, and Andy and his mom are moving to a new house. Woody and Buzz have just missed the moving truck. They try to catch up to the truck, but it seems hopeless.

11. The Resurrection

- *Star Wars:* Luke and the rebels prepare to take on the Death Star. Luke is the only pilot that is able to fly within the trenches. Just as Darth Vader is about to destroy Luke, Han Solo returns and clears the way. Luke uses the Force to guide his aiming as he fires upon the Death Star's sole weak point and destroys it.

- *Toy Story:* As Woody and Buzz find themselves separated from their toy friends, Woody gets a brilliant idea: use the magnifying glass to ignite the rocket that's tied to Buzz. They "resurrect" by flying and catching up to Andy's car and the moving truck.

12. Return with the Elixir

- *Star Wars:* Luke and Han return to the Rebel base, where Princess Leia welcomes them. Luke, Han, and Chewbacca receive medals for the heroic journey. There is peace in the galaxy. Luke has gone from farm boy to hero.
- *Toy Story:* Woody is reunited with his toy friends and is back in Andy's room. It's Christmas Day, but Woody doesn't worry about the toys Andy will receive as presents. Woody becomes much more confident and wiser from the journey.

THE SEQUENCE METHOD

Another unique way to structure a screenplay is using the sequence method. Screenwriter, director, and professor Frank Daniel developed the sequence method to compartmentalize the screenwriting process while helping to increase the dramatic tension in a screenplay. Writing a screenplay can be overwhelming, especially when you are learning the craft. Even if you know your theme and premise and have a thorough story outline with strong characters and compelling story elements, it can be challenging to write a 90–120 page script.

Daniel served as a dean of the Film and TV School of the Academy of Performing Arts in Prague (FAMU), American Film Institute and USC School of Cinema-Television. He was also an artistic director at the Sundance Institute and a co-chair of the Film Department at the Columbia University School of the Arts. Daniel worked with students for many years and saw how they struggled to keep the dramatic tension in their screenplays. He developed a new structure to help the students with the rigorous task of completing a feature-length screenplay. He said: "Most anyone can write a 120-page screenplay, but not everyone can keep the audience captive for 120 pages."

Daniel's teachings have been incorporated into the screenwriting curriculums at the institutions where he taught over the years. While attending graduate film program at Columbia University, I was fortunate to have learned the sequence method from Malia Scotch-Marmo, a screenwriter and professor. The sequence method had a ripple effect in the screenwriting community, and more and more screenwriters have become aware of this approach and used it in their scripts. His teaching has had an impact on his students and as they have become professionals in the industry, his approach has been proven to work. Daniel's students include directors Milos Forman, David Lynch, and Terrence Malick, to name but a few. In 2004, Paul Joseph Gulino, a former student, published a book, *Screenwriting: The Sequence Approach*, where he discusses the sequence method and provides examples.

The Three-Act Structure and the Sequence Method

The three-act structure provides a sense of order. It gives the writer a clear purpose of what needs to happen in each act. Let's take the first act. We know that the characters, the world and settings, the inciting incident, and the protagonist's objective have to be introduced in the first act. Now, instead of writing the first act, what if we went further and broke down the same first act into two different sequences? Instead of writing a 30-page first act, what if you wrote two 15-page sequences? Keeping the same narrative three-act structure, the sequence method allows the screenwriter to compartmentalize a segment of the story in a sequence. Each sequence has a beginning, a middle, and an end, and the screenplay's main tension (dramatic tension) stays intact throughout each sequence.

The sequence method consists of breaking down the three-act structure into eight sequences.

* Act 1 is divided into two sequences.
* Act 2 is divided into four sequences.
* Act 3 is divided into two sequences.

First Sequence: Act 1, Sequence 1

The first sequence exposes the world in which our main character resides. It exposes the political, sociological, and cultural settings, where the audience can identify with the world of the story. It introduces the main characters and the supporting characters. The sequence is generally composed of a beginning, a middle, and an end, and at the end of the first sequence, there is a "hook" that engages the audience. The "hook" is generally referred to as the inciting incident.

Second Sequence: Act 1, Sequence 2

The second sequence establishes the main character's want and need. The inciting incident provokes a strong desire to accomplish a goal, or pursue an objective. The protagonist wants and needs something they didn't have before – a dramatic need. As their objective is realized, there is a turning point in the story at the end of the second sequence – aka the end of the first act. The protagonist moves from the first act to the second act. In the process, the main tension is raised.

Main Tension

Can the protagonist attain his or her objective?

Third Sequence: Act 2, Sequence 1

During the third sequence, the protagonist takes the first step on the journey to attain their goal, leaving their ordinary world. As they move toward their goal, new challenges surface. The protagonist is pushed out of their comfort zone and forced to learn, cope, and adapt to this new environment.

Fourth Sequence: Act 2, Sequence 2

In the fourth sequence, the protagonist confronts another layer of difficulty, and something unexpected happens. The antagonist's presence is strong in this sequence. The protagonist's conflict with the antagonist escalates. The protagonist's initial plan to move toward the goal has a setback and starts to move in the wrong direction.

Fifth Sequence: Act 2, Sequence 3

In the fifth sequence, the protagonist faces their greatest fear and/or confronts their weakness. The conflicts escalate into a crisis. The protagonist may overcome the fear or be defeated by it. Regardless of the outcome, there is a moment of self-reflection and the protagonist continues to move toward their objective again.

Sixth Sequence: Act 2, Sequence 4

The sixth sequence is the final sequence in the second act. In this sequence, the story moves toward answering the main tension raised at the end of the first act. Usually, there is a confrontation with the antagonist. There is always an event or occurrence at the end of the sequence, such as a battle, a wedding, a graduation, or a championship fight.

Answer to the Main Tension

Yes, the protagonist achieves their goal, or no, they don't attain their goal.

Seventh Sequence: Act 3, Sequence 1

As the main tension is answered in the last sequence of the second act, a new tension builds up in the third act. The aftermath or the consequence of either attaining the goal or failing to attain the goal surfaces, and the protagonist is confronted with a new challenge.

Eighth Sequence: Act 3, Sequence 2

The eighth and final sequence provides a resolution to the story. The protagonist reveals how they have transformed over the course of their journey (character transformation). In this sequence, the screenwriters tie up all the loose ends. Whether it's the supporting character's journey or a subplot, every storyline comes to an end. Finally, the final sequence reveals the protagonist's final emotional state, allowing the audience to conclude the psychological experience following the protagonist's emotional arc.

The Sequence Elements

Each sequence is approximately 15 pages long, with a beginning, a middle, and an end. Each sequence is composed of the following sequence elements:

1. What is the sequence title?
2. Whose sequence is it?
3. What does he/she want?
4. What's the conflict?
5. Who is in the way?
6. Who helps?
7. What is the emotional arc of the main character in the sequence?

- *Sequence Length:* If you divide a 120-page screenplay into eight sequences, it comes out at 15 pages per sequence. This is not a rule but a guiding principle, so the number of pages for each sequence can vary. Writing eight sequences approximately 15-pages long is much more manageable than writing a 120-page screenplay.
- *Sequence structure:* As in any narrative structure, a sequence must have a beginning, a middle, and end.

1. *What is the sequence title?* The sequence title is an important summarization of what the sequence is about.
2. *Whose sequence is it?* In a single-protagonist screenplay, the story follows the journey of a protagonist; therefore, every sequence belongs to the protagonist.
3. *What does he/she want?* The protagonist's objective (want/need) drives the sequence forward. For each sequence, the protagonist must pursue an objective. The sequence's objective can be a secondary or smaller objective to accomplish the main objective.
4. *What's the conflict?* Similar to the sequence's objective, each sequence must have a conflict of its own.
5. *Who is in the way?* We must identify who the antagonist is for the sequence. In most cases, it is the same antagonist, but there are times where other supporting characters besides the antagonist preventing the character from achieving the sequence's objectives.
6. *Who helps?* We need to identify the supporting characters who help the protagonist through the sequence.

7. *What is the emotional arc of the main character in the sequence?* For each sequence, the protagonist goes through an emotional change. When applying the sequence method, the screenwriters clearly define the emotional arc for each sequence. They map out the entire screenplay's emotional arc before writing the screenplay. Therefore, when you put the emotional arcs of the eight sequences side by side, you'll get the protagonist's emotional arc for the entire story.

CASE STUDY III

The Sequence Method: *Get Out* (2017)

Screenwriter/Director: Jordan Peele

FIRST SEQUENCE: ACT 1, SEQUENCE 1

1. *What's the sequence title?* Chris and Rose.
2. *Whose sequence is it?* Chris, the protagonist, is an urban photographer. The sequence begins as he gets ready in the morning in his apartment.
3. *What does he want?* Chris wants to know if Rose's parents know if he is black, and if they don't, perhaps she should tell them. They are preparing to spend the weekend at Rose's parents' house.
4. *What's the conflict?* Chris wants Rose to inform her parents of his race. He doesn't want to surprise them, but Rose doesn't want to tell them. Rose assures him that her parents are not racist, that everything will be fine. One important clue that gets mentioned during their conversation is that she hasn't been in an interracial relationship prior to dating Chris. This is a lie, and the truth will be revealed during the crisis of the film.
5. *Who is in the way?* Rose is in the way. Chris wants to inform her parents, but Rose won't tell them.
6. *Who helps?* Rose completely assures Chris that everything will be all right.
7. *What is the emotional arc of the main character in the sequence?* Chris starts the sequence worried about the weekend trip. But after the reassurance from Rose, Chris feels at ease. In the first sequence, the protagonist's emotional arc goes from being worried to feeling at ease.

SECOND SEQUENCE: ACT 1, SEQUENCE 2

1. *What is the sequence title?* The Drive.
2. *Whose sequence is it?* It's Chris's sequence. Rose drives and Chris is in the passenger seat.

3. *What does he want?* Chris wants to have a nice drive to Rose's parents' house. He wants to smoke a cigarette, but Rose won't let him. Chris makes a call to his friend, Rod, and gives him final dog-sitting instructions.
4. *What's the conflict?* Rose hits a deer, and the car comes to a stop. Chris walks back to the side of the road and looks at the dead deer, foreshadowing what is to come.
5. *Who is in the way?* The cops. Rose called the police, and Rose reports the incident to the police officer. Holding Rose's driver's license, the cop looks at Chris and asks for his identification.
6. *Who helps?* When Chris is about to give the cop his identification, Rose confronts the cop about racially profiling her boyfriend and asks why he needs Chris's ID when he wasn't even driving. The cop tries to defend himself, but it's too late. In the end, the cop doesn't check Chris's ID.
7. *What is the emotional arc of the main character in the sequence?* At the beginning of the sequence, Chris is a little nervous as they drive up to Rose's parents' house. His nervousness is shown when he takes out a cigarette. At the end of the sequence, Chris feels safe with Rose by her side. Chris goes from feeling nervous to feeling safe.

Main Tension

Can Chris make a good impression on Rose's parents and spend a quality weekend with her family?

THIRD SEQUENCE: ACT 2, SEQUENCE 1

1. *What is the sequence title?* Meet the Armitages.
2. *Whose sequence is it?* It's Chris's sequence. He is introduced to Rose's parents, Dean and Missy; the groundskeeper, Walter; and the maid, Georgina. Later, Jeremy, Rose's brother, joins the family dinner.
3. *What does he want?* He wants to make a good impression and get to know Rose's family.
4. *What's the conflict?* Chris feels something strange with Walter and Georgina. Rose's parents seem nice and welcoming, but there is something creepy about them.
5. *Who is in the way?* Jeremy gets hostile toward Chris during dinner, ruining the evening for everyone.
6. *Who helps?* Rose helps. Rose rescues Chris from the awkwardness and takes his side during the family dinner. When they are back in their room, she is embarrassed about her family's behavior during dinner and again puts Chris at ease.
7. *What is the emotional arc of the main character in the sequence?* Chris' emotional arc changes. He goes from feeling welcomed to feeling strange.

FOURTH SEQUENCE: ACT 2, SEQUENCE 2

1. *What is the sequence title?* The Sunken Place.
2. *Whose sequence is it?* It's Chris's sequence. Chris can't sleep, and he goes out for a smoke in the middle of the night. But he gets scared by Walter and Georgina, and on the way back, he runs into Missy, Rose's mother, who hypnotizes him against his will.
3. *What does he want?* He wants to smoke a cigarette.
4. *What's the conflict?* When Chris goes outside for a smoke, he is terrorized as he sees someone in the distance running toward him. Chris becomes paralyzed. The runner passes by him, and it's Walter. Then he comes face to face with Georgina, who looks out the window. When Chris reenters the house, he encounters Rose's mother, Missy. He is unwillingly hypnotized, and the conversation turns to when Chris's mother passed away on a rainy night, a backstory. Missy learns about Chris's deepest fears.
5. *Who is in the way?* When Chris goes to have a cigarette, Walter and Georgina prevent him from having a peaceful smoke. Missy hypnotizes Chris. She sends him into the Sunken Place, a place where his mind is detached from the physical body.
6. *Who helps?* No one helps.
7. *What is the emotional arc of the main character in the sequence?* Chris's emotional arc goes from being nervous to devastated.

FIFTH SEQUENCE: ACT 2, SEQUENCE 3

1. *What is the sequence title?* The Party.
2. *Whose sequence is it?* It's Chris's sequence. In the early morning, the sequence begins with him out on a walk, taking pictures of nature. Chris senses there is something wrong with Walter when he has a brief encounter with him on his way back. Back inside, he talks to Rose about Missy hypnotizing him the previous night, and he feels like throwing up when he thinks about smoking. Then the guests arrive. Chris and Rose greet every guest. Chris meets two interesting characters, Logan and Jim Hudson. Logan is the only other black man at the party. He acts and talks like an old white man. The other man, a blind white man, is Jim Hudson, who owns the Hudson Art Gallery.
3. *What does he want?* Chris wants to be a good boyfriend and help greet the guests.
4. *What's the conflict?* There are two major conflicts taking place in this sequence. First, Chris discovers that his phone's power cord was unplugged by Georgina. He informs Rose of the incident, but she doesn't believe him. Second, Logan attacks Chris, telling him to "get out" when he takes a photo using a flash.
5. *Who is in the way?* Georgina and Logan. Georgina comes to the bedroom and apologizes to Chris for accidentally unplugging his phone. Logan apologizes to Chris and the other guests for his behavior earlier.

6. *Who helps?* Rod and Rose. Chris speaks to his friend Rod and tells him that Missy hypnotized him, and Rod half-jokingly says something is not right. And Rose tries to comfort him.

7. *What is the emotional arc of the main character in the sequence?* Chris goes from peacefully taking pictures at dawn to getting attacked by Logan at the party. Chris's emotional arc goes from peaceful to confused.

SIXTH SEQUENCE: ACT 2, SEQUENCE 4

1. *What is the sequence title?* Let's Go Home.
2. *Whose sequence is it?* It's Chris's sequence. He and Rose go for a walk and have a conversation by the lake.
3. *What does he want?* Chris wants to go home.
4. *What's the conflict?* Back at the Armitage estate, the guests are gathered by the gazebo as Dean, Rose's dad, conducts an auction. He takes bids from guests in front of Chris's portrait. Jim Hudson, the blind man, wins the auction. When Chris and Rose return home to pack their belongings, Chris finds a shoebox with a pile of photos of Rose, who is with a different black man in each photo. Chris realizes that Rose has been lying to him.
5. *Who is in the way?* The entire Armitage family, Dean, Missy, Jeremy, and Rose. As Chris is about to leave, the Armitage family appears in the foyer, blocking his path in every direction. Chris learns his fate as Rose reveals her true identity to Chris. As Chris tries to fight his way out of the foyer, Missy sends him to the Sunken Place with the clinking sound of the teacup and spoon.
6. *Who helps?* Rod. Chris texts Rod the picture he snapped at the party while packing his belongings. Rod calls him, telling him he recognizes Logan. His actual name is Andre and not Logan. Rod tells him to get out as soon as possible. The tension builds as he hurries to get out of the house.
7. *What is the emotional arc of the main character in the sequence?* When he has a conversation about going home, he feels hopeful. Then he gets trapped in the Sunken Place. In this sequence, Chris's emotional arc goes from feeling hopeful to feeling trapped.

Answer to the Main Tension

The main tension is: "Can Chris make a good impression on Rose's parents and spend a quality weekend with her family?" The answer to the main tension is: No, Chris hasn't met his objective. Chris's objective was insignificant, because the Armitage family had a different agenda all along. Chris was fooled into believing his objectives mattered to Rose's family.

SEVENTH SEQUENCE: ACT 3, SEQUENCE 1

1. *What is the sequence title?* The Game Room.
2. *Whose sequence is it?* It's Chris's sequence.

3. *What does he want?* Chris wants to escape from the game room and from the house.
4. *What's the conflict?* Chris's arms and legs are tied to a leather chair.
5. *Who is in the way?* The Armitage family. First, Roman, Rose's grandfather, appears on the television in front of him. Chris discovers his fate. He explains the Coagula procedure, where the Armitage family takes his body and gives it to someone else because of his physical superiority. Later, Jim Hudson appears on TV. Chris has a videoconference with Jim. Chris discovers that Jim will take over his body, and Chris will remain in the Sunken Place. Chris freaks out.
6. *Who helps?* Rod worries about Chris not coming home from the weekend trip. Rod also performs an internet search and discovers that Andre/Logan has gone missing. Rod starts to worry about Chris and goes to the police, but he is laughed at because no one wants to believe him. The second person who helps Chris is himself at the end of this sequence. Chris sees the torn arm of the leather chair, revealing the cotton stuffing, and he gets an idea.
7. *What is the emotional arc of the main character in the sequence?* Chris's emotional arc goes from feeling scared to feeling empowered.

EIGHTH SEQUENCE: ACT 3, SEQUENCE 2

1. *What is the sequence title?* The Exit.
2. *Whose sequence is it?* It's Chris's sequence.
3. *What does he want?* He wants to escape.
4. *What's the conflict?* Chris is still tied up and hypnotized.
5. *Who is in the way?* Jeremy, Dean, Missy, Rose, Walter, and Georgina. First is Jeremy, who comes to get Chris for the operation. Chris attacks Jeremy, knocking him unconscious, then takes out the earplugs he's made out of cotton stuffing from the chair arm. Chris only pretended to be hypnotized. Then Chris uses a deer's head to kill Dean. When he comes up from the basement, Missy attacks him, and Chris kills her. As Chris is trying to drive away from the house, he runs over Georgina, and he goes back to save her. Rose starts to shoot at Chris and Walter comes to help Rose, but at the last minute, everything changes.
6. *Who helps?* Walter and Rod. First, Walter, the groundskeeper, regains consciousness in the Sunken Place, and helps Chris by shooting Rose. Walter kills himself. Then Rod comes to the rescue. Rod comes to the Armitage estate and helps Chris escape.
7. *What is the emotional arc of the main character in the sequence?* Chris's emotional arc goes from feeling trapped to feeling liberated.

Screenplay structure helps organize and design the story. Whether it is the three-act structure, the sequence method, or any other commonly used screenplay structure, it always helps the writer craft the story to have a comprehensive storyline where the audience can follow and experience what the story has to offer.

5

SETTING

A film's setting is a topic that often gets overlooked when studying screenplays, but I believe it's essential to understand why the writer sets the story in a specific time and place. At times, the story dictates the location and the era, but there are times when the writer considers setting the story in a specific world and period. Films dealing with historical facts or real-life characters don't have much room to change for obvious reasons, but in an original screenplay, the writer has the freedom to choose where and when the story will take place.

A film's setting facilitates an environment for the characters to exist, and they also lay out the sociocultural and sociopolitical setting where the plots are constructed with story elements. Four attributes help to define the setting in a screenplay:

1. Geographic location
2. Time period
3. The world of the story
4. The sociocultural setting

GEOGRAPHIC LOCATION

Where is the story taking place? Is it in Pearl Harbor? Napa Valley? The Amalfi coast? Buenos Aires? In an imaginary world? Some screenwriters do intensive research on the locations where the story will take place, and some writers use a familiar or well-known setting. A geographic location helps the audience to identify where the story is taking place. The geographic location is so vital for some screenwriters that they treat the location as they would treat a character. The amount of location information a writer provides in each scene adds a backdrop in which the characters can interact with each other and take action. Therefore,

DOI: 10.4324/9781003138853-7

screenwriters only provide the necessary information that is required to keep the audience attentive and engaged.

All geographic locations have characteristics. When you think of Paris, London, New York, or anywhere else, you may think of a street. Each place has specific characteristics that are unique to each location. The film *Sabrina* (1954) takes place in the Hamptons in Long Island, New York, which is known as a summer destination for affluent NYC residents. The film follows the journey of a chauffeur's daughter, Sabrina. As she returns home from Paris, she confronts a dilemma. She is in love with her father's wealthy employer's son, David Larrabee. The social class difference exposition between the two families is shown by their employer–employee relationship and where they live. Sabrina lives with her father in a humble apartment above the multiple-car garage on the Larrabee estate, while David lives in a mansion's main building. This geographic location's characteristics help establish the challenges Sabrina must overcome if she decides to follow her heart.

In *Lady Bird* (2017), the geographic location is a dramatic element in the story instead of a backdrop for the characters. The film's premise deals with the protagonist's leaving her hometown in California and arriving in NYC to attend college. The protagonist, Christine, realizes the value of the moment after she leaves them behind. She finally realizes the precious moments she had back in Sacramento with her family when alone and miles from home.

TIME PERIOD

The time period in which the story takes place gives away important information about the story. As it did with geographic location, a specific period in time can expose many details and facts about when the story takes place. For example, is the story taking place during the past, present, or future? Is the story taking place during the Roman Empire, medieval times, World War II, or the 1990s? Is the story taking place during the present time or the future? As the audience learns when the story is taking place, they will learn to expect certain things from the story, as the time period reveals the era's characteristics. For example, the narrative time period of the film *Parasite* is set in 2019, the same era as when the film was released. *Parasite* is a satire treating the social class difference by displaying a lifestyle contrast between the destitute Kim and the wealthy Park families. This South Korean film did well at the global box office and received awards from international film festivals, as well as the Cannes Film Festival, British Academy Film Awards, and the Academy Awards. The theme and premise of the film are so specific and particular that they resonate a universal truth with the global audience. Because the film's premise mirrors the period's global socioeconomic setting, the ramification of social class differences shown in the film is felt in every culture worldwide. Everyone who watched *Parasite* or read the screenplay can sympathize with the main characters as they struggle to escape poverty.

As you saw in the *Parasite* example, there are three factors to consider when analyzing time in a screenplay.

1.   What is the time period of the story?
2.   When was the screenplay written?
3.   When is the film being watched or the screenplay being read?

You are perhaps asking: Why do we need to explore the three different time elements existing in a screenplay? First, as stories in films mimic our lives and experiences, they also document our cultures and traditions, so seeing the story's time period can help us to ground the audience in the era. Second, when was the screenplay written? Was the screenplay reflecting a story that happened in the past (a period film)? Was the story taking place in the future? Or is the story taking place in the same era as when the screenwriter wrote the screenplay? Knowing when the screenwriter wrote the screenplay and comparing that to the film's time period can provide information to understand the writer's intentions for setting the story in a specific time.

Third, when was the film watched, or when was the screenplay read? Was it when the film was first released, or several years later? Stories in a film do not have an expiration date; however, the relevancy or takeaway from the film might vary when the audience consumes the story.

When analyzing a screenplay, the three different time factors can help us grasp a deeper understanding of the film and the period in which it was made. The great films remain classics, and we analyze their screenplays to understand how they became classic films. We need to look into the three different time factors, because the film speaks to the audience, conveying a universal truth about what was current and compelling for that period of time when the film was released.

The Dark Knight, released in 2008, was received very well by critics and audiences. It's about a well-established superhero character, Batman, and deals with a character, the Joker, disturbing the social order and creating chaos, fear, and injustice. *The Dark Knight* was released several years after the catastrophic events of September 11, 2001, when the United States was attacked by al-Qaeda, who killed nearly 3,000 people. In 2008, when the film was released, the wars in Afghanistan and Iraq were still creating uncertainty in the minds of the global population. As the world leaders and the United Nations were at war with the Taliban and Iraq, terrorism gained momentum, creating global fear and chaos. During this period of time, it wasn't rare to see terrorist attacks in the news. Even though *The Dark Knight* is a fictional story, the screenplay speaks about a subject matter that was pressing to audiences of the time. What the audience was facing in real life was similar to what Batman was facing with the Joker in *The Dark Knight*: terror, chaos, and fear. As the audience goes through the psychological journey, with Bruce Wayne catching the Joker, there is a great emotional fulfillment that comes from watching the film. "Good" goes against "evil," and the "good" prevails in this film. Obviously, this is not the only reason why the film did well at the box office – it had a great screenplay, and the execution was flawless – but we can't deny the fact that the timing of the film's release had an impact on the audience. In this film, you can see so much about pressing issues after 9/11: terrorism, the economy, wars, and politics. No one wants to see a film about terrorism, but when you put the idea into a Batman film – a superhero crime epic film – the audience is much more receptive to the story. Therefore, when studying a screenplay, you should break down each time factor to see how the film was received during its release. We must revisit the time period to see the sociocultural and sociopolitical setting of that era.

THE WORLD OF THE STORY

Every story takes place in a particular world – the story world, to be more specific. Normally, the story world is associated with the protagonist's professional life. In *Whiplash*, the Shaffer conservatory is the world in which the story revolves around. It's the world of a music school and music students. By identifying the story world, we now understand the world the protagonist has to navigate through to attain the goal. So the geographical location and time period of where and when the story is taking place is important, but we also have to consider the world of the story. Each world has a specificity that is relevant to the story. For example, a film like *Goodfellas* (1990) deals with the Italian-American gangster's world in NYC during the 1960s. In *Boogie Nights* (1997), the story revolves around the porn industry in the late 1970s in California. Unlike the geographical location, the story world provides a specific condition in which the character coexists, and it also grounds the audience to the specificity of the world.

THE SOCIOCULTURAL SETTING

The sociocultural setting in a screenplay provides a framework for people's attitudes, opinions, beliefs, and perspectives. Therefore, choosing the right sociocultural setting that best serves the story is crucial for the screenwriters to make. It could be a historical setting, where the screenwriter does a lot of research for a specific time period in our history, a sci-fi setting where the screenwriter creates a fictional/imaginary setting in the future, or it could be a sociocultural setting in the present. The setting provides a set of rules and laws of the world where the story is taking place, and it shows the boundaries and limitations of a given society.

When Denis Villeneuve was hired to direct *Blade Runner 2049* (2017), he asked his filmmaker colleagues to make three short films to bridge the 35-year gap between the original *Blade Runner* (1982) and the sequel. Each of the three short films served as a key backstory for the sequel and helped set up the film's sociocultural setting.

The first short film, *Black Out 2022*, is an animated film that reveals the incident where a group of replicants fights for survival as humans hunted and killed by accessing the central database to identify them. The rebel replicants plan to erase the database and the backups. An electromagnetic pulse causes a global blackout that has massive and destructive implications all over the world.

The short film *2036: Nexus Dawn* introduces one of the antagonists in the sequel, Niander Wallace, who showcases a new line of superior replicants. The final short film, *2048: Nowhere to Run*, introduces Sapper Morton, a replicant who lives in hiding among humans. While he is protecting a little girl, his identity is revealed, and someone notifies the police.

An interesting fact about these short films is that *Black Out 2022* was written and directed by Shinichirō Watanabe, but the other two short films were written by *Blade Runner 2049* screenwriters Hampton Fancher and Michael Green. These short films helped to bridge the sociocultural gap of 35 years between the original and the sequel. The first short film informs us of the blackout that took place in 2022. The sequel makes several important references to the blackout of 2022. The second short film reveals that after the blackout, the production of replicants has become illegal, but now, in the year 2036, Niander Wallace is approved to manufacture a new line of replicants that are far more obedient than their processors. The third short film takes place in 2048, a year before the sequel begins. This short film sets up the setting for the sequel. There are still awakened replicants living in hiding, like Sepper Morton, who fights the thugs in order to save a girl's life, knowing that he will be making a scene and someone might notice him. But he is willing to protect the girl because she is someone special. She is believed to be born from a replicant. If the truth is revealed, it will change the course of the replicants' existence on Earth, which sets up the sequel, *Blade Runner 2049*.

Director Denis Villeneuve took a similar approach to the Wachowskis's first sequel to *The Matrix*. After the massive success of the first installment, and in preparation for the sequel, *The Matrix Reloaded*, the Wachowskis produced nine animated films, *The Animatrix*, to help the audience understand the setting of *The Matrix*. These films explain how machines started to take over the world.

Some filmmakers go the extra mile in constructing the story's setting because it is in this environment where the characters and plots coexist.

Let's switch gears and talk about the impact the film's sociocultural setting has on the audience. Why is it important to understand the setting when studying a screenplay? A perfect example of the point I want to make took place when WarnerMedia Studios and Networks launched a streaming service, HBO Max, in the United States. The film *Gone with the Wind* (1939) was listed in their film library as the new platform was launched. Soon after, a well-known screenwriter in Hollywood wrote an article saying that HBO Max should remove *Gone with the Wind* from their list for the horrific portrayal of black slavery in the film. As this topic became controversial, HBO Max removed the film from the library.

Let's stop here for a moment and think about what happened. A film was removed from a streaming service because of a portrayal of slavery – a historical fact in America. As films mimic our lives, our real life's sociocultural settings are documented in films. Since the Lumière brothers invented the motion picture in 1895, we've been documenting our progress as human beings, and the changes we face are reflected in the sociocultural setting. Films like *Gone with the Wind* (1939) or *Birth of a Nation* (1915) should be studied instead of being purged from our memories. All the horrific things mankind has committed are part of who we are as human beings. Whether we like it or not, whether we agree with it or not, whether we tolerate it or not, it is our history. We should learn from our past, and we should not make the same mistakes again. HBO Max restored *Gone with the Wind* in their library with a disclaimer two weeks after it was taken down.

6

TECHNIQUES AND TOOLS

Professional screenwriters learn to master screenwriting techniques and tools like any other professional artist. Like sculptors who use carving tools to bring a vision alive in stone, or a pianist who uses fingers to express feelings through the piano as an extension of himself or herself, all artists have practiced and mastered the techniques and tools for their respective crafts. For screenwriters, the tools at their disposal are words, including scenes, description, and dialogue. The techniques at their disposal include the story's arrangement – what is the information, and when and how is it presented to the audience. Now, the use of screenwriting tools and techniques can and will affect the audience's involvement in the story. They control the audience's expectations and guide them through the story.

A screenwriter uses numerous techniques and tools to complete a screenplay. Most screenwriters will use a specific technique in conceptualizing the idea of the story and using tools to develop the story framework to meet the initial vision. It would be difficult to assess all the techniques and tools a screenwriter uses to write the script, but we can analyze what has been presented to us. We can study how they are keeping the audience engaged and captivated with the following:

1. Events/occurrences
2. Reversal
3. Dramatic irony
4. Setup and payoff

EVENTS/OCCURRENCES

Screenwriters use events and occurrences to bring the characters together. Events and occurrences can be an integral part of the protagonist's achieving the objective and affect the protagonist's emotional arc throughout the story. Usually, there is a

DOI: 10.4324/9781003138853-8

significant event or occurrence at the end of the first act and another significant event taking place at the end of the second act. Events or occurrences can be birthdays, national holidays, or characters gathering together to speak about an important matter. Or an event or occurrence can be a sporting event, graduation, wedding, award night, concert, or election night. The main plot point in the story shifts from these events; there is an event that sets the protagonist's quest for their goal, and there is an event that wraps the journey to attain their goal.

At the end of the first act, an event or occurrence sets the story in motion, allowing a pathway to the second act. If you recall our discussion of three-act structure, at the end of the first act, we often see a plane taking off, the character preparing to start a semester, or characters getting ready to embark on a journey. The protagonist participates in an action to pursue their objective, and the screenwriter uses an event to set the motion for the second act. In *Star Wars: A New Hope*, the event that sets the story in motion at the end of the first act is Luke Skywalker and Ben Kenobi hiring Chewbacca and Han Solo so that they can flee Tatooine. This event allows Luke Skywalker to pursue his objective of helping Ben Kenobi to rescue Princess Leia and ultimately becoming a Jedi, as his father did before him. In *The Godfather* (1972), the event that set the motion at the end of the first act is the second murder attempt on Vito Corleone at the hospital, which Michael prevents from happening. The attack on his father becomes a personal fight for Michael Corleone, and he decides to join the family business so that he can protect the family.

At the end of the second act, the event or occurrence is usually the final confrontation between the protagonist and the antagonist. This final confrontation usually reveals the answer to the main tension of the story. In *Star Wars: A New Hope*, the event at the end of the second act is the battle between the Rebel Alliance and the Galactic Empire. Luke Skywalker takes a stand against the Empire's attack by joining the fight with the Alliance. During the battle, Luke Skywalker destroys the Death Star and helps to save the Rebel base. In *The Godfather*, the event that sets off the third act is Vito Corleone's funeral. Now, Michael is fully in charge of the family business. Before his death, Vito meets Michael. They talk about how Vito never wanted Michael to be in this role. Vito wanted Michael to be a senator or congressman. He tells Michael that the other families will try to kill him, and lets Michael know that whoever set up a meeting with Barzini, a rival gangster, is the traitor. At the funeral, Salvatore Tessio arranges the meeting between Michael and Barzini. Michael, knowing that he will get killed at the meeting, acts first. Michael issues an order to kill everyone involved: Barzini, Tattaglia, Moe Greene, Strachi, Cuneo, Tessio, and even his brother-in-law, who betrayed the Corleone family.

Now, screenwriters do not limit the use of events/occurrences to the end of the first and second acts. They use events or occurrences throughout the story. In the film *Get Out*, Chris, the protagonist, goes on a weekend trip to meet Rose's parents for the first time. This event takes place at the end of Act One. Chris meets Rose's parents outside the house, and the story is set in motion for the second act. As

Chris speaks to Rose's parents for the first time, inside the house, Chris enters the extraordinary world. "Will Chris make a good impression and get to know Rose's parents?" is the main tension. Without this event, there is no story. Therefore, this event plays a key function. Another event is the party the Armitage family is having in honor of Rose's grandfather on the same weekend Chris and Rose are visiting. At this important event, Rose introduces Chris to the guests, who are eager to meet him. During this gathering, there is another crucial event planned for the evening. "Bingo" is a code name for the Armitage family's auction for the guests, where they bid to win Chris.

In *The Godfather* (1972), the film starts with an event: the wedding of Vito Corleone's daughter, Connie. The wedding brings together the Corleone family and friends. The protagonist, Michael Corleone, is introduced, as well as the world of the story he is about the enter. Vito Corleone takes a business meeting with some of the guests, and the audience is let into Corleone's family business and the gangster world. In *Toy Story*, Andy's birthday is an essential event in the first act that helps to introduce Buzz Lightyear, an important supporting character. When Woody accidentally pushes Buzz out the window sets the story in motion. Woody and Buzz are forced to enter the extraordinary world together. Another significant event in the story is the "moving day" at the end of the second act. The screenwriters set this up at the beginning of the screenplay. Finally, the screenwriters end the screenplay with another event, Christmas, to provide a resolution to the story.

Every screenwriter relies heavily on setting up the events or occurrences to bring the characters together and move the story forward.

REVERSAL

One of the tools a screenwriter can use in a screenplay is a reversal. It changes the direction of the story 180 degrees and causes new developments. A reversal always surprises the audience with a sudden and drastic change in a character or a plot point. Normally, the screenwriter withholds certain character or plot information until the right moment to release them, surprising the audience and altering the direction of the story. This screenwriting technique is commonly used in genre films, including mystery, suspense, thriller, and horror. There are two types of reversal in a screenplay: a character reversal and a story reversal.

Character Reversal

A character can change themself to become someone else in the story or reveal their true identity. For example, in *The Dark Knight*, Harvey Dent transforms from a district attorney to a villain, Two-Face. He goes from being a supporting character to an antagonist. Another example is Rose Armitage in *Get Out*. She reveals her true self – a villain – to Chris during the climax of the film. Until this point, she had two identities: one that seduced Chris, and one that is cold-hearted, brainwashed by her family heritage. When she tells Chris that she can't give him the car keys, the audience feels her betrayal, even though they saw it coming. In *Toy Story*, the mutant toys in Sid's room have a character reversal – at first, they are a threat to Woody and Buzz, but later, mutant toys help Woody save Buzz during the ordeal and help them escape from Sid's backyard. Films like *The Usual Suspects* (1994) and *Knives Out* (2019) have character reversals. We the audience believe a character's objective is one thing, but later find out the objective is something else, pulling the rug out from underneath us. By applying reversal, screenwriters surprise the audience and twist the story's trajectory. Screenwriters use character reversal to dramatize the story by deepening or alleviating the conflict.

Story Reversal

A story's path can change as the plot twists to reveal a new direction. The short film, *Pigalle*, directed by Richard LaGravenese in the anthology film *Paris Je t'aime* (2006), gives us a perfect example of how a plot twist suddenly changes the direction. In *Pigalle*, a man enters an adult entertainment shop in Paris. The man sits at the bar and orders a drink. Next to him is a woman sipping her drink. They exchange smiles and chitchat. Then the man enters a small room in the back. Inside the room, the man negotiates a deal with a stripper. Suddenly the woman from the bar enters, surprising the man and seducing him. All seems to be going well when the woman gets upset and slaps the man. In doing so, she reveals their true identities. They are a couple, and they were role-playing to spice up their sex life, but something didn't go the way it was supposed to, and she got upset. The screenwriter withheld the truth about their relationship until the right moment. Now, the story of the man and woman takes a different turn. It's a new development, a reversal. Had we known they were a couple from the start, we would have had different expectations for the film.

Another example is *In the Mood for Love* (2000). When the two main characters find out that their spouses are cheating on them, they start building a friendship to cope with loneliness, but they end up falling in love in the process – a true reversal in the story.

A reversal changes the story's direction. The audience thinks the story moves in one direction, but it shifts into a new direction, and a new dramatic tension is raised.

DRAMATIC IRONY

The use of dramatic irony in a narrative story has been engaging the audience, spectators, and readers for centuries. If the audience didn't know Oedipus's fate from the start in Oedipus Rex, a play by Sophocles, how would the audience's experience change? Oedipus's fate – killing his father and marrying his mother – would have come as a surprise at the end when his true identity is revealed as the son of King Polybus. But knowing Oedipus's fate through Oracle's prophecy at the beginning adds suspense to the story. The audience is curious to foresee the protagonist's tragic future. They want to see how the tragic events will turn out and discover how Oedipus will confront the truth.

Dramatic irony occurs when the audience knows more than the characters in a story. At times, the audience is let into the story or character's secret, an important backstory, or a crucial plot point in hindering or achieving the goal. Dramatic irony cultivates curiosity about what the future will hold for the characters. The audience gets emotionally invested in the story.

If a friend confesses to you that he cheated on an exam, or better yet, you saw him cheat, wouldn't you want to know what happens next? Did he get caught? Did he get a good grade? Did he feel guilty, or is he planning to do it again? By letting the audience in on a secret, they indirectly become part of the story; their thoughts are invested in the story and in the character.

I have yet to watch a film or read a narrative book without the use of dramatic irony in a story. This technique is most commonly used by writers, and it is a very effective tool to bring the audience close to the heart of the story. Sometimes writers apply dramatic irony without a conscious effort. It's a technique that they are very familiar with, and it's embedded in their storytelling skills. It's almost second nature in distributing or withholding character and story information across the screenplay to raise tension for the audience. The screenwriter uses dramatic irony for the main plot but also in subplots, so it is very common to see several dramatic ironies used in a screenplay.

For example, in *The Dark Knight*, a noticeable dramatic irony in the film takes place during the "social experiment" scenes with the ferries, which I will discuss in a moment. Before I explain what the screenwriters did with these scenes, we need to revisit director Alfred Hitchcock's suspense vs. surprise example. Hitchcock said that if a group of people is gathered at a table and a bomb goes off, then the audience will be shocked. They will be surprised for 5–10 seconds. But suppose the same group of people are gathered at the table and the audience knows that there is a bomb underneath. In that case, it will create suspense for the duration of their conversation – a dramatic irony in which the audience knows more than the characters. The audience will be emotionally invested in the characters surrounding the table, and the tension will rise over time. Hitchcock says that the bomb should never go off. You must release the tension by ensuring that the bomb doesn't explode. If the bomb goes off, the audience will get upset.

Now, based on what Hitchcock said with the bomb analogy, let's look at the "social experiment" scenes in *The Dark Knight*. Two ferries leaving Gotham City have been rigged with bombs, and each bomb detonator has been placed on the opposite ferry. Now, the Joker tells the passengers on each ferry to blow up the other ferry if they want to live. Otherwise, at midnight, the Joker will blow up both of them. In this sequence, the screenwriters added a second bomb to Hitchcock's suspense vs. surprise bomb example.

Two dramatic ironies are going on in these scenes. The people on each ferry don't know what the people on the other ferry will do. The audience sees what is taking place on both ferries, and the suspense intensifies as double dramatic ironies press the audience. The release comes when the audience discovers that the passengers on either ferry cannot blow up the other ferry. They won't dare to kill the others. The citizens have spoken, and the moral decision has been made. Now, just as Joker is about to blow up the ferry, Batman intervenes, and the bombs on the ferries never go off.

In *Toy Story*, Buzz Lightyear thinks he is a space ranger, but the rest of the toys know he is just like one of them – a toy – and so does the audience. The suspense builds as the audience predicts disappointment when Buzz finds out about his true identity.

In *Get Out*, we saw what the Armitage family is planning behind Chris's back. The audience is let in on a secret, and now, the audience wants to know what will happen to Chris. The audience feels the tension and the suspense by knowing what the Armitage family is planning to do with Chris's consciousness and his body.

Dramatic irony is a great tool for writers to engage the audience. It helps the audience participate in the story, engaging them emotionally to the characters and to their objectives.

SETUP AND PAYOFF

The story's natural progression is to set up an objective for the protagonist, and then have them go on a journey to attain the objective. At the end of the story, the payoff is what they learned or gained along the journey, whether they accomplish or fail to attain the objective. There is a setup and payoff in the grand scheme of the main plot. In Chapter 3, "Story," I explained how the screenplay's story elements cause the main storyline to progress. Now, setup and payoff techniques are used to craft the plot as well as in subplots. A character's actions have cause and effect. Most action is premeditated and then executed. Therefore, a character's action has preparation and aftermath, a setup and payoff. Most screenwriters use this technique to make the audience anticipate an outcome from the character's actions – not just the protagonist's actions, but the actions of all characters in the screenplay.

The screenwriters for the film *The Apartment* (1960), Billy Wilder and I.A.L. Diamond, were masters of using setup and payoff techniques. They used it with every story element possible. They not only applied these techniques for plots and subplots, but they used this technique with dialogue, activities, and objects. For example, let's look at the setup and payoff used in a subplot. The screenwriters use Baxter's relationship with his neighbor, Dr. Dreyfuss, as a setup and payoff. Dr. Dreyfuss is introduced as a doctor who worries about Baxter's health because he thinks Baxter is the one who is partying every night, when actually he is just lending his apartment to executives in his firm for extramarital affairs, in exchange for his promotions. When Baxter finds Ms. Kubelik unconscious after taking sleeping pills in his apartment, he rushes to get Dr. Dreyfuss, and the neighbor helps Ms. Kubelik recover. Thus, there is both a setup and a payoff. Furthermore, Dr. Dreyfuss's honest plea for Baxter to have a decent life play into Baxter's moral consciousness. It helps him to remove himself from the toxic corporate environment later in the screenplay.

As Dr. Dreyfuss plays an important supporting character in *The Apartment*, Rod plays an important supporting character in *Get Out*. Rod helps to move the story with a setup and payoff. Rod, a T.S.A. agent and Chris's best friend, is skeptical about Chris visiting Rose's parents. Rod thinks it is a bad idea for Chris to visit his white girlfriend's parents over the weekend. What started as a joke becomes a reality, and Chris's life is threatened. The writer sets up this supporting character, Rod, to be used as comic reliefs in the story. He's also in a subplot, helping Chris at the end of the film. Rod's persistence in finding out what has happened to Chris pays off when he saves him at the end. From Chris's point of view, in the main plot, there is a payoff when he escapes the Armitage estate alive. This is an example of a subplot having a payoff, but it also explains how the subplot's payoff helps the main plot's payoff.

Now, let's look at Wilder and Diamond's use of an object as a setup and payoff in *The Apartment*. The confusion between the corporate executive washroom key and Baxter's apartment key is the setup in the first act. One of the executives leaves the wrong key under the doormat and Baxter is locked out of his apartment for the night. The confusion with the keys is then used in the third act, when Mr. Sheldrake asks for the keys to his apartment. Baxter returns the key to the executive washroom instead of giving the key to his apartment on purpose, and Mr. Sheldrake, his boss, gets confused. Baxter states that he won't be needing the executive washroom as he quits the job. Another example with the use of an object as both a setup and payoff is in *Lady Bird*. Marion, the mother, writes a letter to Lady Bird, her daughter, who is going away to college. We see crumpled sheets of paper lying all around the kitchen table and the floor as Marion tries to write the perfect letter. Larry, Marion's husband and Lady Bird's father, slips a folder into Lady Bird's luggage before she departs for New York City. When Lady Bird arrives at the dorm and unpacks, she notices the folder. She finds all the different versions and drafts of the letters her mother wrote. Actions speak louder than words. The writer sets up the sequence by showing how much Marion loves her daughter, despite how much she was against her daughter going away for college. The screenwriter shows Marion's feelings through actions. Now, the payoff takes place when Lady Bird gets to see Marion's love for her through the attempts of writing one perfect letter. The screenwriter uses a character's intent to show love for her daughter as a setup, and introduces Larry as a mediator who connects Marion's action to the payoff when Lady Bird sees the letters. The screenwriter uses a letter as both a setup and payoff to show Marion's love for her daughter.

Now, the use of activity as a setup and payoff in *The Apartment* is the card game Baxter and Ms. Kubelik play. When she is staying over to recover from taking the pills, Baxter and Ms. Kubelik play a card game, setting up the payoff. Ms. Kubelik returns to his apartment on New Year's Eve, and they pick up the card game where they left off. The payoff provokes a strong emotional reaction from the audience. Baxter confesses his love for Ms. Kubelik while he is holding the deck of cards, and

Ms. Kubelik replies, "Shut up and deal." The subtext of her dialogue carries strong meaning: she already knows how much Baxter loves her. She realized it when he refused to give the key to his apartment to Mr. Sheldrake. This ending wouldn't have worked without the setup of the card game during an earlier encounter.

Finally, let's look at the use of dialogue as a setup and payoff. In *The Apartment*, Dr. Dreyfuss thinks Ms. Kubelik has taken the pills because of Baxter. He tells Baxter to become a "mensch," a man with honor and integrity. During the film's climax, Baxter tells Mr. Sheldrake that he has decided to become a mensch. The use of this word, "mensch," was planted early in a passing comment by Dr. Dreyfuss, but when Baxter mentions it to Mr. Sheldrake, it has a strong payoff, as we see Baxter's transformation.

These are just a few examples of how the screenwriters used the setup and payoff techniques to engage the audience. Wilder and Diamond didn't waste a single moment: every character, every action, every encounter, every conflict had a purpose in the screenplay, and they were all shown through the use of setup and payoff. Most screenwriters rework the setup and payoff during the revision and rewrite of their screenplays.

Part III
SCRIPT ANALYSIS

To put our discussions into practice, I have selected seven films to illustrate the deconstruction of screenplay elements by applying the script analysis techniques discussed in this book. These analyses are not meant to be definitive breakdowns of each screenplay, but rather they are intended as demonstrations of the ways how screenplays can be deconstructed and studied. To get the most out of these analyses, it is very important to be familiar with each screenplay. I suggest you find the latest versions of these screenplays and read them with an analyst's mindset. Think about the writer's intentions and try to understand how the screenplay elements are working together throughout the story.

These screenplays were carefully chosen with four different criteria in mind:

- One, it must be a good story well told, with solid screenwriting fundamentals, and it must have received both critical acclaim and box-office success.
- Two, they must have diverse voices. These screenplays were written by a diverse group of filmmakers. I wanted to include works written by various genders and works from writers outside the United States. I also wanted to include screenplays in different genres and made on various budgets – from low-budget films to Hollywood blockbusters.
- Three, I wanted to focus on contemporary screenplays, not classics, except for *The Apartment*. It is imperative to know how screenplays have been evolving and learn from classics as well.
- Four, I wanted the screenplays I chose to be easily accessible for educational purposes.

The screenplays I've chosen to analyze are as follows:

- *The Apartment* (Romance/Comedy/Drama), 1960

DOI: 10.4324/9781003138853-9

- *Toy Story* (Animation/Family), 1995
- *The Dark Knight* (Action/Crime/Drama/Thriller), 2008
- *Whiplash* (Indie/Music/Drama), 2014
- *Get Out* (Horror/Mystery/Thriller), 2017
- *Lady Bird* (Comedy/Drama), 2017
- *Parasite* (Comedy/Drama/Thriller), 2019

SCRIPT ANALYSIS QUESTIONS

The following questions are based on the material presented in each chapter. I've provided answers to these questions to help you analyze the seven screenplays.

I. Theme and Premise

1. What is the theme of the screenplay?
2. What is the premise of the story?

II. Character Study

1. Who are the major characters in the screenplay, and what are their character types?
2. What are the backstories in the screenplay, and how are they relevant to the story?
3. How is the protagonist introduced in the film, and what do we learn about them?
4. What are some of the protagonist's psychological, physical, and social attributes?
5. How does the protagonist see the world?
6. How does the antagonist see the world?
7. What are the protagonist's work/professional, family/personal, and secret/private lives?
8. What are the different personas the protagonist wears throughout the screenplay?
9. What is the protagonist's main objective?
10. What is the antagonist's main objective?
11. What are the protagonist's external and internal conflicts?
12. How does the protagonist transform over the course of the screenplay?

III. Story Elements

1. Who is the protagonist?
2. What is the inciting incident in the screenplay?
3. What is the protagonist's objective?
4. What is the main tension in the screenplay?
5. What is the action taken by the protagonist in achieving their goal?

6. What is the main conflict in the screenplay?
7. What is the crisis in the screenplay, and how does the protagonist overcome it?
8. What happens during the climax of the screenplay?
9. What is the answer to the main tension? Did the protagonist achieve their goals?
10. What is the resolution in the screenplay?

IV. Structure (Three-Act Structure)

1. How is the story set up in the first act?
2. How does the first act end?
3. How does the story complicate/develop in the second act?
4. How does the second act end?
5. How does the story resolve in the third act?

V. Setting

1. Where is the geographic location of the story?
2. In which time period does the story take place?
3. What is the world of the story?
4. What is the sociocultural setting of the screenplay?

VI. Techniques and Tools

1. What are some of the important events/occurrences in the screenplay?
2. What are some of the instances of dramatic irony used in the screenplay?
3. Are there any uses of reversal in the screenplay?
4. What are some of the instances of setup and payoff used in the screenplay?

THE APARTMENT
(Romance/Comedy/Drama), 1960

Writers: Billy Wilder and I.A.L. Diamonds

I. THEME AND PREMISE

Theme

Let's go back to an earlier example from Chapter 1. The theme of *Groundhog Day* is: "People can change, and when they change, they can get the rewards they want in life." Now, let's look at the theme of *The Apartment*. Doesn't Baxter transform at the end of the film? When he transforms, he wins over Ms. Kubelik's heart, doesn't he? *Groundhog Day* and *The Apartment* share similar themes, including dignity over greed and integrity over dishonesty. When people change, they can be rewarded in life.

Premise

A young and ambitious corporate worker tries to move ahead in the firm by arranging favors for the executives. In return, he wants a promotion.

II. CHARACTER STUDY

Characters

Protagonist: C.C. "Bud" Baxter
Antagonist: Mr. Sheldrake
Supporting characters: Ms. Fran Kubelik, Dr. Dreyfuss, Mildred Dreyfuss, Ms. Olsen, Joe Dobisch, Al Kirkeby, Mr. Vanderhoff, Mr. Eichelberger

Backstory

Several backstories are mentioned throughout the screenplay. Some backstories reveal characters' pasts, and some backstories pertain to the plot of the film. One

DOI: 10.4324/9781003138853-10

of the most important backstories that explain how everything started is revealed when Baxter meets Mr. Sheldrake for the first time. Baxter, who lives in a one-bedroom apartment on the Upper West Side of Manhattan, lends his apartment to his coworker, who needs to change into a tuxedo. The word gets out about his apartment, and whenever someone needs a place in the city, they ask Baxter. Now the executives are using his bachelor pad as their secret place to conduct extramarital affairs with their mistresses.

Protagonist's Introduction

The screenplay introduces Baxter through his own voice-over. He gives insurance statistics, talks about his job as an insurance clerk, and says he works late a lot because he can't always get into his apartment. Baxter is introduced at his office as one of the hundreds of workers crunching numbers at their desks. After everyone goes home, he works alone on the 19th floor. The introduction provides an opening into his professional life and personal life. Baxter presents a conflict about his apartment at the beginning when he states: "The only problem is: I can't always get it when I want to." Baxter waits for his "guests" to clear out of his apartment. Once they leave, Baxter finally goes in, cleans up, heats up a frozen meal, flips through the TV channels as he eats, and then goes to bed. As he is about to fall asleep, he gets a call from another executive demanding that he clear out of the apartment, as he is coming over with a date.

Psychological, Physical, and Social Attributes

Wilder and Diamond describe Baxter as "serious, hard-working, and unobtrusive." As you get to know Baxter, he seems to be a genuinely nice guy. He is considerate, polite, and caring. He may be ambitious and greedy in his efforts to climb the corporate ladder, but he's also a pushover. Baxter throws away his moral codes and even his own comfort to please the executives. All we know about his physical attributes is that he is about 30, and he has a scar on his knee from shooting himself in a car, which is exposed through a backstory. Socially, he doesn't have much going on in his life, as he recently moved to New York from Cincinnati. He doesn't have many friends and is lonely. On Christmas Eve, he goes out drinking alone. His neighbor, Dr. Dreyfuss, thinks he is partying every night and sometimes has two dates in one night. But Baxter doesn't reveal the truth.

Protagonist's Worldview

Baxter's point of view of the world is optimistic, unethical, and selfish. He is optimistic because he believes that pleasing the executives might get him a promotion, and he will gain esteem and respect. That is why he lets his superiors walk all over him, and that is why he has a hard time saying "no" to them. He is so wrapped up in this corporate world that he struggles to choose between his ambitions and the woman he loves. He bends his moral code for his future, facilitating his superiors' extramarital affairs. He is selfish and greedy for wanting to take advantage of the scheme in order to advance in the firm.

Antagonist's Worldview

Mr. Sheldrake's point of view of the world is corrupt. He feels entitled to abuse his powers as a director of personnel. When he discovers Baxter's scheme, instead of firing him for his unethical code of conduct, he decides to join in, promising Baxter a bright future.

Protagonist's Life

Baxter's life consists of having a career at an insurance company. He has no social life. The only encounters he has outside of the office are with his neighbor, Dr. Dreyfuss, and in his private life, he is a lonely man.

Protagonist's Personas

Baxter has a professional persona that he wears at the office and around the executives. He is just a pushover, someone who bends to his superiors' will. In his personal life, he wears a different persona with his neighbors; he acts like a womanizer to cover up for the fact that he is letting others use his apartment. In his private life, he gets to be himself. When he interacts with Ms. Kubelik, he is charming, funny, and caring.

Protagonist's Objectives

Baxter has his sights set on becoming a young executive for the firm, and the only advantage he has in this world is his apartment. In his personal life, Baxter wants privacy and time to himself, as he is forced to spend a lot of time outside of his apartment. In his private life, Baxter has a huge crush on Fran Kubelik, an elevator operator at the company. He wants to win her over.

Antagonist's Objectives

Mr. Sheldrake wants to maintain his extramarital affair with Ms. Kubelik by using Baxter's apartment. He abuses his power as the director of personnel and manipulates his employees to get what he wants.

Protagonist's Conflicts

Baxter's most significant conflict is an internal conflict. He wants a promotion, and he also wants to win over Ms. Kubelik. This is a conflict of interest because the man responsible for his promotion is having an affair with the woman he loves. At first, he decides to suppress any feelings he has for her in order to achieve his main objective. His external conflict, the character vs. character conflict, is with the director of personnel. Mr. Sheldrake has the power to give him the promotion he wants, but he is also using Ms. Kubelik for their extramarital affair. Baxter doesn't have the courage to come in between them. The character vs. environment conflict is Baxter's conflict with the toxic corporate environment.

Protagonist's Transformation

Baxter goes through a clear character transformation. At the beginning of the screenplay, he is miserable, but at the end of the screenplay, he is happy with himself – a change in his emotional arc. Baxter becomes a man of dignity and integrity, a total contrast to who he was at the beginning of the film when he was willing to overlook the unethical behaviors of his supervisors. Furthermore, Baxter stops being a pushover and stands up for himself and for what he wants.

III. STORY ELEMENTS

Protagonist

C.C. "Bud" Baxter is in his 30s. He is a low-level employee at a gigantic insurance company in New York City. A.O. Scott, a film critic for the *New York Times*, described Baxter as a "genuinely nice guy with a timid soul."

Inciting Incident

The time has come for Baxter to receive his reward after letting the four executives borrow his apartment. As the year's end is approaching, the executives send employee performance reports to the director of personnel, Mr. Sheldrake, the antagonist. Baxter has collected enough "points" from the four executives to get a promotion, but Mr. Sheldrake discovers an abnormality in the reports, even as the four executives are praising Baxter's productivity. Mr. Sheldrake calls Baxter into his office to question him, but Baxter thinks he is getting a promotion. When Baxter arrives, Mr. Sheldrake intimidates him and asks him to reveal the truth. Baxter confesses to the illicit apartment scheme he is running for the executives. Baxter promises that he will give it up. There is a reversal we didn't see coming in Mr. Sheldrake's reaction to Baxter's scheme: instead of firing him, Mr. Sheldrake wants the same arrangement for himself. Baxter finally has met the person with powers to give him the promotion he wants. Now, all he has to do is to please the director of personnel.

Jack Lemmon, the actor who plays Baxter, discussed his character in an interview:

> It's not that Baxter was a nice guy who's gone wrong, it's that he's hysterically naïve. . . . He'd been taught that success was how far you could get in

a company and how much money you could earn, and he's surrounded by these leeches who just use him to have assignments in his apartment. We know damned well that people in big business still behave like that.

Protagonist's Objective

Baxter's main objective is to accommodate Mr. Sheldrake's request in exchange for promotions. After encountering Mr. Sheldrake, Baxter gets a promotion, becomes a second administrative assistant, and moves into an office. Now nothing is stopping him – Baxter has cleared a path for success; he just needs to make arrangements for Mr. Sheldrake. Baxter's secondary objective is his desire to win over Fran Kubelik's heart. He makes arrangements to go on a date with Ms. Kubelik, but he is stood up.

Main Tension

The main tension that arises at the end of Act One is: "Can Baxter move up the corporate ladder by making arrangements for Mr. Sheldrake?" This is the main tension that carries the story in the second act. Besides the main tension, a second through-line gets raised at the end of the first act: Baxter's love interest for Ms. Kubelik, which raises the question: "Can Baxter win her heart?"

Action

The main action begins when Baxter decides to give the key to his apartment to Mr. Sheldrake. Instead of standing up for himself, he ignores his need to sleep off a terrible cold. He is obsessed with achieving his goal. At the beginning of the second act, Baxter immediately gets a promotion from Mr. Sheldrake, but Baxter's aspiration doesn't end there. Baxter keeps making arrangements for Mr. Sheldrake to stay in his apartment twice a week. So Baxter's actions reflect his desire to move up the ladder.

Main Conflict

The main conflict is the dilemma Baxter has when he discovers the woman Mr. Sheldrake is having an affair with is Fran Kubelik, the elevator operator at the firm, whom Baxter has a crush on. Baxter's main conflict is dealt with externally and internally. His external conflict is with Mr. Sheldrake. Previously, Baxter did not have a problem with Mr. Sheldrake using his apartment for affairs, but now that the woman Mr. Sheldrake is seeing is the woman Baxter cares for, he faces a big dilemma. Baxter is presented with a conflict of interest, an internal conflict. If he wants to advance in the firm, he must let go of his interest in Ms. Kubelik. If he wants to go after her, he cannot allow Mr. Sheldrake to use her anymore.

The screenwriters first let us, the audience, in on a secret by showing Mr. Sheldrake meeting Ms. Kubelik before Baxter finds out they are together – a dramatic irony. The screenwriter makes us feel sympathy for Baxter as Ms. Kubelik decides to stay with Mr. Sheldrake, breaking her promise of meeting Baxter that evening. Meanwhile, Mr. Sheldrake takes Ms. Kubelik to Baxter's apartment. Baxter stood up, waited at the theater for her to arrive. What a tragic evening for Baxter, but perhaps it's better that he didn't find out the truth that evening.

Crisis

At the Christmas office party, Baxter invites Ms. Kubelik to show off the new junior executive hat he has recently purchased. Ms. Kubelik hands him the compact with the fleur-de-lis pattern with a broken mirror inside so that he may check himself in the mirror. But Baxter's expression changes when he sees the broken mirror. It is the same makeup compact kit Baxter gave to Mr. Sheldrake to return to the woman who left it behind in his apartment. Baxter discovers that the woman he is after is having an affair with the person who has power over his promotion. That evening, Baxter goes out to a bar alone to drink the night away. During the Christmas party on the 19th floor, Ms. Olson, Mr. Sheldrake's assistant, reveals that Ms. Kubelik has been played by her boss, listing the women Mr. Sheldrake has had affairs with, including herself. Ms. Kubelik discovers how little she means to him, and that evening, she takes an overdose of sleeping pills.

When Baxter returns home, he finds Ms. Kubelik unconscious in his bed and asks his neighbor, Dr. Dreyfuss for help. First, the doctor pumps her stomach, then forces her to drink coffee and prevents her from falling asleep by walking her around the living room. In the early hours of the morning, Ms. Kubelik finally recovers from the overdose. She is in stable condition and can finally rest.

Baxter makes a conscious choice to overcome the crisis he is confronted with. Instead of standing up for Ms. Kubelik, Baxter's action is to keep working toward his promotion, and that means he has to do everything he can to cover up her suicide attempt and leave Mr. Sheldrake out of it. First, Baxter hides the envelope Ms. Kubelik left for Mr. Sheldrake, which looks like a suicide note. Then Baxter notifies Mr. Sheldrake of the incident, and Mr. Sheldrake asks Baxter to take care of the situation. He says that he is counting on him, and Baxter follows his orders.

In the next two days, Baxter makes sure she recovers not only physically, but also emotionally. In the process, they connect on a level they haven't before. They enjoy each other's company. Ms. Kubelik realizes how caring and nice Baxter is to her, and Baxter falls deeper in love with her and realizes she is the woman he wants to be with. As he did with Dr. Dreyfuss, Baxter takes the blame for the situation when Mr. Kubelik's angry brother-in-law comes to pick her up. The brother-in-law knocks Baxter down with a punch in the face. Ms. Kubelik realizes what Baxter is doing to cover up the incident. She calls him a "fool" and kisses him on his forehead.

Now let's look at this crisis from Baxter's point of view. First, Baxter comes home and finds Ms. Kubelik in his bed. He thinks she has fallen asleep and tries to kick her out of the apartment. His voice shows resentment toward her because he discovered that Ms. Kubelik was the woman Mr. Sheldrake was having an affair with. When he realizes she has overdosed on his sleeping pills, his attitude changes. He is in a horrible situation, and he is in shock to see the woman he loves attempt suicide in his apartment. Because he wants the promotion, he is willing to help cover up the incident instead of standing up for her.

Baxter's main objective has always been a promotion. The crisis of finding Ms. Kubelik in this apartment affects him personally, but he puts his feelings aside and overcomes challenges by protecting Mr. Sheldrake from a possible scandal. Baxter's action shows his desire for his main objective. However, in spending two days with her, Baxter realizes his affection for Ms. Kubelik is getting stronger, and he desires to win her over.

Climax

Baxter's final confrontation with Mr. Sheldrake at the office on New Year's Eve is the climax of the story. His transformation is shown through his actions. When Mr. Sheldrake asks for the keys to Baxter's apartment so that he can take Ms. Kubelik there, Baxter refuses. He stands up for himself and firmly rejects Mr. Sheldrake, saying, "You are not going to bring anybody into my apartment. . . Especially not Ms. Kubelik. . . No key." Mr. Sheldrake threatens to fire him, and Baxter throws a key onto the desk and walks out. As Mr. Sheldrake marches into Baxter's office to tell him that it's the wrong key – that it's the key to the executives' washroom – Baxter tells him he won't be needing it anymore and gathers his belongings. Before walking out, Baxter tells Mr. Sheldrake that "I decided to become a mensch. Do you know what that means? A human being."

Now, there is a buildup leading up to the climax. When Baxter goes to see Mr. Sheldrake after Christmas break, it feels like a final confrontation. From the moment Baxter arrives at his office until he enters Mr. Sheldrake's office, Baxter practices his lines, saying how Mr. Sheldrake's troubles are over, he is going to take Ms. Kubelik off his hands, how he loves her very much. But when he arrives at the office, Mr. Sheldrake beats him to the punch, saying that Baxter doesn't need to worry about Ms. Kubelik anymore. Mrs. Sheldrake, his wife, has kicked him out of the house for cheating and that he is going to take Ms. Kubelik off Baxter's hands. Again, Baxter doesn't stand up for himself. He is not brave enough to tell Mr. Sheldrake the lines he has been practicing. A coward, he informs Mr. Sheldrake that Ms. Kubelik returned home last night. Mr. Sheldrake gives Baxter a huge unexpected promotion for taking care of the matter when he wasn't able to, and Baxter becomes Mr. Sheldrake's right-hand man as assistant director. This is a significant reversal in the story, as what we thought would be the climax of the film takes a turn and complicates the plot even more.

Answer to the Main Tension

The main tension of the film is: "Can Baxter move up the corporate ladder by making arrangements for Mr. Sheldrake, director of the personnel?" The answer to the main tension is: Yes. Baxter gets a huge promotion as assistant director for facilitating the affair and helping to cover up for Mr. Sheldrake. As part of his promotion, Baxter moves up to the 27th floor. However, during the climax, Baxter gives up his promotion and quits the job. This is a reversal we weren't expecting, which leads to the resolution of the screenplay, answering the other through-line of the film: "Can Baxter win over Ms. Kubelik's heart?" The answer to the second through-line is: yes, he wins her heart.

Resolution

The resolution begins as Baxter packs up to move out of his apartment on New Year's Eve. Dr. Dreyfuss comes over, asking for ice, as he has guests. Dr. Dreyfuss plays a significant role as a supporting character. He is the one who tells Baxter to be a "mensch." The screenwriters are tying up loose ends and providing Dr. Dreyfuss an exit from the film. Meanwhile, Mr. Sheldrake and Ms. Kubelik are back in their regular booth at the Chinese restaurant, celebrating New Year's Eve. During their casual chat, Ms. Kubelik discovers why Baxter gave up his job: Baxter refused to give the keys to his apartment to Mr. Sheldrake. Baxter was against his boss taking Ms. Kubelik to his place, and he was willing to walk out of the office for it. She realizes how much Baxter cares for her, and she runs to his apartment. When she arrives, Baxter confesses his love for her while playing the card game. She knows it, though, and tells him to just "shut up and deal."

And that's how it ends – with a fresh start for this couple. *The Apartment* is the story of Baxter's moral transformation from being a goal-oriented corporate pushover/yes-man to a self-respecting man. The conscious change he makes at the end of the story helps him go from being a pushover to being someone who stands up for himself. Baxter does the right thing. He transforms himself into a man of dignity.

IV. STRUCTURE (THREE-ACT STRUCTURE)

The screenplay has six instances of "FADE-OUT," indicating that the screenplay has six acts. In a conventional three-act structure, the first two fade-outs would be grouped together and be considered the first act. The third and fourth fade-outs would be grouped into the second act. The fifth and sixth fade-outs would be grouped into the third act.

Six-Act Structure

- First Act: The setup. In Baxter's ordinary world, the scheme he runs is exposed.
- Second Act: The conflict. Baxter is in love with the boss's mistress. His objective – to please Mr. Sheldrake in exchange for a promotion – is established

early on in the story, but a complication arises when the audience discovers the man Ms. Kubelik is dating is the man responsible for giving Baxter his promotion.

- Third Act: The crisis. Baxter gets the first promotion but at a high price. He discovers that the woman he loves is dating his boss. To make the matter worse, Ms. Kubelik overdoses on sleeping pills in Baxter's apartment after Mr. Sheldrake leaves her.
- Fourth Act: The complication. Ms. Kubelik recovers and Baxter helps to cover up the incident for his boss.
- Fifth Act: The final push, or the climax. Mr. Sheldrake fires Ms. Olsen, his secretary, for causing trouble for him. Ms. Olsen had told Ms. Kubelik about Mr. Sheldrake's previous affairs, which caused Ms. Kubelik to take the pills. Baxter falls deeper in love with Ms. Kubelik during this time and gains the courage and confidence to tell his boss.
- Sixth Act: The resolution. Once again, Baxter doesn't stand up for himself. He never mentions his feelings for her to Mr. Sheldrake. Instead, he gets a promotion, but Baxter quits when Mr. Sheldrake asks for the keys to his apartment. He becomes a "mensch." And when he transforms, he is rewarded in life.

V. SETTING

The *geographic location* of the story is set in New York City, and the *time period* is 1959. The story world is set in a large insurance company in downtown Manhattan. The *sociocultural setting* in this film documents the social, cultural, and traditional aspects of our lives, and this story contains inappropriate social behaviors, which were commonly accepted in the 1950s. Women in this story were mistreated within the corporate environment.

VI. TECHNIQUES AND TOOLS

Events/Occurrences

The screenwriters chose to end the first act with a meeting between Baxter and Mr. Sheldrake, director of personnel. Baxter thinks he is getting a promotion, but instead, he almost gets fired when Mr. Sheldrake discovers the scheme he is running. Baxter has been lending his apartment to the executives for their extramarital affairs in exchange for a great performance review, so that he may climb up the corporate ladder and become the youngest executive in the firm. However, Mr. Sheldrake wants to use Baxter's apartment in exchange for a promotion. Finally, Baxter has met the person with the powers to give him the actual promotion. The second act is about Baxter working to accommodate and please Mr. Sheldrake to achieve his objective.

The event/occurrence at the end of the second act is another meeting between Baxter and Mr. Sheldrake. Baxter has been taking care of Ms. Kubelik, who has taken an overdose of sleeping pills. During this time, Baxter spends days and nights taking care of Ms. Kubelik and falls further in love with her. Baxter decides to let Mr. Sheldrake know about his feelings for her when he returns to the office. However, during the meeting, Baxter learns that Mr. Sheldrake has been kicked out of the house for cheating and that he is going to take Ms. Kubelik away – a complete reversal from Baxter's plan. Mr. Sheldrake thanks Baxter for taking care of her and breaks more news: he promotes Baxter to assistant director of personnel and offers him the office next to his. Baxter gets the promotion he wants, but he doesn't get the girl.

Other important events/occurrences in the story include Christmas Eve and New Year's Eve. In the story, one of the most dramatic events takes place during the holiday office party. Baxter discovers what the audience has known all along, a dramatic irony: Ms. Kubelik is the woman Mr. Sheldrake has been seeing. Furthermore, Ms. Kubelik finds out through Ms. Olsen, Mr. Sheldrake's secretary, the truth about Mr. Sheldrake's previous affairs and how he has no plans to leave his family. Baxter drinks the night away, and Ms. Kubelik takes the pills in Baxter's apartment after Mr. Sheldrake leaves. All of these occurrences take place on Christmas Eve.

Now, New Year's Eve is another important day in the screenplay. Baxter seems to have given up on pursuing Ms. Kubelik and is focusing on his work when Mr. Sheldrake asks for the keys to his apartment to take Ms. Kubelik away on New Year's Eve. Baxter refuses to give the keys to his boss, and when given an ultimatum, Baxter quits his job. When Ms. Kubelik finds out what has happened from Mr. Sheldrake during the New Year's Eve party, she runs toward Baxter's apartment.

Dramatic Irony

The audience knows the woman Mr. Sheldrake is having an affair with is Ms. Kubelik, but Baxter doesn't know. The writer uses this dramatic irony to raise the audience's interest in future events. The audience knows Baxter has the biggest crush on Ms. Kubelik and also knows that he wants the promotion. The mixed feelings the audience gets by knowing what the protagonist doesn't create dramatic irony. The writers let Baxter discover the truth when he returns a compact makeup case with a broken mirror to Mr. Sheldrake; the compact belongs to the woman with whom he is having an affair. Then Baxter sees Ms. Kubelik with the same compact case. Baxter puts two and two together and figures out their relationship. How did the dramatic irony work for the audience? Because the screenwriters kept this information from the protagonist, Baxter, and let the audience in on the secret, they created a sense of sympathy toward him. The question "It's really unfortunate, but what is he going to do when he finds out?" is raised in the audience's mind.

Another dramatic irony happens when the neighbors, Dr. Dreyfuss and Mrs. Dreyfuss, think Baxter is the bachelor making all the noise at night. But Baxter doesn't reveal the truth because it might not work in his favor. Having his neighbors know the scheme he is running will never go well, so Baxter keeps it a secret. His lies grow when Ms. Kubelik takes the pills. Baxter asks Dr. Dreyfuss for help. His neighbor thinks Ms. Kubelik took the pills because of Baxter. Dr. Dreyfuss tells Baxter to become a "mensch," a person with integrity and honor – a real human being. Baxter doesn't reveal the truth to Dr. Dreyfuss until the end. The audience knows more than the supporting character, and the writer decides not to reveal this secret.

Reversal

I mentioned this earlier, but Baxter thinks he is getting a promotion when he meets Mr. Sheldrake for the first time. However, when he gets there, Mr. Sheldrake questions him about a key that has traveled through the company mail system and confronts Baxter about the key being to his apartment. Baxter tells the truth, explaining that the key is his, and tells him that executives have been scheduling his apartment for affairs. He pleads for forgiveness and asks Mr. Sheldrake to let him keep his job. There is a story reversal here: Baxter thought he was getting a promotion, but now he is on the verge of getting fired. Now, as Mr. Sheldrake finds out what Baxter is doing, there is a dramatic shift in the scene. Mr. Sheldrake wants to be part of the scheme. He swaps a pair of tickets to a musical with the key to Baxter's apartment for the evening and informs him that there will be personnel changes around the office, saying that Baxter is executive material.

Another use of reversal in the story takes place at the end of the film when all seems to have gone back to normal. After Baxter quits, he starts to pack up to move out of New York City. Mr. Sheldrake and Ms. Kubelik are back together, enjoying the New Year's Eve party. Mr. Sheldrake tells the story of how he couldn't get the key to Baxter's apartment for the night and how Baxter refused to give it to him, especially because he was going there with Ms. Kubelik. Mr. Sheldrake tells her that Baxter has quit his job. Ms. Kubelik realizes that Baxter did it for her; he didn't give the key to Mr. Sheldrake to protect her. At that moment, Ms. Kubelik runs toward Baxter's apartment. When she arrives, they pick up a card game they didn't get to finish the last time they were together. It is a happy ending, a reversal in their story arc.

Setup and Payoff

Wilder and Diamond were masters of using setup and payoff techniques. They used it with every story element possible to have a setup and payoff. They not only applied these techniques in subplots, but they also used them with dialogue, activities, and props.

For example, let's look at the use of subplot: the screenwriters use Baxter's relationship with Dr. Dreyfuss as having a setup and payoff. Baxter's neighbor is introduced as a doctor who worries about Baxter's health because he thinks Baxter is the one who is partying every night. Furthermore, when Baxter finds Ms. Kubelik unconscious, he rushes to get Dr. Dreyfuss, and the neighbor helps Ms. Kubelik recover after taking sleeping pills. Dr. Dreyfuss and his honest plea for Baxter to have a decent life play into Baxter's moral quandary, which helps him to remove himself from the toxic corporate environment.

Let's look at the use of a prop as a setup and payoff. The confusion between the corporate executive washroom key and Baxter's apartment key is the setup in the first act. One of the executives left the wrong key under the doormat, and Baxter was locked out of his apartment for the evening. This confusion is then used in the third act when Baxter returns the key to the executive washroom instead of giving Mr. Sheldrake the key to his apartment.

Let's look at the use of activity as a setup and payoff. The card game Baxter and Ms. Kubelik play when she is staying over to recover becomes a setup, which pays off when she returns to his apartment on New Year's Eye, and they pick up the card game again.

Finally, let's look at the use of dialogue as a setup and payoff. Dr. Dreyfuss tells Baxter to become a "mensch," a man with honor and integrity, when he thinks Ms. Kubelik has taken the pills because of Baxter. During the resolution of the film, Baxter tells Mr. Sheldrake that he has decided to become a "mensch."

These are just a few examples of how the screenwriters used the setup and pay-off techniques to engage the audience. Wilder said: "If you have a problem with the third act, the real problem is in the first act." If you have problems with resolution at the end of the story, then the real problem is in the story's setup.

TOY STORY
(Animation/Family), 1995

Original Story by: John Lasseter, Pete Docter, Andrew Stanton, and Joe Ranft

Screenwriters: Joss Whedon, Andrew Stanton, Joel Cohen, and Alec Sokolow

I. THEME AND PREMISE

Theme

Egotism leads to the loss of friends and isolation. Woody has been Andy's favorite toy for some time, but now self-interest takes over Woody's emotions as Buzz Lightyear becomes Andy's favorite toy. Now, Woody must let go of his ego and learn to work together with his adversary, Buzz, to reunite with Andy and his friends.

Premise

Toys come alive when humans are not around. Woody, the leader and Andy's favorite toy, becomes jealous of Buzz, as he becomes Andy's new favorite toy. Woody tries to find ways to become the number-one toy again, but in the process, he is separated from Andy and his friends. Now he must find a way back with the help of his adversary.

II. CHARACTER STUDY

Characters

Protagonist: Sheriff Woody
Antagonist: Sid
Supporting characters: Human: Andy, Mrs. Davis (Andy's mom), Molly (Andy's sister) Toys: Buzz Lightyear, Mr. Potato Head, Sarge, Slinky Dog, Rex, Hamm, Bo Peep, and the mutant toys

DOI: 10.4324/9781003138853-11

Backstory

An important backstory in the screenplay is that Woody has been Andy's favorite toy. As the other toys are put back in their bins each day, Woody always stays on Andy's bed. Another backstory important to the plot comes from Andy's exposition. As Mrs. Davis hangs up the "Happy Birthday" sign. Andy says: "Can we leave this up till we move?" Furthermore, seeing the "House for Sale" sign at the beginning of the film tells the audience that Andy's mom plans to move.

Protagonist's Introduction

Andy introduces Sheriff Woody as he plays with his toys. Mr. Potato Head is robbing a bank, and Woody comes to the rescue, capturing him and putting him in jail. Andy tells Woody he saved the day again. As the opening credits roll, Andy plays with Woody around the house. The introduction establishes Andy's relationship with the protagonist: Woody is Andy's favorite toy. The second introduction occurs when Woody comes alive when Andy and Molly, his sister, are not around. Woody calls a staff meeting, and Slinky helps gather every toy that has come alive in the room. Woody plans a mission to spy on the humans, as it is their ritual to see if Andy gets a new present for his birthday.

Psychological, Physical, and Social Attributes

Woody, a cowboy and sheriff, is brave, and he has charming qualities that help to bring everyone together. He is positive and kind-hearted. But when Buzz arrives, jealousy takes over. Woody is affected psychologically by the lack of affection he once used to get from Andy. Woody confronts Buzz and tries to hide him from Andy. He becomes self-centered and insecure. Physically, Woody is an old-fashioned pull-string cowboy doll, but when humans are not around, he comes alive. Socially, Woody is a natural leader. He plans and executes missions with the other toys.

Protagonist's Worldview

Woody's point of view of the world revolves around his playtime with Andy. Being Andy's favorite toy made Woody believe he is irreplaceable. Woody is very possessive of Andy and can't accept that Buzz is becoming the number-one toy. When Buzz threatens his reason for existence, Woody takes action to restore order but learns an important lesson in the process.

Antagonist's Worldview

Sid entertains himself by torturing his toys. Instead of playing with them, he likes pulling them apart or blowing them up with explosives. Sid is a mean kid, and the toys in Andy's room are scared of his malicious acts.

Protagonist's Life and Personas

Woody's work/professional life is being a toy. He waits for Andy to play with him. In his personal life, he is friends with every toy in Andy's room, and he is the group leader. In his private life, Woody has the heart set on Bo Peep, the porcelain doll. Woody is first introduced to us as a calm, confident, and collected leader in front of the other toys, but when Buzz takes his spot, Woody changes, he becomes self-centered, insecure, and unconfident. But at the end of the adventure, he changes again. Woody knows Andy loves him; his insecurity fades away, and he goes back to being his usual self but a little wiser.

Protagonist's Objectives

At first, Woody wants to become Andy's favorite toy again. When Buzz falls out the window, Woody wants to prove that he didn't intend to push him out the window and clarify the misunderstanding with the other toys. In order to present his case, he must bring Buzz with him to Andy's room.

Antagonist's Objectives

Sid's objective is to torture the toys. Sid takes pleasure from mutating them as all of his toys are deformed. Sid's room is a torture chamber for the toys.

Protagonist's Conflicts

Woody's inner conflict is whether to do something about Buzz Lightyear. Woody intends to push Buzz behind the desk to hide him from Andy, but it goes terribly wrong. He accidentally pushes Buzz out the window. This action leads to an unforeseeable event, which takes the story into the second act, where Woody and Buzz must navigate through the human world and return to Andy's room. Woody's inner conflict in the first act occurs because of his insecurity and jealousy.

Protagonist's Transformation

Woody learns to share Andy with Buzz and the other toys as he is reunited with his friends in Andy's room. He becomes less possessive of Andy as he learns that Andy still loves and cares for him. Woody goes from being insecure about being replaced to feeling assurance of his relationship with his owner. The journey has helped Woody understand his owner's affection toward him.

III. STORY ELEMENTS

Protagonist

Sheriff Woody is a pull-string cowboy doll, who comes alive when humans are not around.

Inciting Incident

Woody sees the preparations for Andy's birthday party preparation when he is on the first floor, and he gathers all the toys for a staff meeting when he returns to Andy's room. It is a ritual to spy on birthdays and Christmas to see if Andy gets a toy. The film establishes from the beginning that the toys want Andy's affection, and they fear being replaced and abandoned. If a new toy comes to replace them, they don't want to be sold at a garage sale. The inciting incident takes place when Andy gets Buzz Lightyear as a birthday present. Woody is pushed to the side, and Buzz takes center stage. Woody is jealous of Buzz as he becomes Andy's favorite new toy.

Protagonist's Objective

As Andy's room converts from a cowboy theme to a space theme with Buzz's arrival, Woody confronts Buzz.

```
Woody approaches the skateboard, grabs hold of Buzz's
foot and rolls him out from under the ship.

                    WOODY
          Listen, Lightsnack, you stay away
          from Andy. He's mine, and no one
          is taking him away from me.

                    BUZZ
          What are you talking about?
          (to Robot)
          Where's that bonding strip?!

Buzz rolls himself back under.
```

Woody wants to take back what he thinks is his. When Andy's mom allows Andy to bring one toy to Pizza Planet, Woody gets an idea. He wants to hide Buzz behind the desk, and uses a remote racer car to push him there. But Buzz falls out the window. The toys in the room blame Woody and question his motive. Mr. Potato Head turns against him, saying Woody can push any of them out the window if anyone comes between Woody's playtime with Andy. As Woody is pressed against the wall, Andy comes into the room, looking to take Buzz. When he can't find Buzz, he takes Woody instead. Buzz, who has fallen into the driveway, sees Andy take Woody into the minivan. He hops on the rear bumper of the car. Woody's objective is to bring Buzz back with him to solve any misunderstandings with his friends.

Main Tension

How can Woody convince his friends that pushing Buzz out the window was an accident? Can they reunite with Andy when they fall out of the minivan at the gas station?

Action

Woody realizes that he must bring back Buzz with him in order to clear up any misunderstandings that arose from Buzz falling out the window. The toys in Andy's room believe that he pushed Buzz on purpose because he is taking Woody's place. So Woody's first action is to keep Buzz by his side and try to return to Andy's room. When Woody sees the Pizza Planet delivery car arrive at the gas station, he convinces Buzz to go with him. As they arrive at Pizza Planet, Woody looks for Andy, but Buzz gets distracted by the space-themed arcade and enters the crane game through the "prize" slot. Woody misses the chance to be united with Andy and goes after Buzz. Sid, the neighbor boy, comes to play the crane game and grabs Buzz as a prize. Horrified, Woody tries to prevent Buzz from getting lifted by the crane, but he is pulled up with Buzz. Now both of them are in Sid's hands. Woody's action in Sid's room is to find a way to escape. Sid plans to launch a rocket with Buzz attached to it. Woody gathers the mutant toys, threatening Sid. Once free, Woody and Buzz make it back over the fence, but it's too late: Mrs. Davis's minivan and the moving truck have left the house. Woody's action is to catch up to the moving car to reunite with his friends and Andy.

Main Conflict

Woody's main conflict is with Buzz, which triggers a series of conflicts until all is resolved and they are reunited with Andy. The first conflict is Woody losing his spot as Andy's favorite toy. The second conflict comes from a misunderstanding, where the other toys in Andy's room believe Woody has pushed Buzz out the window on purpose. The third conflict occurs when they fall out of the minivan at the gas station and become stranded when they are left behind. The fourth conflict comes from being trapped in Sid's room; Woody must find a way back to Andy's room with Buzz. The fifth and final conflict is introduced when they have to catch up to the moving truck to be reunited with their friends and Andy.

Crisis

The crisis begins as Woody and Buzz enter Sid's house. Buzz accidentally sees a TV commercial and discovers he is just a toy, not a real space ranger. In disbelief, Buzz tries to prove that he is not a toy and launches himself from the second-floor staircase, but he lands flat, breaking his arm. Meanwhile, Woody has made contact with toys from Andy's room and tries to cross over by using a line made of Christmas tree lights. Mr. Potato Head asks to prove that he is still with Buzz, but Woody can't get Buzz to come to the window. Mr. Potato Head drops the line, and all hope is lost. Woody has been abandoned by his friends and awaits his destined future.

Climax

Sid prepares to blow up Buzz, who is tied to a rocket. Woody can't allow this to happen. He gathers the mutant toys and asks for their help. They plan a rescue mission as Sid gets ready in the backyard. The toys decide to come alive in front of Sid, scare him, and rescue Buzz before he is launched. Woody has a final confrontation with Sid and comes out on top. Woody and mutant toys help Buzz to escape. When Woody and Buzz make their way back, they are confronted with a new challenge: It's moving day, and the moving van has just left the driveway as they cross the fence. Woody and Buzz join forces and work as a team to make it back. It's not easy catching up to the moving van, so Woody uses Buzz's helmet as a magnifying glass to ignite the rocket. Woody and Buzz fly in the air. They detach from the rocket before it explodes. As they descend, they make it to the minivan. As they land through the minivan's sunroof, Andy finds them, and they are both greeted with love and affection.

Answer to the Main Tension

Yes, Woody and Buzz are reunited with their toy friends and Andy. And yes, Woody clears up all misunderstandings after Buzz falls out the window.

Resolution

It's Christmas Day, and all the toys are gathered with Buzz, who is leading the spy operation, to see if Andy is getting a new toy. Woody is not concerned about Andy's new present, as he has learned a lesson. Woody is confident about Andy's affection toward him, and he has learned to share Andy with other toys.

IV. STRUCTURE

Three-Act Structure

The *first act sets up* the story with the introduction of the characters on the day of Andy's birthday party, and the first act ends with Buzz hopping onto the minivan as Andy and Woody go to Pizza Planet. The protagonist has entered the extraordinary world – the world outside of Andy's room.

The *second act begins* as they arrive at the gas station. As Buzz sees Woody, they get into a fight falling out of the minivan. The second act ends with Woody and the mutant toys saving Buzz from Sid.

The *third act begins* with their quest to catch up to the moving van. The third act ends on Christmas Day when Woody shows his transformation: he no longer worries about Andy's presents.

The Sequence Method

First Sequence: Act 1, Sequence 1

1. *What's the sequence title?* Andy's Room – Woody's Ordinary World.
2. *Whose sequence is it?* It's Woody's sequence.
3. *What does he want?* This is a world where the toys want their owner's affection, their happiness has a direct correlation with playtime. Woody and his toy friends want to know if Andy is getting a new toy for his birthday.
4. *What's the conflict?* The toys are living in the human world. It is a difficult environment to navigate for them, especially when humans are around. The most important conflict in this sequence is the news of Andy receiving a new toy present, Buzz Lightyear.
5. *Who is in the way?* Andy's mom is in the way of spying.
6. *Who helps?* Sarge and his army go on a mission to spy on the birthday party.
7. *What is the emotional arc of the main character in the sequence?* In the beginning, Woody is happy and secure, but he starts to feel a little insecure as Buzz Lightyear threatens to take Andy's affection from him.

Second Sequence: Act 1, Sequence 2

1. *What is the sequence title?* "It Was an Accident."
2. *Whose sequence is it?* It's Woody's sequence.
3. *What does he want?* Woody wants to become Andy's favorite toy again.
4. *What's the conflict?* And y's room goes from having a cowboy-themed to a space-themed bedroom. Andy's blanket and bedroom decorations are all about the space. Woody feels rejected. Buzz becomes Andy's favorite toy.
5. *Who is in the way?* As Woody tries to reclaim his place, Buzz is in the way. Buzz takes away from Woody's playtime with Andy. And when Andy decides to play with Woody, he is the secondary character in Andy's imaginary world. Buzz is the new hero.
6. *Who helps?* No one helps, so he decides to take matters into his own hands. Woody tries to hide Buzz behind the desk and gets Andy's attention while they take a trip to Pizza Planet, but it all goes terribly wrong and Buzz falls out the window. The other toys blame Woody, thinking that he did it on purpose. This misunderstanding is carried into the second act.
7. *What is the emotional arc of the main character in the sequence?* Woody's emotions go from feeling insecure to feeling dispirited and devastated.

Main Tension

Can Woody make it back to Andy's room, clear the misunderstanding with his friends, and reclaim his place as Andy's favorite toy?

Third Sequence: Act 2, Sequence 1

1. *What is the sequence title?* Road to Planet Pizza.
2. *Whose sequence is it?* It's Woody's sequence.
3. *What does he want?* Woody feels the need to bring Buzz back with him to clear any misunderstanding he has with the other toys.
4. *What's the conflict?* Buzz is extremely angry with Woody, as he thinks Woody intentionally pushed him out the window. They fight and fall out of the minivan.
5. *Who is in the way?* Buzz is in the way. Buzz wants to go separate ways. Buzz still thinks he is a space ranger on a mission.
6. *Who helps?* The Pizza Planet delivery guy. After seeing the Pizza Planet delivery car stop at the gas station, Woody convinces Buzz to come with him, and they get in the car.
7. *What is the emotional arc of the main character in the sequence?* Dispirited and devastated to hopeful.

Fourth Sequence: Act 2, Sequence 2

1. *What is the sequence title?* The Crane Game.
2. *Whose sequence is it?* It's Woody's sequence. They arrive at Pizza Planet, but instead of being reunited with Andy, they are picked up by Sid.
3. *What does he want?* Woody wants to reunite with Andy and bring Buzz with him.
4. *What's the conflict?* Buzz gets sidetracked, and Woody misses the opportunity to reunite with Andy. The space-themed arcade at the Pizza Planet distracts Buzz, and he goes in search of a spaceship. Woody is forced to follow him.
5. *Who is in the way?* Buzz and Sid. Buzz goes inside the crane machine, thinking it is a spaceship. Sid plays the crane game and wins Buzz and Woody as prizes.
6. *Who helps?* No one helps.
7. *What is the emotional arc of the main character in the sequence?* Hopeful to frightened.

Fifth Sequence: Act 2, Sequence 3

1. *What is the sequence title?* Sid's Room.
2. *Whose sequence is it?* It's Woody's sequence. The sequence begins with Woody and Buzz arriving at Sid's house.
3. *What does he want?* Woody wants to escape with Buzz.
4. *What's the conflict?* The house is well guarded by Sid's dog. Buzz finds out he is a toy and not a space ranger when he sees a TV commercial. Disappointed, Buzz loses the will to live. While Woody makes contact with his friends in Andy's room, he misses the chance to reunite with his friend, as he can't

convince Buzz to come to the window and clear any misunderstanding he has with his friends.

5.   *Who is in the way?* Sid, Hannah (Sid's sister), and Scud (Sid's dog). Woody and Buzz attempt to escape from the house, but Sid, Hannah, and Scud get in the way.
6.   *Who helps?* Nobody.
7.   *What is the emotional arc of the main character in the sequence?* Terrified to hopeless.

Sixth Sequence: Act 2, Sequence 4

1.   *What is the sequence title?* The Mutant Toys.
2.   *Whose sequence is it?* It's Woody's sequence.
3.   *What does he want?* Woody wants to prevent Sid from blowing up Buzz, who is attached to a dangerous rocket.
4.   *What's the conflict?* Woody is trapped inside a milk box container.
5.   *Who is in the way?* Sid and Sid's dog.
6.   *Who helps?* Woody and Buzz help each other. The mutant toys come to help when Woody asks. Woody plans to scare Sid with the mutant toys and free Buzz from the ordeal.
7.   *What is the emotional arc of the main character in the sequence?* Woody goes from being hopeless to hopeful to make it back to Andy's room with Buzz.

Seventh Sequence: Act 3, Sequence 1

1.   *What is the sequence title?* To Infinity and Beyond.
2.   *Whose sequence is it?* It's Woody's sequence.
3.   *What does he want?* Woody and Buzz want to catch up to the moving truck.
4.   *What's the conflict?* If Woody and Buzz don't make it to the moving truck, they will never be reunited with Andy and his friends.
5.   *Who is in the way?* The truck driver and Andy's mom have no idea Woody and Buzz are trying to catch up to them.
6.   *Who helps?* The other toys from Andy's room. When Woody makes it to the moving truck, he takes the remote racer car to get Buzz, who was left behind. The toys from Andy's room witness Woody's attempt to save Buzz, which clarifies any misunderstandings they have about Woody. As the remote racer's battery runs out, they lose all hope of being united with the moving truck. Suddenly, Buzz has an idea: use the rocket. Woody ignites the rocket. They fly, catching up to the moving van.
7.   *What is the emotional arc of the main character in the sequence?* Woody's emotional arc goes from feeling worried to feeling relieved as they land inside the minivan.

Answer to the Main Tension

The main tension is: Can Woody make it back to Andy's room and clear up the misunderstanding with his friends? The answer to the main tension is: Yes, Woody and Buzz are reunited with Andy and their friends.

Eighth Sequence: Act 3, Sequence 2

1. *What is the sequence title?* Christmas Day.
2. *Whose sequence is it?* It's Woody's sequence.
3. *What does he want?* He just wants to be left in peace, as the other toys are spying to see if Andy is getting a new toy. Woody is confident that no other toy will replace him or his friends. So, now Buzz leads the spy operation instead of Woody.
4. *What's the conflict?* Andy gets a Mrs. Potato Head and a puppy dog as presents.
5. *Who is in the way?* The other toys from Andy's room. Woody doesn't want to bother with spying on Andy, but the other toys are still insecure.
6. *Who helps?* Bo Peep takes Woody to the side and kisses him under the mistletoe, leaving lipstick marks all over his face.
7. *What is the emotional arc of the main character in the sequence?* Woody's emotional arc goes from being relieved to feeling secure and wiser.

V. WORLD AND SETTING

The *geographic location* of the story takes place in a neighborhood with houses. Perhaps the writers are referring to a universal location, implying that this story can take place anywhere. The *time period* of the story takes place during modern times. Andy's mom drives a minivan, and there is a pizza restaurant with an arcade. The *world of the story* is a fictional world made out of living toys. They come alive when the humans are not around. This group of toys wants the owner to play with them – the basis of their *sociocultural setting*. The toys want to drive their actions, their desires, and their existence as beings. And the writers seamlessly expose their culture through a ritual of spying on Andy when he gets new toys for birthdays and Christmas. They are afraid of the new toys because they worry about being replaced and sold at a garage sale. However, what's familiar in this fictional world are the human characteristics and traits in toys. They all have human emotions such as love, jealousy, and guilt.

VI. TECHNIQUES AND TOOLS

Events/Occurrences

- In *Toy Story*, Andy's birthday is an essential event in the first act that helps to introduce Buzz Lightyear, an important supporting character.
- When Woody accidentally pushes Buzz out the window, this occurrence sets the story in motion, and Woody and Buzz are forced to enter the extraordinary world together.
- When Woody and Buzz are trapped in Sid's room, Sid plans to launch Buzz tied to a dangerous rocket. This incident sets up the climax of the film, and during the same event, Woody plans to scare Sid by coming alive with the mutant toys.
- Another significant event in the story is the "moving day" at the end of the second act. The screenwriters set this up at the beginning of the screenplay. When Andy sees the "happy birthday" sign, he says, "Can we leave this up till

we move?" Then, when we see the outside of the house, there is a "House for Sale" sign in the front.

- Finally, the screenwriters end the screenplay with another event, Christmas, to provide a resolution to the story.

Dramatic Irony

- The audience knows about the toys coming alive when humans are around, but the human characters in the story do not know.
- The audience knows that Buzz's falling out the window was an accident, but the other toys in the story do not know.
- Buzz Lightyear thinks he is a space ranger, but the rest of the toys know he is just like one of them – a toy – and so does the audience. The suspense builds as the audience predicts disappointment when Buzz finds out about his true identity.

Reversal

In *Toy Story*, the mutant toys in Sid's room have a character reversal. At first, they threaten Woody and Buzz, but later, they help Woody save Buzz during the ordeal and help them escape from Sid's backyard.

Setup and Payoff

Setup: The story set up a future moving day at the beginning of the screenplay.
Payoff: Andy and his family move to a new house as Woody and Buzz make their way back.
Setup: Andy leaves Woody on top of his bed.
Payoff: Andy leaves Buzz on top of his bed and throws Woody to the side.
Setup: Woody and Buzz argue about Buzz not being able to fly when they first meet.
Payoff: Woody and Buzz fly attached to a rocket at the end of the story.
Setup: Sid is introduced strapping a toy soldier to an explosive.
Payoff: Sid ties Buzz to an explosive rocket to launch it into the air.
Setup: Introduction of mutant toys. Woody and Buzz are terrified by their appearance.
Payoff: The mutant toys help Woody save Buzz.
Setup: Sid burns Woody's forehead with a magnifying glass.
Payoff: Woody uses Buzz's helmet as a magnifying glass to ignite the rocket.

THE DARK KNIGHT
(Action/Crime/Drama/Thriller), 2008

Written by Christopher Nolan, Jonathan Nolan, and David Goyer

I. THEME AND PREMISE

Theme

The Dark Knight does not have a conventional superhero theme, such as self-sacrifice, responsibility, or redemption. The film goes a step further. Although the superhero themes are embedded in the story, the genre in which the story is told is what separates *The Dark Knight* from previous superhero films.

The Dark Knight is a crime drama, and the screenwriters set up the dramatic elements to support and fulfill the serious undertone of this genre. At the heart of a superhero film is always the good overcomes the evil, but in *The Dark Knight*, the theme deals with ethics and morality, which is put to the test in an anarchic state. At the end, orders triumph over chaos, and justice is served.

Premise

When the Joker, a psychopath and anarchist, threatens Gotham City with chaos, fear, and destruction, Batman joins forces with Lieutenant James Gordon from the police department and district attorney Harvey Dent to fight the criminals. Complications arise as the Joker gains power and momentum by taking over the mob and its fortune.

II. CHARACTER STUDY

Characters

Protagonist: Bruce Wayne/Batman

DOI: 10.4324/9781003138853-12

Antagonists: The Joker, The mob (Lau, Maroni, Chechen, Gambol, and more), Detective Ramirez and Detective Wuertz (the traitors), Harvey Dent (third act)

Supporting characters: Lt. James Gordon, Harvey Dent, Rachel, Alfred, and Lucius Fox

Backstory

The Dark Knight is the second installment of Christopher Nolan's *The Dark Knight* trilogy. In the first installment, *Batman Begins*, the screenwriters introduce the major characters, establish the world in the story, and define key relationships between characters. In *The Dark Knight*, the screenwriters don't spend too much time setting up characters' backstories or the world of the story. They dive right into the story, as the world has already been established in the previous installment.

However, in *The Dark Knight*, several backstories are revealed throughout the film. One of them is Batman's ongoing relationship with the Gotham City police department and his friendship with Lt. Gordon. Another is the exposition of the mob's criminal operation. All the mobs in Gotham City have united, and their money is being handled by one entity, Lau Security Investments. Mr. Lau, the CEO of the investment company, helps the mob launder their money and keeps it in a safe place. Finally, one more important backstory worth noting is Bruce's interest in Rachel.

One interesting use of backstory is how the Joker misleads the audience with his lies. The screenwriters have the Joker tell different versions of the story of how he got the scars on his face. The Joker first tells the story to Gambol, the mobster who puts a price on his head. The Joker holds a knife to Gambol's face and says that the scars are from his abusive father for being "too serious." This is the first time the Joker reveals a story from his past – a backstory – which helps us understand a little about his background. He talks about his scars a second time when he speaks to Rachel during Harvey's fundraiser. He reveals a different version of the story, saying he cut himself to please his wife. This technique is different from how backstory is usually incorporated into screenplays. Without any explanation, the screenwriters have shown the readers the Joker's psychopathic characteristics and dishonest traits. He changes the story depending on his opponent. The third time the Joker asks, "Do you know how I got these scars?" is during the final confrontation with Batman. But Batman doesn't give him an opportunity to tell the story – he doesn't care, and the audience doesn't either. The Joker's actions help us learn who he is as a character.

When the Joker is taken into custody by Lt. Gordon, the police run the Joker's fingerprints and find no record of him. He is not in the system, and nobody knows what his name is and where he is from. It is no coincidence that we don't know about the Joker's past. The screenwriters purposely decided not to include his backstory and keep him mysterious. Jonathan Nolan, one of the screenwriters, discussed the Joker in an interview:

> To me, the most interesting version of that character – The Joker – is one who's elemental, almost like he's conjured out of thin air, so the idea that he has a backstory, there are different ways to do it, but in this world. It feels like it would be reductive for him.

Protagonist's Introduction

Before Batman is introduced, a bank robbery sequence during the opening introduces the antagonist, the Joker. He doesn't say much, but we can feel his presence. The intense opening sequence introduces a carefully choreographed robbery, revealing the Joker as the mastermind behind a perfectly timed heist with a great exit plan. Then a sequence of criminal activities in Gotham City is shown, followed by a scene with Lt. Gordon in the police crime unit with Detective Ramirez and Detective Wuertz. The two detectives will betray the police unit later in the screenplay, so the screenwriters briefly introduce these two important supporting characters. The three of them watch the Gotham City mayor being interviewed on TV. He says:

> Like this so-called Batman. A lot of people say he's doing some good, that criminals are running scared. . . . But I say no. What kind of hero needs to wear a mask? You don't let vigilantes run around breaking the law . . . where does it end? Yet, we hear rumors that instead of trying to arrest him, the cops are using him to do their dirty work.

Even before Batman is introduced, the screenwriters are introducing the perception of who Batman is in the eyes of the public.

Finally, Batman is introduced when he disrupts a business meeting between two criminals. Scarecrow makes an appearance, linking the criminal world between the first installment, *Batman Begins*, and the second installment, *The Dark Knight*. Before the real Batman is introduced, the business deal is interrupted by Batman wannabes with guns. The introduction of these copycats is a subplot setup that will be revisited later in the screenplay with a payoff. As a fight breaks out between the wannabes and the criminals, the Batmobile makes a grand entrance. Batman fights the criminals and captures them in action-packed scenes. Batman's introduction gives us a glimpse of what to expect from these action sequences.

It is hard to perceive Bruce Wayne's emotional state as Batman. So when Bruce is introduced without a mask, we have an insight into his emotional state. Bruce is concerned with the current threat Gotham City is facing from the mob and the Joker, but also, through his interactions with Alfred, we see his interest in getting to know Harvey Dent, a district attorney who is becoming popular for his brave and fearless actions in fighting crime. Furthermore, Alfred reveals Bruce's affection for Rachel, but Bruce ignores it, changing the subject, assuring the audience that his feeling for Rachel is real. Lastly, Alfred helps reveal Bruce's devotion to protect the city. Alfred sees the scars and bruises on Bruce's body and says:

ALFRED
Know your limits, Master Wayne

BRUCE
Batman has no limits

ALFRED
Well, you do, sir

BRUCE
I can't afford to know them

Bruce Wayne reveals his willingness to fight without limits, creating anticipation for what may come later in the screenplay. In an online interview, *The Dark Knight*'s co-writer/director Christopher Nolan said:

> In the beginning of *The Dark Knight*, you see that Bruce Wayne and his Batman persona have matured. He's really the fully-formed Batman from the comics, but he's also in a place where he's having to question, having engaged the response to his presence in Gotham that he's seeing the rise in copycats and vigilantism, all kinds of things going on, and an escalation of the war with organized crime, and so there are a lot of potentially negative consequences all of his crusade brewing in Gotham at the beginning of the film. With all of the major story movements of *The Dark Knight*, we've tried to imbue them with a sense of inevitability. We really want kind of in the first reel to set up a set of expectations and feelings about the type of story that you're going see in the way in which these things are going to play out for these characters, but hopefully, we're trying to surprise people in terms of how those things come to pass.

Batman is not introduced during a random day in his life. The screenwriters chose to build this moment to showcase who Batman is as a character. When Bruce Wayne is introduced – the superhero behind the mask – he reveals his objective by interacting with Alfred.

Psychological, Physical, and Social Attributes

Bruce doesn't have the physical attributes of a superhero, and he doesn't have any superpowers. When Bruce is first introduced without a mask, he is stitching up a deep cut in his arm. He is human, after all. However, he has wealth – he is a billionaire. Bruce has limitless resources and the latest technology at his disposal to fight crime.

In the trilogy's first installment, *Batman Begins*, Bruce Wayne witnesses the murder of his parents as a child, and it leaves a permanent psychological scar on him. When Bruce gets older, he wants to kill his parents' murderer. In the process, he learns about the difference between justice and revenge, thanks to his childhood friend, Rachel. Bruce confronts Falcone, the mob boss who ordered the killing of Bruce's parents, but he is ridiculed and humiliated by the mobsters. Bruce travels and learns more about the criminal world. He builds physical and mental strength by learning martial arts and training to be a fighter. When he returns to Gotham, he reclaims his inheritance of his father's company, Wayne Enterprises, conquers his fear of bats, and begins to fight the criminals as Batman.

Bruce Wayne believes in justice. He will hurt enemies, but he never kills them and always brings them to law enforcement. He is "incorruptible," as the Joker states. His objective is always to protect Gotham City from the criminals. Bruce is a selfless person, always putting his life in danger to save the lives of innocent people. His heart is always in a good place, and he has faith in people. In addition to his psychological attributes, Bruce exposes a different set of psychological traits: he hopes to live a normal life since Gotham City demands a hero without a mask.

Bruce's social attributes as a CEO and billionaire remain the same as in previous versions of Batman films. Bruce always misleads others about his persona – one that is far from his real self – to protect his secret identity. Only three people know he is Batman: Alfred, Rachel, and Mr. Fox. Bruce trusts each one of them, and they always help him with his goals.

Bruce Wayne's appeal as a character comes from his confidence, drive, sense of humor, flaws, antiheroic traits, and his willingness to protect innocent people from criminals. He is also appealing because the audience can relate to his goals. The audience is led into Bruce Wayne's psychological journey, following the ups and downs of his emotional arc through the different stages in the story. From Bruce's intention to turn Harvey Dent into a new Gotham City hero to his desire to live a normal life with Rachel and the sacrifice he makes to cover up the damage Harvey Dent left behind. Bruce is a brave, responsible, and selfless character. He is a hero. In an online interview, Christopher Nolan says:

> The interesting thing about Batman as a figure is that he's driven by very dark things. There's a lot of rage, a lot of anger that really motivates him. He's trying to channel it into something good, but he's really playing with fire, he's working outside the law, he's doing all kinds of very questionable things, but in the service of good. That really is playing with fire, that really is riding this knife-edge, so what we do in *The Dark Knight* is we just sort of test that, using the character of the Joker.

Protagonist's Worldview

Bruce's point of view of the world is a world without crime – a world where justice prevails. This point of view can be seen through various actions, but it is clearly revealed to the readers in the last sequence of the screenplay when Batman decides to take the blame for Harvey's criminal actions. Even though the Joker has turned the district attorney, Harvey Dent, into a villain, Batman can't let the people of Gotham find out. Harvey was a public figure who represented hope for Gotham City. Bruce will not allow the spirit of the city to die with Harvey's transformation. So, Batman and Lt. Gordon conspire to hide the truth. Thus, Harvey Dent dies a hero, and Batman runs away from the law. The action of sacrificing himself for the greater good reveals how Bruce sees the world.

Antagonist's Worldview

The Joker has a unique point of view of the world, a worldview that neither Batman nor Gotham City has ever encountered before. The Joker does not want money or power; he pours gasoline on the millions of dollars he stole from the mob. The Joker is unpredictable – he doesn't follow the rules, obey the law, or have ethical codes. The Joker's point of view is dark and evil, governed by hatred, anger, and chaos. He wants to demoralize and destroy the city. In the same interview, Christopher Nolan says of the Joker:

> I had an idea of what the Joker would be in the world we created of *Batman Begins*, and to me, it was creating a sort of psychologically credible anarchist, a force of anarchy, a force of chaos, a purposeless criminal, a psychopath. To me, that is the most frightening form of evil: the enemy who has no rules, the enemy who's not out for anything, who can't be understood, who can only be fought.

Protagonist's Personas

Bruce Wayne has several personas in *The Dark Knight*. His professional and social persona is a billionaire, the CEO of Wayne Enterprises, and Gotham's most eligible bachelor. He portrays himself as dating gorgeous women, driving fast cars, and showing no interest in his business. But underneath his professional persona, he strives to help and protect Gotham City.

Bruce's personal persona is shown through his interactions with Alfred and Lucius Fox, the only characters who know Batman's true identity besides Rachel. Bruce can be himself when he is interacting with these characters. With Alfred, Bruce is someone who's not afraid to show his weaker side or share thoughts on matters pressing to Batman. Bruce knows Alfred is someone who will always give it to him straight, as a good mentor would do. With Mr. Fox, Bruce shows his witty side – a lighter side of his personality.

Bruce's private persona is revealed through his encounters with Rachel. With Rachel, Bruce comes across as an assertive and competent man and doesn't shy away from revealing his vulnerable side.

Bruce's superhero persona – Batman – projects a fearless, courageous, heroic, frightening, and intimidating presence to the criminals and hides his true identity under the mask to protect his professional and personal lives. When Batman interacts with Lt. Jim Gordon and district attorney Harvey Dent, he speaks in a lower tone of voice. He doesn't waste time but talks only about pressing matters and then disappears, minimizing his interaction with them.

Protagonist's Objectives

Bruce's personal objective remains true to its original story. He wants to keep Gotham City safe from criminals. In Christopher Nolan's first installment of the trilogy, *Batman Begins*, we see how Bruce Wayne becomes Batman. Christopher Nolan has said that he wanted to take a "realistic" approach to this story, putting the characters into a real-life setting while following the predefined storyline of the Batman franchise.

In his private life, Bruce's objective is to be with Rachel. Bruce and Rachel had previously talked about getting together when Gotham City no longer needed Batman. Bruce decides to find a replacement because he wants a new hero for Gotham City so that he can fulfill his private life objective. As Harvey Dent, the district attorney, gains popularity in the city, Bruce decides to support him and helps Harvey to become the new hero of Gotham City.

Because he is a billionaire, Bruce Wayne can financially support the cause of his personal want. He organizes a fundraiser to give Harvey financial support, promising him that he will never have to raise a cent for his future campaigns. Bruce not only helps Harvey as a billionaire, but also contributes as a superhero. Batman captures Mr. Lau from Hong Kong and brings him back to Gotham City so that Harvey and Rachel can get the evidence they need to prosecute members of the mob. Bruce takes action because there is something greater at stake: his chance of a normal life with Rachel. There are only a few scenes in the screenplay where Bruce is alone with Rachel, and each time, he reveals his desire.

> BRUCE
> You know that day that you once told me about when Gotham would no longer need Batman? It's coming.

> RACHEL
> Bruce, you can't ask me to wait for that.

> BRUCE
> It's happening now. Harvey is that hero. He locked up half of the

```
            city's criminals, and he did it
            without wearing a mask. Gotham
            needs a hero with a face.

        Later in the screenplay:

                        BRUCE
            You once told me that if the day
            came when I was finished that
            we'd be together.

                        RACHEL
            Bruce, don't make me your one
            hope for a normal life.

                        BRUCE
            Did you mean it?

                        RACHEL
            Yes.
```

Bruce's private objective works on different levels. First, he is revealing his human side as a superhero character, where the audience can empathize with the character's needs. Second, Bruce's private objective of wanting to be with Rachel raises the stakes in wanting to attain his main objective – to catch the Joker and make Harvey the hero Gotham wants.

Antagonist's Objectives

The Joker wants chaos. First, the Joker fights the mob, then moves on to his main target: Batman. The Joker always disturbs order, causing destruction and creating fear. From the moment he is introduced until the final confrontation with Batman, the Joker is a dangerous threat to Gotham City. As the antagonist, the Joker knows Batman's weak spots and attacks him where it hurts the most, abducting the two central figures in his life, Harvey and Rachel. By killing Rachel, the Joker takes away Bruce Wayne's "one hope for a normal life" and the Joker turns the White Knight of Gotham, Harvey Dent, into a villain. Rachel's death sends Bruce Wayne into his lowest emotional point in the story, and the Joker brings Batman down to his level, provoking violent, unethical, and antiheroic behaviors. If it weren't for the Joker, we would have never seen Batman's dark side and how far he will go to protect the city. Even when the Joker is captured, his victory seems empty.

In an interview, Christopher Nolan discussed the Joker's objectives:

> I think you feel that the Joker has the drive to tear the world down. The line we gave Alfred to sort of summon [this] up really well is: "Some men just want to watch the world burn." That, to us, was the most frightening way

of approaching the character, that he isn't someone who can be in any way negotiated within him in a material sense or legal sense or a political sense. He is just somebody who wants to tear everything down around him. . . [he is] somebody who just lives and delights in taking people's rulesets and turning them against themselves.

Supporting Character's Objectives

Out of all the supporting characters in *The Dark Knight*, Harvey Dent's objective directly affects the protagonist. Harvey Dent is a fearless new district attorney in Gotham City, an ally to Lt. Gordon and Batman. He is a strong supporting character, but he becomes an antagonist during the last stretch of the screenplay. Harvey wants two things before the transformation in the story: one, to prosecute the mob associated with organized crime in Gotham City; two, he wants to marry Rachel. Now, because of the Joker, Harvey loses Rachel. To make matters worse, the Joker converts Harvey into a villain. Harvey Dent, now called Two-Face, wants to take revenge, a new objective. He goes after the corrupt detectives who betrayed the unit and jeopardized his life and killed Rachel. The consequences of Harvey's action have a detrimental effect on the protagonist's objective to protect Gotham City. Although he is a supporting character, he has the biggest character transformation in the story.

Here's Christopher Nolan on Harvey Dent:

Very often, [film noir is] centered around a protagonist who's either an unreliable narrator, which is what we played with very much in *Memento* or simply someone who has some flaw in them, some tragic flaw that you know early on there's an indicator in the story that this is going to snowball into something catastrophic. In *The Dark Knight*, I found a lot of interest in the character of Harvey Dent for myself. He is a very heroic figure at the beginning. He's the guy that Bruce Wayne sees as being able to take over for him. He's a hero without a mask, he's a positive figure for Gotham to rally behind who can take over for Batman, but in the way that Aaron Eckhart plays him, there's something right from the beginning you see in him that's questionable. You see a sort of a vaulting ambition, you see a germ of darkness there that can – and of course, therefore, will – in this kind of story rise up and turn into something ugly.

Protagonist's Conflict

The protagonist's conflict comes from his physical limitation in fighting the criminals. Bruce is constantly confronted with physical limitations because he is always outnumbered. Even with advanced gear and armor, he is constantly searching for stronger, lighter, and faster gadgets and gears. Mr. Fox at Wayne Enterprises always helps Bruce in this department.

Batman's biggest conflict is with the Joker: It's a character vs. character conflict. They only have a handful of encounters, but they have detrimental outcomes each time. During the first encounter, the Joker learns of Batman's connection to Rachel. Without hesitation, Batman launches himself after Rachel when Joker pushes her out the window. In the second encounter, Joker learns that Batman lives by a set of rules. Batman could have killed the Joker, but he does not. In the interrogation room, the Joker gets under his skin and provokes him. Even when Batman has the upper hand, he is still losing: the Joker has abducted both Harvey and Rachel, thus gets the last laugh in the third encounter. In the final encounter, Batman captures the Joker, but not before saving the lives of the hostages, and preventing the bombs from going off in the ferries.

Bruce Wayne's internal conflict deals with his desire to protect Gotham vs. his self-interest. He can't have both, so he decides to focus on his self-interest rather than Gotham City, but not before replacing himself with a new hero that will protect Gotham. As much as Bruce is fighting for Gotham, he is also fighting for himself and his future.

Protagonist's Transformation

This screenplay has a tragic ending for Bruce Wayne. His emotional arc fluctuates – from the hope of a normal life, to the death of his love interest, to breaking his own ethical code to catch the enemy, to sacrificing himself at the end to protect the white-knight image for Gotham City. Bruce Wayne's emotional arc goes from being hopeful to hopeless. While he is able to bring back peace and restore order, he has lost two important people in his life. Bruce had hoped for a new hero for Gotham City, Harvey Dent, and he had hoped to have a normal life with Rachel.

Bruce's last action as Batman defines his transformation in the screenplay. Batman decides to take the blame for Harvey's criminal activities, including the killing of Detective Wuertz, the corrupt cop. Bruce sacrifices himself in order to protect Harvey's image from the citizens of Gotham City. To Bruce, Harvey Dent must die as a hero. Batman is no longer a hero, but a cop killer: the Dark Knight. Batman goes from being a hero to being an outlaw.

Bruce Wayne is a complex character with multiple personas. The screenwriters shape the protagonist with a very specific want and need, and his objective resonates with the audience because it encompasses a universal theme. What makes him appealing is his human characteristics of wanting justice, fighting for a good cause, and displaying his desire to live a life with the person he loves. As Bruce embarks on his journey in pursuing his goals, the audience engages with his psychological experience because they have access to his emotional arc. As the story shifts into a tragic phase, Bruce has to make an unethical choice and break his moral codes for the right reasons – protecting the city and its citizens. Bruce Wayne stays true to his character, demonstrating heroic actions throughout the screenplay. The sacrifice he makes at the end is a secret. Bruce knows his transformation from a hero to a criminal is a small price for what the citizens of Gotham City will get in return: a true heroic act.

III. STORY ELEMENTS

Protagonist

Bruce Wayne, a billionaire and the CEO of Wayne Enterprises, has a secret identity as Batman, fighting criminals in Gotham City.

Inciting Incident

The inciting incident is the Joker robbing the bank in the opening sequence. The Joker doesn't rob the bank for the money, but to get the attention of the mob, who owns the bank. This inciting incident sets the story in motion, creating Bruce's objective of wanting to catch the mob and the Joker.

Protagonist's Objective

Batman's main objective of protecting Gotham City is intertwined with the objectives in his personal and private lives. Bruce's main objective is to catch the Joker, but he also wants to retire Batman (personal life objective) and be with Rachel (private life objective). As the audience starts to care about all aspects of the character's life, they connect that much more with the protagonist and his goals.

Main Tension

Can Batman catch the mob and Joker to bring order and justice back to Gotham City?

Action

Batman and Lt. Gordon decide to first get the mob off the street and then deal with the Joker. Batman informs Lt. Gordon and Harvey Dent of Lau's Investment Firm's involvement with the Gotham City mob, and the three of them collaborate to take down the criminals and put them behind bars. When Mr. Lau feels the heat and leaves Gotham City's jurisdiction, Batman goes to Hong Kong to bring him back. Harvey collects evidence from Mr. Lau to put the criminals behind bars with the help of Lt. Gordon.

Bruce Wayne also takes action to obtain his personal and private objectives. As Harvey Dent, the new district attorney, starts to gain popularity with the people, he decides to support him so that he can become the new hero in town, and Batman can hang up his cape for good. Bruce throws a fundraiser for Harvey, so he may have a great political career in the future. Also, because he wants to be with

Rachel, he makes sure she knows how he feels about her and promises her that it will happen sooner than later.

Main Conflict

The main conflict is the fight between Batman and the Joker. They each want different things – a perfect example of the unity of opposites. The Joker wants chaos, and Batman wants order. The conflicts reveal information about the characters and story. Without conflict, we wouldn't have known how much Bruce Wayne loves Rachel. And without Rachel's death, Harvey Dent would never turn into a villain. Without conflict, we wouldn't know how much Bruce cares for Gotham City.

The unity of opposites between the Joker and Batman is so strong that it can only be broken when one of the characters is emotionally and/or physically transformed at the end. The Joker goes from being a villain to a prisoner.

Crisis

The crisis occurs when the Joker's men kidnap Rachel and Harvey, and Batman has time to save only one of them. He chooses to save Rachel, but when he gets there, he finds Harvey. The Joker has switched addresses on purpose. You never get straight answers from the Joker. This is a crisis for Bruce Wayne because Rachel dies, and Harvey becomes a villain, ruining his future goals. Bruce not only loses the woman he loves but loses the future he could have had with her.

After Rachel's death, Bruce grieves. In this scene, there is a voice-over of Rachel reading the letter she left for Bruce. At the last minute, Alfred decides to hide the letter. Alfred makes this decision in order to protect Bruce's memories of Rachel, as the letter concerns Rachel's rejection of Bruce's offer and her plans to marry Harvey Dent. To overcome the crisis of losing Rachel and continue with his main objective, Batman must find the Joker and stop him from harming the people of Gotham City. The death of Rachel pushes him to take action that goes against his moral and ethical code. In an attempt to capture the Joker, Batman decides to use the latest sonar technology as a last resort to locate the Joker. He accesses every mobile phone in Gotham City and invades the privacy of millions of civilians to track down the Joker's whereabouts. His actions are clear: Batman's main objective is stronger than his moral and ethical codes. Batman overcomes the crisis and confronts the antagonist one last time.

Climax

The climax takes place during the final confrontation between Batman and the Joker. Until this point in the story, the Joker has been gaining ground in Gotham City. Because the mob is losing control without a leader, the Joker starts to gain power in the underworld: "This town deserves a better criminal, and I'm gonna give it to them." The Joker continues with his objective, creating chaos. He traps every citizen in Gotham City without giving them an exit. All bridges and tunnels have been blocked off, except for the two ferries leaving the city. The Joker plans to conduct a "social experiment." He has rigged both ferries with bombs and has placed a bomb detonator for each ferry inside the other. The Joker asks the passengers on both ferries to blow up the other ferry before they get both blown up. If both ferries are still standing by midnight, he plans to blow up both of them.

Before Batman gets to the Joker, he has another challenge to overcome. He has to save the people kidnapped from the hospital. Batman figures out the villains are dressed the hostages with fake guns taped to their hands, and the real thugs pretend to be the victims. After locating the Joker's whereabouts, Batman informs Lt. Gordon, and a SWAT team assembles in the building opposite. As the SWAT move in, Batman doesn't have time to tell Gordon; he only has time to react. Batman immobilizes the SWAT team, fights the villain pretending to be the hostage, and saves the real victims.

Now, as Batman closes in on the Joker, there is still a pending matter: the "social experiment." The passengers on both ferries can't trigger the detonator; they all have made their moral choices. By midnight and the people on both ferries have sent a clear message: they will not hurt each other. As the fight between Batman and the Joker continues, the Joker tries to blow up both ferries, but Batman captures him.

Answer to the Main Tension

The main tension is: Can Batman catch the members of the mob, as well as the Joker, and restore order? The answer to the main tension is: Yes, Batman catches the mob members and the Joker. But Bruce pays a high price to attain his goal.

Resolution

In *The Dark Knight*, even after Batman attains the main objective of catching the Joker, he still has to clean up Harvey Dent's mess. Bruce's other objective of wanting to turn Harvey into a white knight needs to have a conclusion. Batman decides to take the blame for Dent's actions of killing the police officers, and projects a false image of who Harvey Dent has become in order to keep him as a symbolic figure for the citizens of Gotham City. Now, as a consequence of this action, Batman becomes an outlaw. He has to live in hiding.

IV. STRUCTURE

Three-Act Structure

The first act sets up the story with the inciting incident. The Joker robs the bank. Aside from the main plot of going after the criminals, Bruce Wayne/Batman establishes his personal and private want and need; he wants Gotham City to have a hero without a mask, Harvey Dent. The first act ends with a meeting, an event, a turning point. Harvey Dent, Lt. Gordon, and Batman meet on the rooftop and discuss their plan to capture the mob, Mr. Lau is at the center of the investigation, but he has fled the country. Batman plans to bring him back. Harvey Dent will prosecute him, and Lt. Gordon will arrest the mob members.

The second act begins with Bruce Wayne and Lucius Fox, who have traveled to Hong Kong to bring Mr. Lau back to Gotham City's jurisdiction. The second act ends with a defeat: the Joker manages to turn Harvey Dent into a villain, blows up Gotham General Hospital, and traps the citizens in Gotham City by blocking the bridges and tunnels – another turning point in the story.

The third act begins with Batman wanting to catch the Joker once and for all. He uses sonar technology to find the Joker's whereabouts, and during the "social experiment," he has the final confrontation with the Joker. The third act ends with Batman saving Lt. Gordon's family from Harvey Dent, and dealing with the aftermath of Harvey's death.

V. WORLD AND SETTING

The *geographic location* of the story is Gotham City, a fictional city. The story's *time period* is contemporary, the same time period as when the film was made. *The Dark Knight* was released several years after the catastrophic events of September 11, 2001, when the United States was attacked by al-Qaeda, who killed nearly 3,000 people. In 2008, when the film was released, the wars in Afghanistan and Iraq were still creating uncertainty in the minds of the global population. As world leaders and the United Nations were at war with the Taliban and Iraq, terrorism gained momentum, creating global fear and chaos. During this period of time, it wasn't rare to see terrorist attacks in the news. Even though *The Dark Knight* is a fictional story, the screenplay speaks to a subject that was pressing to audiences of the time.

What the audience was facing in real life was similar to what Batman was facing with the Joker in *The Dark Knight*: terror, chaos, and fear. As the audience goes through the psychological journey, with Bruce Wayne catching the Joker, there is a great emotional fulfillment that comes from watching the film. "Good" goes against "evil," and "good" prevails in this film. Obviously, this is not the only reason why the film did well at the box office – it had a great screenplay, and the execution was flawless – but we can't deny the fact that the timing of when the story was released had an impact on the audience. In this film, you can see so much about pressing issues after 9/11: terrorism, the economy, wars, and politics. No one wants to see a film about terrorism, but when you put the idea in a Batman film – a superhero crime epic film – the audience is much more receptive to the story.

Therefore, when studying a screenplay, you should break down each time factor to see how the film was received during its release. We must revisit the time period to see the *sociocultural and sociopolitical* setting of that era.

VI. TECHNIQUES AND TOOLS

Events/Occurrences

- *The bank robbery:* The screenplay starts with a bank robbery, revealing the Joker as the mastermind behind the heist.
- *The restaurant:* Bruce and his date join Rachel and Harvey for dinner. Bruce gets to know Harvey Dent.
- *The rooftop meeting:* Batman, Lt. Gordon, and Harvey Dent meet at the roof, and they join forces to fight the mob.
- *The mob meeting:* Joker crashes the meeting, offering to kill Batman for half of the money.
- *The Hong Kong trip:* Batman captures and brings Mr. Lau back to Gotham City's jurisdiction.
- *The fundraiser:* Bruce Wayne believes in Harvey Dent and decides to throw him a fundraiser.
- *The press conference:* Harvey turns himself in, proclaiming to be Batman, and uses this event as a trap to catch the Joker.
- *Commissioner Loeb's funeral service:* The Joker tries to kill the Major in broad daylight, and Lt. Gordon takes the bullet, trying to protect the mayor.
- *The interrogation:* The Joker reveals that he had kidnapped Rachel and Harvey Dent. Batman rescues one of them, but Rachel dies, and Harvey turns to the dark side.
- *The social experiment:* The Joker plans to blow up the ferries leaving the city, but Batman catches Joker before he can detonate the bombs.

Dramatic Irony

An apparent dramatic irony in the film takes place during the "social experiment" scenes with the ferries. But before I explain what the screenwriters did with these scenes, let's revisit director Alfred Hitchcock's suspense vs. surprise example. Hitchcock said that if a group of people is gathered around a table and a bomb goes off, the audience will be shocked for 5–10 seconds. But suppose the same group of people is gathered at the table, and the audience knows that there is a bomb underneath. it will create suspense for the duration of their conversation – a dramatic irony – because the audience knows more than the characters. The audience will be emotionally invested in the characters surrounding the table, and the tension will rise over time. Hitchcock says that the bomb should never go off, and that you must release the tension by exploding the bomb. If the bomb goes off, the audience will get upset.

Now, based on what Hitchcock said with the bomb analogy, let's look at the "social experiment" scenes in *The Dark Knight*. Two ferries leaving Gotham City have been rigged with bombs, and each bomb's detonator has been placed on the opposite ferry. Now, the Joker tells the passengers on each ferry to blow up the other ferry if they want to live. Otherwise, at midnight, the Joker will blow up both of them. In this sequence, the screenwriters added a second bomb to Hitchcock's suspense vs. surprise bomb example. There are two dramatic ironies happening simultaneously. The people on each ferry don't know what the other will do. The audience sees what is taking place on both ferries, and the suspense intensifies as double dramatic ironies press the audience. The release comes when the audience discovers that the passengers on either ferry cannot blow up the other ferry. They won't dare to kill the others. The citizens have spoken, and the moral decision has been made. Now, just as Joker is about to blow up the ferry, Batman intervenes, and the bombs on the ferries never go off.

Another important dramatic irony that lets the audience in on a secret takes place during the last sequence of the film. The audience knows Batman was not the one who killed the cops. It was Harvey Dent, but in order to protect Harvey's image and what he represents for the city, Batman decides to take the blame, and the screenplay ends with dramatic irony.

Reversal

- When the Joker threatens to kill innocent people until Batman reveals his true face, Bruce Wayne goes to a press conference to reveal himself as Batman. But Harvey pretends to be Batman.
- Lt. Gordon dies protecting the Mayor during the commissioner's funeral service. But we discover that his death was a cover-up to catch the Joker.
- Batman goes to save Rachel, but finds Harvey instead. The Joker switched the addresses where Rachel and Harvey were being kept. As a result, Rachel dies, and Harvey is hospitalized.
- The Joker wants to reveal Batman's identity at first, then changes his mind and wants to keep a secret. When Coleman Reese, a financial officer at Wayne Enterprises, learns who Batman is and threatens to reveal Batman's identity, the Joker puts a price on Coleman's head and threatens to blow up a hospital.
- Harvey turns from an ally into an enemy. The Joker convinces him to turn into the dark side.

Setup and Payoff

Setup: Lucius Fox uses sonar technology to help Batman capture Mr. Lau from Hong Kong.

Payoff: Batman links the sonar technology to every mobile phone in Gotham City to locate the Joker for the final confrontation.

Setup: Batman brings Mr. Lau back from Hong Kong.

Payoff: The mob members are prosecuted and then arrested.

Setup: Harvey Dent's anger toward Lt. Gordon for having snitches in his unit at the beginning of the story.

Payoff: Detective Ramirez and Detective Wuertz were working for the Joker's men, which is revealed when Harvey goes to find the traitors after Rachel's death.

Setup: Bruce wants to turn Harvey Dent into a hero with a mask.

Payoff: Batman pays a high price to make Harvey Dent become the hero: he takes the blame for Harvey's crime.

Setup: "You either die a hero or live long enough to see yourself become the villain."

Payoff: Harvey Dent becomes a villain at the end of the film. He becomes Two-Face.

Setup: Even before Batman is introduced in the story, Gotham City's Mayor is on television, asking whether Batman is a criminal or a hero.

Payoff: At the end of the film, Batman turns out to be a villain in the eyes of Gotham City.

WHIPLASH
(Indie/Music/Drama), 2014

Written and directed by Damien Chazelle

I. THEME AND PREMISE

Theme

The story's theme speaks to the challenges and difficulties an artist goes through in pursuing their dreams: Do you have it in you to become the greatest? And what is the price you are willing to pay? These are the constant questions that are asked throughout the screenplay, testing the protagonist, putting them in the worst possible situation.

Premise

The premise is about a freshman student who gets scouted to play for the best jazz ensemble band in the school and in the nation but finds an abusive teacher constantly pushing him to perform at his best. The protagonist rises to the challenge, meeting the teacher's expectations but refusing to be bossed around.

II. CHARACTER STUDY

Characters

Protagonist: Andrew Neiman
Antagonist: Terence Fletcher
Supporting characters: Jim Neiman, Nicole, Carl Tanner, and Ryan Connolly

Backstory

On Andrew's first day with the studio band, Fletcher casually asks about Andrew's parents. From this interaction, we learn that Andrew's parents are not musicians;

DOI: 10.4324/9781003138853-13

his father is a high school teacher and his mom left the family when he was a baby. When Fletcher asks the question, it feels like he wants to get to know his student, but later Fletcher uses Andrew's backstory to humiliate and insult him in an attempt to push Andrew past his limitations. Now, by exposing Andrew's backstory, the screenwriter is telling us about his family story and his past, helping us understand a little bit more about the protagonist. At the same time, the writer is using this opportunity to show the antagonist's characteristics as an abusive teacher.

Protagonist's Introduction

Andrew Neiman is introduced playing the drums alone late at night at the rehearsal studio. He rehearses, trying to perfect the strokes, maintaining a constant beat. His practice is interrupted by Fletcher, who enters the room. Andrew, noticing Fletcher, stops playing. Andrew is intimidated by the man standing in front of him. Fletcher seems to have an interest in Andrew's talent and asks for his name. Andrew knows Fletcher looks for talented players to join his jazz studio ensemble band, one of the best in the nation.

The scene introduces Andrew's ordinary world. It shows the audience who he is, what he does, and what he wants from the start. The writer/director of *Whiplash*, Damien Chazelle, discussed the opening scene in an interview:

> The movie was going to be about a drummer, so literally it opens with a guy drumming and the story itself is really about the drummer's relationship with the teacher. So what the first scene had to introduce was the drummer, the teacher, and tell you exactly what that relationship was going to be, and then the rest of the movie could basically vary [and] riff on that, but I like the idea of basically having the entire movie within the opening scene.

Psychological, Physical, and Social Attributes

Andrew's psychological attributes show him to be driven, hardworking, ambitious, competitive, impulsive, self-centered, and pretentious. Physically, there is nothing extraordinary about him except his talents in playing the drums. Socially, he is awkward, a loner. Andrew doesn't see the use of having friends around him.

Protagonist's Worldview

Andrew believes hard work always pays off. He has a great work ethic and he is passionate about his goal.

Antagonist's Worldview

Fletcher is a perfectionist, unforgiving, ruthless, and forces the students to their limits to obtain the results he wants from them. He abuses the students emotionally and physically to the point where some just break down. Fletcher's actions are justified in his mind, because he wants to discover the next great jazz musician, like Charlie Parker.

Protagonist's Life and Personas

Andrew is a college student at Schaffer Music Conservatory. That is his professional life: he is a music student who dreams of being the greatest musician in the twentieth century. In his personal life, he doesn't have much going on; he only meets his dad on their movie nights. And before getting obsessed with becoming the greatest drummer, he goes out with Nicole, the cashier girl at the popcorn stand from the movie theater. With her, he is sweet and funny, but soon he breaks up the relationship to dedicate more time to his practice. In his private life, he only thinks of music, listens to music, and practices his drums. Andrew takes his mattress from his dorm room to the school's practice room so that he can practice day and night. He practices until his fingers bleed.

Protagonist's Objective

Andrew's world evolves because of music, and becoming the best drummer he can be is his pursuit in life. Nothing else matters. During a family dinner, Andrew's uncle asks:

> UNCLE FRANK
> And what's your idea of success, then?

> ANDREW
> Becoming the greatest musician of the
> twentieth century would be anyone's
> idea of success.

Antagonist's Objective

Fletcher is on a mission to discover the next great jazz musician. In Fletcher's world, only the most talented and strongest musicians are worthy of his time. He aggressively pushes the students to be the best they can be. That is how Fletcher operates – by getting inside the brain of his students and forcing them to overcome his dominance to perform at their best.

Protagonist's Conflicts

Andrew's external conflict, character vs. character, is with Fletcher. The character vs. environment conflict is the competitive environment between the musicians in Fletcher's studio band. Andrew's internal conflict is fighting his limitations, always pushing to improve and perfect his skills as a drummer.

Protagonist's Transformation

Andrew goes from being a timid freshman student to becoming a confident and talented jazz drummer. At the beginning of the screenplay, he is apologetic when Fletcher shows up in the rehearsal room and Fletcher is very much in control of the situation. At the end of the film, Andrew is not apologetic; on the contrary, he takes what he came to get. Andrew is very much in control of the stage during the final performance at Carnegie Hall.

III. STORY ELEMENTS

Protagonist

The protagonist is Andrew Neiman, a freshman jazz drummer at a prestigious music academy, Schaffer Conservatory, in New York City.

Inciting Incident

The inciting incident takes place at the beginning of the screenplay, along with the character introduction. Fletcher walks into the rehearsal studio where Andrew is practicing late at night. Andrew knows that Fletcher is a conductor/teacher for the studio band. He wants to show off his skills and talents as a jazz drummer. This character introduction establishes their power dynamics: Fletcher is the teacher and Andrew is the student. Fletcher humiliates Andrew for his indecisive behaviors, and then asks him to play. Andrew starts to play drum rudiments, one after another. Fletcher demands more, a "double-time swing." Andrew tries his best, but he is out of his comfort zone. He closes his eyes to concentrate. Suddenly, the door slams shut. Andrew looks up. Fletcher is gone. Andrew is not sure if Fletcher liked or disliked his rudiments. From the opening scene, we know each character's dramatic needs. Andrew's want is to be in Fletcher's jazz ensemble band, and Fletcher's want is to find the best performers for his band.

Protagonist's Objective

Andrew has his heart set on becoming one of the greatest jazz drummers of the twentieth century.

Main Tension

As Andrew gets scouted by Fletcher to join the studio band, the first act comes to an end, and the main tension raises in the back of the audience's mind: "Can Andrew become the lead drummer for Fletcher's jazz ensemble band and learn to be a great jazz drummer?"

Action

Andrew's action is to learn as much as possible and practice as much as he can to impress Fletcher and stay in his band. Andrew takes action to achieve his goal by giving up any distractions such as dating that may disturb his goals. Andrew even breaks up with his girlfriend to dedicate more time to his music.

Main Conflict

Andrew's external conflict is with Fletcher and his ruthless teaching method. Fletcher abuses his power and creates a hostile environment to push the students around. He demands perfection. Fletcher humiliates, intimidates, and insults the students to motivate them to perform at their best. Andrew must push himself to the limit each time, or else he will be replaced. He lives in constant fear and stress, and it takes a toll on him. First, there is nothing more important than getting into Fletcher's band. Once he is in the band, nothing is more important than practicing hard, so that when the time comes, he can take the lead drummer's seat. Once he becomes the lead drummer, there is nothing more important than keeping the seat. Andrew is pushed around and constantly tested by Fletcher throughout this process. Finally, Andrew breaks down. He gets into a car accident on the way to a competition, and instead of going to the hospital, he resists the pain and goes onstage. As the band starts to play, he slowly falls apart and can't keep up with the rest of the band.

Andrew endures physical and psychological humiliation from Fletcher because his desire is greater than Fletcher's abuse, and Andrew knows Fletcher holds the keys to his future. The story is always about pursuing greatness – both Andrew and Fletcher have the same objective, but they're standing on opposite sides. As a student, Andrew has a goal of becoming a great drummer, and as a teacher, Fletcher has a goal to generate the next generation of great musicians.

Crisis

The crisis occurs when Andrew arrives late to a jazz band competition. Then he has an argument with Fletcher, and to make the matter worse, he doesn't have his drumsticks to go on stage. Andrew is determined to keep the lead drummer seat, and rushes to get the drumsticks he left at a car rental place. Now, on the way back, Andrew gets into a car accident. Hurt from the car crash, he still has his heart set on keeping the lead drummer's seat, leaving the accident scene to make it to the stage on time. Andrew's willpower to get to the concert hall is so strong that he is willing to endure the shock and pain from the accident. Andrew's abnormal behavior clearly shows how psychologically unstable he is. Bleeding and in pain, Andrew sits on the drummer's seat. As the band starts to play, Andrew seems to keep up with the song, but soon enough, he falls apart. His body can't take it, he can barely hold the drumsticks, and finally, he gives up. He stops playing. To make matters worse,

Fletcher comes over and tells Andrew that he is "done." Andrew kicks the drum in front of him and goes after Fletcher, tackling and punching him.

Andrew is forced to indict Fletcher – the choice to make Fletcher accountable for his abusive behavior. Furthermore, Andrew is dismissed from school and puts his drum set in a closet. He tries to find normalcy in his life. Then Andrew sees Fletcher performing in a jazz bar. Andrew overcomes challenges from the crisis by reconciling with Fletcher and agrees to play for Fletcher at the JVC Jazz Festival at Carnegie Hall.

Climax

The climax takes place at the Carnegie Hall jazz festival. Andrew goes onstage to find out that Fletcher has switched the song. Instead of playing "Caravan," they play "Upswingin." Fletcher wants to take revenge on Andrew and ruin his life, and Andrew tries to improvise, but he can't. Humiliated in front of a live audience, Andrew walks backstage.

Resolution

The resolution takes place during the final performance in the film. After seeing his dad, Andrew goes back onstage. The final confrontation isn't over. Andrew plays the beats to "Caravan," surprising everyone. He takes the lead and asks the band to join in. He is no longer the shy freshman wanting to be in Fletcher's band, and he won't take the humiliation and abuse from Fletcher anymore. He takes control of the situation. Fletcher is forced to follow Andrew's lead and conduct the band. Andrew rises to the challenge.

Answer to the Main Tension

The answer to the main tension is shown through action as Andrew takes control of a difficult situation where he was ridiculed and humiliated in front of a live audience. He storms backstage, but doesn't give up, and walks back onstage to reveal who he has become. The answer to the main tension is: Yes, Andrew becomes a great jazz drummer.

IV. STRUCTURE

Three-Act Structure

In the first act, the story is set up with Andrew meeting Fletcher in the first scene. They establish their power dynamics and each of their objectives from the very beginning of the story. Then we follow Andrew into his ordinary world, where we meet his dad for their movie night, and then return to his crowded dorm hallway, without greeting anyone on the way to his room. He is a loner. Andrew peeks through the studio band rehearsal room's window. As he looks at the drummer, it is clear what he wants. Then he looks around the room and meets Fletcher's eyes, who is looking right at him, and immediately pulls away from the door. Andrew listens and studies his idol, becoming more passionate and practicing to get better. The event at the *end of the first act* is when Andrew gets scouted by Fletcher to join the studio band.

The *second act starts* with the subplot between Andrew and Nicole. Andrew asks her out and they agree to go on a date. As for the main plot, Andrew wakes up late and rushes to get to the studio band rehearsal room by 6:00 A.M., but he steps into an empty room when he gets there. The rehearsal doesn't start until 9 A.M. Fletcher gave him the wrong time on purpose. During the rehearsal, Andrew gets crushed by Fletcher for the first time, and is ridiculed and humiliated in front of the rest of the band members for rushing the beat to the song. Fletcher orders Andrew to practice harder. Now, Andrew moves his dorm mattress to his practice room and practices until his fingers bleed. At the Overbrook Jazz Competition, the studio band finishes the first set, and Carl Tanner, lead drummer, asks Andrew to hold on to the music folder until the second set. Andrew misplaces the folder by mistake and ends up losing it. Carl confesses to Fletcher that he doesn't know the song by heart, but Andrew does, so Fletcher gives Andrew the opportunity to play. The Schaffer Conservatory studio band wins the competition. The next day, Fletcher names Andrew the lead drummer at the beginning of the studio band rehearsal.

The *first half of the second act* is about Andrew becoming the core member, the lead drummer for Fletcher's studio band. The *second half of the second act* starts with Andrew losing the core member seat to Ryan, another drum alternative who has joined the band. Andrew breaks up with Nicole to dedicate more time to his music. Now, Carl, Ryan, and Andrew compete to be the core member as the studio band prepares for the next competition. After a brutal session to determine who can play the double-time swing tempo to Fletcher's liking, Andrew finally earns the part. Now, Andrew is expelled from Schaffer Conservatory from the Dunellen Jazz Competition incident. Andrew attacked Fletcher onstage. Jim, Andrew's father, asks Andrew to tell the truth about the physical and emotional abuse to a lawyer, and Fletcher gets fired from the school. Thus, there is no more studio band, and no more dream of becoming the greatest jazz drummer. Andrew puts his drum set in a closet, and gets ready to move on with his life without music. The event that *concludes the second act* is when Andrew runs into Fletcher playing the piano at a jazz bar. The two of them have a drink and Fletcher invites him to play at the JVC Jazz Festival at Carnegie Hall.

The *third act begins* with Andrew arriving at Carnegie Hall. Fletcher, knowing that Andrew testified against him, takes revenge by changing the song they will play onstage. Andrew is humiliated onstage and heads backstage, but he takes control of the situation instead of walking away. Andrew goes back onstage to perform the song he has been perfecting throughout the screenplay, "Caravan." As the band joins in, Fletcher is forced to conduct the piece. Fletcher gets into it and likes what he hears from Andrew and the band. Andrew gives all he's got, and all the late-night practices and the sacrifices he made finally pay off. He is no longer the timid freshman at the beginning of the film; he is an artist, performing at the top of his game.

V. SETTING

The *geographic location* of the story takes place in NYC during 2014 when the film was released. The world of *Whiplash* consists of the highly competitive world of musicians, and concentrates on the power dynamics between students and a ruthless instructor, who pushes abuse on the students to get the best performances out of them.

VI. TECHNIQUES AND TOOLS

Events/Occurrences

*   *The first encounter:* At the beginning, Andrew and Fletcher meet and establish their dramatic needs for the first time.
*   *Movie night:* Andrew meets his father, Jim, for movie night.
*   *Getting scouted:* Fletcher interrupts the Nassau band rehearsal and scouts Andrew to join his band.
*   *The first date:* Andrew goes out on a date with Nicole.
*   *The first day at studio band:* Andrew joins the best jazz ensemble, where he gets ridiculed and humiliated by Fletcher.
*   *The Overbrook Jazz Competition:* Andrew accidentally misplaces a music folder that belongs to Carl, the lead drummer. Because Carl can't play without the music sheets, Andrew gets to play as a lead drummer.
*   *The family dinner:* Andrew goes to have dinner with his uncle's family, exposing his current psychological state.
*   *The breakup:* Andrew breaks up with Nicole to dedicate more time to his passion.
*   *The tryouts:* Andrew, Carl, and Ryan try out to become the lead drummer for the next competition.
*   *The Dunellen Jazz Competition:* Andrew gets into an accident and then tries to maintain the lead drummer seat, but fails.
*   *The meeting with the lawyer:* Andrew is forced to tell the truth about Fletcher's abusive behaviors, and Fletcher is fired from the Schaffer conservatory.
*   *JVC Jazz Festival at Carnegie Hall:* Onstage, Andrew displays his character transformation.

Dramatic Irony

*   The audience knows Andrew left his drumsticks at the car rental place. The tension builds as time is ticking and the band is about to go onstage. Fletcher won't let him play without his own drumsticks.

- Another use of dramatic irony is when we know Andrew was the cause of Fletcher getting fired, but Fletcher doesn't know, and the tension starts to escalate while they are having a drink at the jazz bar.

Reversal

- There are two reversals taking place in the third act of the film. The first reversal takes place when we find out Fletcher has switched the song they will be performing onstage. They are supposed to play "Caravan," but Fletcher and the band play "Upswingin." Andrew is completely caught off-guard and fails to keep up with the band.
- The second reversal in the third act is Andrew's deciding to go back onstage. The course of the story changes from his desire to take control. Andrew's action displays his character transformation.

Setup and Payoff

The biggest setup and payoff in this screenplay is the use of the song "Caravan." It is a difficult and demanding song to master for a drummer, with very fast drumbeats. Andrew practices the song throughout the film. The payoff takes place during the final scene, where Andrew performs brilliantly, revealing his talents as a great jazz drummer.

GET OUT
(Horror/Mystery/Thriller), 2017

Written and directed by Jordan Peele

I. THEME AND PREMISE

Theme

Systemic racism is still embedded in our society. As writer/director Jordan Peele says, the film "expose[s] the lie of post-racial America." The film exposes casual racism: first, Chris and Rose's interracial relationship raises complications from the start. Chris wants to know Rose has told her parents about his race. Second, after hitting a deer on their way to Rose's parents' house, the police officer racially profiles Chris. Rose stands up for him. At the house, Chris deals with subtle and casual racism from Rose's parents and the guests at the party. Walter and Georgina, the two workers at the estate, are black. Later, we find out they are Rose's grand-parents, whose consciousness has been placed into the bodies of black people.

Premise

A group of people decides to take over black people's bodies while keeping their own minds and consciousnesses intact. The cult members believe in the physical superior-ity of black people. They kidnap black people and hold auctions; the cult members bid to take over their bodies while keeping their minds and consciousness intact.

II. CHARACTER STUDY

Characters

Protagonist: Chris
Antagonists: Rose, Dean, Missy, and Jeremy
Supporting characters: Rod, Walter, Georgina, and Jim Hudson

DOI: 10.4324/9781003138853-14

Backstory

When Chris returns to the house after smoking a cigarette at night, he has a conversation with Missy, Rose's mother. Chris reveals his greatest regret: when he was a young boy, he didn't call anyone or do anything when his mother didn't return home from work. At the time, he thought that if he did call someone, his mother's loss would become real. Chris believes it's his fault his mother died. Had he done something about it that night, it might have changed the outcome. This backstory becomes a setup for a payoff that will take place in the third act, when Chris returns to get Georgina after running her over in the Armitage driveway.

Another important backstory revealed during the house tour is the story of Rose's grandfather, Roman Armitage. A black runner, Jesse Owens, defeated Roman in the qualifying rounds for the 1936 Olympics. Dean, Rose's father, says to Chris, "He almost got over it." This incident fueled envy, and became the seed of the new cult. Members of high society seek to transplant their brains into a healthy black person's body. This important backstory explains the existence of the Order of the Coagula, the cult the film's premise is based on.

Protagonist's Introduction

Chris is introduced as he gets ready in the morning. He is a healthy young man. Rose, his girlfriend, comes over to his apartment as Chris starts packing for the weekend trip.

Psychological, Physical, and Social Attributes

Chris is soft-spoken, and is not easily triggered into participating in the conflict. He is quiet, happy to listen, and doesn't have to be the center of attention. Chris's most prominent psychological attribute is the guilt he feels about his mother's death. Missy discovers his weakness during their conversation and uses it to hypnotize him and take him to the "sunken place." What are Chris's physical attributes? He has an athletic body and a keen eye for composition in images, which helps with his career as an urban photographer. What are his social attributes? Chris lives a normal life – he is a talented photographer, he has a place to himself, and he has a dog. He has a best friend, Rod, and he is in an interracial relationship. Chris appeals to the audience because of his kindness and generous qualities.

Protagonist's Worldview

Chris's point of view of the world is optimistic. He gives Rose and her family the benefit of the doubt, even after several awkward incidents, like the unpleasant family dinner where Jeremy goes overboard with his comments and mind-games. Or even when he gets hypnotized against his will and when he endures awkward micro-aggressive racial comments from Rose's family and the guests at the party.

Antagonist's Worldview

Rose and her family, the Armitages, have a very disturbing point of view of the world. For their cult, the Order of Coagula, they seduce, lie, and kidnap black people; they then auction off each victim so that the brain of the white person who wins the auction can be implanted into the victim's body.

Protagonist's Life

The story revolves around Chris's personal and private lives, so his work/professional life isn't mentioned often, but from the information we do get, we can tell that he is a talented urban photographer. In his personal life, he has a strong friendship with his best friend, Rod. He appears to be in a great relationship with his girlfriend, Rose, and he attempts to build a relationship with her parents. But the ordeal he goes through exposes his private self. He is not afraid to defend himself. If it's a matter of killing to survive, he is brave and courageous.

Protagonist's Personas

When Chris is with Rose, he is honest and sweet to her, avoids confrontations, and completely trusts her. When Chris is with Rose's parents, he shows the same persona he presents to Rose: he is polite, attentive, and accommodating, even when he hears micro-aggressive comments like "my man!" When Chris speaks to Walter after coming from a morning walk, or when he approaches Logan, he shows a different persona than when he speaks to the Armitages. He is much more friendly with them. He tries to approach them with sincerity and with a positive vibe. When Chris speaks to Rod, his best friend, he can be completely himself. The tone and demeanor of his voice changes.

Protagonist's Objectives

Chris wants to survive the weekend, first metaphorically, then later, literally. He wants to make a good impression on Rose's parents and spend quality time getting to know them. This is his objective at the beginning of the film, but his objective changes once his life is threatened. At that point, Chris wants to escape the Armitage estate and survive the ordeal.

Antagonist's Objectives

The Armitage family has one mission in the screenplay, to auction Chris's body off to a cult member. Rose seduces Chris and brings him to meet her parents. During their stay, Rose's parents have a gathering where the cult members come to see and get to know Chris. Dean, Rose's father, holds an auction and the winner gets to transplant their brain into Chris's body.

Protagonist's Conflicts

Chris's internal conflict comes from being in an interracial relationship. Even though he loves his girlfriend, and their relationship is serious enough to meet her parents, there is a racial conflict present in his mind, and it is exposed when he asks Rose if her parents know about his race. Even though Rose assures him that her parents are not racist, the conflict never washes away, and internal conflict lingers in his mind.

Chris's external conflict exists in two forms. He has a conflict with the surroundings or the environment he is in and he has conflicts with other characters. First, the environment he is in is a trap. The Armitages seem like they are trying to make him comfortable, but there are strange vibes and behavior, especially at the party. When Logan attacks Chris, that is the tipping point and Chris decides to go home. His conflict is with other characters – with the Armitages. Dean, Missy, Jeremy, and Rose all play their parts in the conflict with Chris. There is a unity of opposites: the Armitages want to take his body, and Chris wants to protect himself.

Protagonist's Transformation

At the beginning of the film, Chris worries about making a good impression, but at the end of the film, he worries about surviving. An urban photographer, he becomes capable of killing others in self-defense. Chris reaches his final transformation when he strangles Rose, but he stops, realizing his act is revenge and not self-defense. As Rose smiles while being strangled, he decides that he will not allow her to turn him into a monster. Chris's emotional arc goes from being optimistic to being liberated. At first, he is optimistic about the weekend he would spend with Rose's family, but by the end, he is liberated from the cruel scheme they were trying to pull off – putting him in the "sunken place" forever.

III. STORY ELEMENTS

Protagonist

The protagonist is Chris Washington. He is a talented urban photographer who is in an interracial relationship.

Inciting Incident

The inciting incident is Chris agreeing to go to meet Rose's parents and spend the weekend at their estate. The screenplay begins after the inciting incident has taken place. Chris and Rose's first encounter in the story exposes their plan – the weekend trip to meet Rose's parents.

Protagonist's Objective

As Chris is about to spend the weekend with Rose's parents, his initial objective is to make a good impression and build a relationship with them. But later on, when his life is threatened, his objective changes: he wants to survive the ordeal and escape the Armitage estate.

Main Tension

Can Chris make a good impression, and build a relationship with Rose's parents?

Action

Chris's action is consistent with his objective – he tries to get to know Rose's parents. First, Chris goes on a house tour with Dean. Later, they have iced tea on the deck. When Jeremy arrives, they all have a family dinner. Chris is attentive and polite as he tries to navigate through unfamiliar terrain in good spirits. Later that evening, after coming back from smoking, he sits with Missy, and is hypnotized without his consent. Next day when the guests arrive, he helps Rose greet the guests who have come to the party to honor her grandfather, Roman Armitage. Chris takes action to fulfill his objectives.

Main Conflict

The main conflict is between Chris and the Armitage family. Rose and her family want to hypnotize Chris and have the highest bidder take his body from the auction. Chris wants to live and survive the ordeal.

Crisis

The crisis for Chris takes place when Logan attacks him after snapping a picture of the only black man at the party. Logan snapped out of the sunken place when the camera flashed him and told Chris to "get out." Now, up to this point, Chris has had weird and unnatural encounters with Walter and Georgina. Chris also feels Jeremy's racial aggression during the family dinner and feels threatened when Missy hypnotizes him without his consent. All the micro-aggressions and racism he experiences with Dean and the guests at the party come to a head when Logan attacks him. Chris overcomes the crisis by deciding to leave. During the conversation at the lake, Chris tells Rose that he wants to go home, and she agrees. While Chris and Rose are at the lake, back at the house, Dean conducts a silent auction. The guests are bidding for Chris. Jim Hudson wins the bid.

Climax

Chris and Rose come back from the lake, and as Chris starts to pack his bag, he finds a shoebox containing photos. As he goes through the pictures, he notices Rose with different black men, posing as if they are in a relationship. All this time, Chris thought he was her first black boyfriend, but he discovers Rose's dishonesty for the first time. Her true self is revealed to Chris in the foyer when he asks for the keys to the car: "You know I can't give them to you, right?" Chris feels the betrayal as every Armitage family member blocks every exit in the foyer. As Chris tries to force himself out of the house, Missy sends him to the "sunken place" by clinking a silver spoon against a teacup. Chris, the protagonist, confronts the Armitages, the antagonists, and he loses.

Answer to the Main Tension

Did the protagonist achieve his goals? No. Chris doesn't get to spend quality time with Rose's family. Although he made an effort to get to know them, that didn't really matter, as the Armitages had a different agenda all along.

Resolution

As Chris is held captive in the game room, his arms and legs are tied up in a leather chair. He uses the cotton sticking out on the armrest to cover his ears to prevent him from going into hypnosis. When Jeremy comes to get him for the brain transplant surgery, Chris pretends to be hypnotized but attacks Jeremy, rendering him unconscious. Then Chris kills Dean, who is getting ready for surgery, with a deer head, and when he comes upstairs from the basement, he attacks and kills Missy before she has a chance to reach for the silver spoon and the teacup. As he hurries to leave the premises, he runs over Georgina with the car. When he goes back to get Georgina, Rose starts shooting, Walter comes to help Rose, but as Chris snaps another photo with the flash, Walter regains consciousness for a brief second, just as he did with Logan during the party. Walter shoots Rose and then kills himself. Rose asks for help, but Chris strangles her. He soon lets her go as a police car enters the driveway. Chris discovers the driver is Rod, who has come to rescue him.

During the resolution, we witness the character transformation. Chris, the soft-spoken, nice guy with a generous spirit, has changed to become a violent man out of necessity and desperation. He is forced to take lives to survive a horrific event.

IV. STRUCTURE

Three-Act Structure

- The first act sets up the story by introducing two characters in love, who are about to pay a visit to meet the girlfriend's parents. Because the couple is in an interracial relationship, Chris, the protagonist, worries that Rose has not disclosed his race to her parents. "Do they know I'm black?" he says. She assures him that they are not racist and says, "My dad would've voted for Obama a third time if he could have. Like, the love is so real." On their drive to Rose's parents' house, they hit a deer and report the accident. The cop who comes to take the report racially profiles Chris, and Rose calls him on it.

- The first act ends as the car pulls into the Armitage estate driveway. Missy and Dean come out to greet them.

- The second act begins with the four inside the house. Chris has entered the extraordinary world. The four of them have a chat, and then Dean takes Chris on a house tour. Throughout their interaction, Dean overacts, calling him, "My man!" These are not the words Dean would normally use, but because Chris is black Dean uses acts of micro-aggression on him. In the second act, Chris tries to stay true to his objective and participates in family functions, having iced tea on the deck, joining the family dinner, and greeting the guests with Rose.

- The second act ends as Chris and Rose decide to leave the house and go back home. As Chris packs his belongings and gets ready to go, he is confronted by every member of the Armitage family, blocking every possible way out from the foyer. As Chris and Jeremy confront each other, Missy sends Chris into the "sunken place."

- The third act begins with Chris waking up, tied up and sitting on a leather chair. Chris discovers his fate after watching an introductory video made by Roman Armitage, Rose's grandfather, for the victims of the procedure. Then Chris has a moment to interact with Jim Hudson, the person who will be taking over his body. When nervous, Chris tends to scratch whatever he is holding; during the hypnosis session, Chris scratches the arm of the sofa with his nails. We see a series of flashbacks of him scratching a wooden arm holder with his nails. We know that writer/director Jordan Peele has been paying attention to detail. In order to justify the cotton sticking out of the leather arm chair, Peele continually shows Chris scratching the armchair with his nails until the cotton underneath the leather starts to appear. When he sees the cotton sticking out of the armchair, he gets an idea.

- The third act ends with the protagonist's exit from the Armitage house. The writer ties up all the loose ends by showing a resolution with every family member of the Armitage family, including Georgina and Walter. Chris goes home with the help of his best friend, Rod.

The Sequence Method

First Sequence: Act 1, Sequence 1

1. *What is the sequence title?* Chris and Rose.
2. *Whose sequence is it?* Chris, the protagonist, is an urban photographer. The sequence begins as he gets ready in the morning in his apartment.

3. *What does he want?* Chris wants to know if Rose's parents know he is black. If they don't, perhaps she should tell them, because they are getting ready to go to spend the weekend at her parents' house.
4. *What's the conflict?* Chris wants Rose to inform her parents of his race. He doesn't want to surprise them, but Rose doesn't want to tell them. Rose assures him that her parents are not racist, that everything will be fine. One important clue that gets mentioned during their conversation is that she hasn't been in an interracial relationship prior to dating Chris. This is a lie, and the truth will be revealed during the crisis of this film.
5. *Who is in the way?* Rose is in the way. Chris wants to inform her parents, but Rose won't tell them.
6. *Who helps?* Rose completely assures Chris that everything will be all right.
7. *What is the emotional arc of the main character in the sequence?* Chris starts the sequence worried about the weekend trip. But after the reassurance from Rose, Chris feels at ease. In the first sequence, the protagonist's emotional arc goes from being worried to feeling at ease.

Second Sequence: Act 1, Sequence 2

1. *What is the sequence title?* The Drive.
2. *Whose sequence is it?* It's Chris's sequence. Rose drives and Chris is in the passenger seat.
3. *What does he want?* Chris wants to have a nice drive to Rose's parents' house. He wants to smoke a cigarette, but Rose won't let him. Chris makes a call to his friend, Rod, and gives him final dog-sitting instructions.
4. *What's the conflict?* Rose hits a deer, and the car comes to a stop. Chris walks back to side of the road and looks at the dead deer, foreshadowing what is to come.
5. *Who is in the way?* The cop. They calls the police, and Rose reports the incident to the police officer. Holding Rose's driver's license, the cop looks at Chris and asks for his identification.
6. *Who helps?* When Chris is about to give his identification to the cop, Rose confronts the cop about racially profiling her boyfriend and asks why he needs Chris's identification when he wasn't even driving. The cop tries to defend himself, but it's too late. The cop doesn't check Chris's identification.
7. *What is the emotional arc of the main character in the sequence?* At the beginning of the sequence, Chris is a little nervous as they drive up to Rose's parents' house. His nervousness is shown when he takes out a cigarette. At the end of the sequence, he feels safe with Rose by his side. In the second sequence, the protagonist's emotional arc changes. Chris goes from feeling nervous to feeling safe.

Main Tension

Can Chris make a good impression on Rose's parents and spend a quality weekend with her family?

Third Sequence: Act 2, Sequence 1

1. *What is the sequence title?* Meet the Armitages.
2. *Whose sequence is it?* It's Chris's sequence. He is introduced to Rose's parents, Dean and Missy; the groundskeeper, Walter; and the maid, Georgina. Later, Jeremy, Rose's brother, joins the family dinner.
3. *What does he want?* He wants to make a good impression and get to know Rose's family.
4. *What's the conflict?* Chris feels something strange with Walter and Georgina. Rose's parents seem nice and welcoming, but there is something creepy about them.
5. *Who is in the way?* Jeremy gets hostile toward Chris during dinner, ruining the evening for everyone.
6. *Who helps?* Rose helps. Rose rescues Chris from the awkwardness and takes his side during the family dinner. When they are back in their room, she is embarrassed about her family's behavior during dinner and again puts Chris at ease.
7. *What is the emotional arc of the main character in the sequence?* Chris's emotional arc changes. He goes from feeling welcomed to feeling strange.

Fourth Sequence: Act 2, Sequence 2

1. *What is the sequence title?* The Sunken Place.
2. *Whose sequence is it?* It's Chris's sequence. Chris can't sleep, and he goes out for a smoke in the middle of the night. But Walter and Georgina scare him, and on the way back, he runs into Missy, Rose's mother, who hypnotizes him against his will.
3. *What does he want?* He wants to smoke a cigarette.
4. *What's the conflict?* Chris goes downstairs and steps out of the house to grab a smoke. Chris is terrorized as he sees someone in the distance running toward him. Chris becomes paralyzed. The runner passes by him, and it's Walter. Then he comes face to face with Georgina, who looks out the window. When Chris reenters the house, he encounters Rose's mother, Missy. He is unwillingly hypnotized, and the conversation turns to when Chris's mother passed away on a rainy night – a backstory. Missy learns about Chris's deepest fears.
5. *Who is in the way?* When Chris goes to have a cigarette, Walter and Georgina prevent him from having a peaceful smoke. Missy hypnotizes Chris, sending him into the "sunken place," a place where his mind is detached from the physical body.
6. *Who helps?* No one helps.
7. *What is the emotional arc of the main character in the sequence?* Chris's emotional arc goes from being fidgety to devastated.

Fifth Sequence: Act 2, Sequence 3

1. *What is the sequence title?* The Party.
2. *Whose sequence is it?* It's Chris's sequence. In the early morning, the sequence begins with him out on a walk, taking pictures of nature. Chris senses there is something wrong with Walter when he has a brief encounter with him on his way back. Inside the house, he talks to Rose about Missy hypnotizing him the previous night, and he feels like throwing up when he thinks about smoking. Then the guests arrive. Chris and Rose greet every guest. Chris meets two interesting characters, Logan and Jim Hudson. Logan is the only other black man at the party. He acts and talks like an old white man. The other man, a blind white man, is Jim Hudson from the Hudson Gallery.
3. *What does he want?* Chris wants to be a good boyfriend and help greet the guests.
4. *What's the conflict?* There are two major conflicts taking place in this sequence. First, Chris discovers that his phone's power cord was unplugged by Georgina. He informs Rose of the incident, but she doesn't believe him. Second, Logan attacks Chris, telling him to "get out" when he takes a photo using a flash.
5. *Who is in the way?* Georgina and Logan. Georgina comes to the bedroom and apologizes to Chris for accidentally unplugging his phone. Logan apologizes to Chris and other guests for his behavior earlier.
6. *Who helps?* Rod and Rose. Chris speaks to his friend Rod and tells him how he got hypnotized by Missy, and Rod half-jokingly says something is not right.
7. *What is the emotional arc of the main character in the sequence?* Chris goes from peacefully taking pictures at dawn to getting attacked by Logan at the party. Chris's emotional arc goes from peaceful to confused.

Sixth Sequence: Act 2, Sequence 4

1. *What is the sequence title?* Let's Go Home.
2. *Whose sequence is it?* It's Chris's sequence. He and Rose go for a walk and have a conversation by the lake.
3. *What does he want?* Chris wants to go home.
4. *What's the conflict?* Back at the Armitage estate, the guests are gathered by the gazebo as Dean, Rose's dad, conducts an auction. He takes bids from guests in front of Chris's portrait. Jim Hudson, the blind man, wins the auction. When Chris and Rose return home to pack their belongings, Chris finds a shoe box with a pile of photos of Rose, who is with a different black man in each photo. Chris realizes that Rose has been lying to him.
5. *Who is in the way?* The entire Armitage family: Dean, Missy, Jeremy, and Rose. As Chris is about to leave, the Armitage family blocks his path in the foyer. Chris learns his fate as Rose reveals her true identity to Chris. As Chris tries to fight his way out of the foyer, Missy sends him to the "sunken place" with the clinking sound of the spoon and tea cup.

6. *Who helps?* Rod. Chris texts Rod the picture he snapped at the party while packing his belongings. Rod calls him, telling him he recognizes Logan. His real name is Andre. Rod tells him to get out as soon as possible. The tension builds as he hurries to get out of the house.

7. *What is the emotional arc of the main character in the sequence?* Logan's attack on Chris makes him feel threatened. When he has a conversation about going home, he feels hopeful. Then he gets trapped in the "sunken place." In this sequence, Chris's emotional arc goes from feeling threatened to being trapped.

Answer to the Main Tension

The main tension is: "Can Chris make a good impression on Rose's parents and spend a quality weekend with her family?" The answer to this main tension is: No, Chris hasn't met his objective. Chris was fooled into believing his objectives mattered to Rose's family.

Seventh Sequence: Act 3, Sequence 1

1. *What is the sequence title?* The Game Room.
2. *Whose sequence is it?* It's Chris's sequence.
3. *What does he want?* Chris wants to escape from the game room and from the house.
4. *What's the conflict?* Chris's arms and legs are tied to a leather chair.
5. *Who is in the way?* The Armitage family. First, Roman, Rose's grandfather, appears on the television in front of him. Chris discovers his fate. He explains the Coagula procedure, where the Armitage family will take his body and give it to someone else. Later, Jim Hudson comes on TV. Chris has a videoconference with Jim. Chris discovers that Jim will take over his body, and Chris will remain in the "sunken place." Chris freaks out.
6. *Who helps?* Rod worries about Chris not coming home from the weekend trip. Rod also performs an internet search and discovers that Andre/Logan has gone missing. Rod starts to worry about Chris and goes to the police, but he is laughed at because no one wants to believe him. The second person who helps Chris is himself at the end of this sequence. Chris sees the torn leather arm, revealing cotton stuffing, and he gets an idea.
7. *What is the emotional arc of the main character in the sequence?* Chris's emotional arc goes from feeling scared to feeling empowered.

Eighth Sequence: Act 3, Sequence 2

1. *What is the sequence title?* The Exit.
2. *Whose sequence is it?* It's Chris's sequence.
3. *What does he want?* He wants to escape.
4. *What's the conflict?* Chris is still tied up and hypnotized.

5. *Who is in the way?* Jeremy, Dean, Missy, Rose, Walter, and Georgina. The first is Jeremy, who comes to get Chris for the operation. Chris attacks Jeremy, knocking him unconscious, then takes out the earplugs he's made out of cotton stuffing from the chair arm. Chris only pretended to be hypnotized. Then Chris uses a deer's head to kill Dean. When he comes up from the basement, Missy attacks him, and Chris kills her. As Chris is trying to drive away from the house, he runs over Georgina, and he goes back to get her to save her. Rose starts to shoot at Chris and Walter comes to help Rose, but at the last minute, everything changes.

6. *Who helps?* Walter and Rod. First, Walter, the groundskeeper, regains consciousness in the Sunken Place, and helps Chris by shooting Rose. Walter kills himself. Then Rod comes to the rescue. Rod comes to the Armitage estate, and helps Chris escape.

7. *What is the emotional arc of the main character in the sequence?* Chris's emotional arc goes from being trapped to being liberated.

V. SETTING

The *geographic location* of the story takes place in two places: in a city, and in suburbia. The screenwriter doesn't specify the actual location, which means it can be anywhere in the United States. The *time period* in which the story takes place is around the same period as when the film was released in 2017. The story takes place in a highly exclusive cult *world*, where the members gather to bid on a healthy human being so that they can transplant their minds and prolong their lives in a healthy body. They believe in the physical superiority of black people, and they only abduct black people to transplant themselves into. For the *sociocultural setting*, the story takes place as President Obama is ending his second term. Dean makes a clear statement to Chris, saying that he would have voted for Obama for a third term if allowed.

VI. TECHNIQUES AND TOOLS

Events/Occurrences

- The first event is the drive Chris and Rose take to get to the Armitage estate.
- The second event is meeting Missy and Dean Armitage.
- The third event is the family dinner, where they all gather to have a meal. The event includes Jeremy, Rose's brother.
- The fourth event is the party, the annual gathering in honor of Dean's father, Roman Armitage.
- The fifth event is where all the guests gather to bid in the auction.
- The sixth event is Chris's attempt to leave the house. Jeremy confronts him and Missy sends him to the "sunken place."
- The seventh event is the escape.

Dramatic Irony

One of the biggest dramatic ironies is that the audience knows what the Armitage family is about to do to Chris, but Chris has no idea. When Logan is first introduced to Chris, the audience immediately knows that Logan is the same man who was attacked and kidnapped at the beginning of the screenplay. The audience, seeing Logan and the man who he has become, can make the connection and foresee what the future might hold for our protagonist. The guests, who have had the chance to meet and greet Chris, gather to bid in an auction. While the bidding is taking place, Chris and Rose are by the lake, trying to process all that has happened and they decide to go back home. The audience knows what Chris doesn't; they know about the auction and know Jim Hudson won the bid.

Reversal

- When Chris is strangling Rose, police sirens can be heard, and they are approaching fast. Chris raises both hands in the air, surrendering to law enforcement, but instead of a police officer, it's Rod, his friend who works as a T.S.A. agent at the airport.
- Rose reveals her true self to Chris. This is a character reversal, where his most trusted ally turns into his worst enemy. He feels used, betrayed, and violated.
- Walter, the groundskeeper, comes to help Rose capture Chris during the final scenes. As Walter starts to win the fight, Chris snaps a photo with the flash on, just like he did it with Logan, and Walter regains his consciousness and helps Chris. Walter shoots Rose, then kills himself with the rifle. Walter helping Chris is an unexpected event, a reversal, that sets the story on a different path.

Setup and Payoff

- The setup of the story lets Chris believe that he is meeting the parents of his girlfriend. The payoff is the Order of Coagula scheme the Armitage family is trying to execute.
- Another important setup and payoff is revealed during Missy and Chris's conversation before he gets hypnotized. Through Missy, the audience finds out Chris's biggest regret in life, which took place when he was a kid, Chris didn't do anything when his mother didn't come home from work. He didn't call anyone, not the police or his aunt, because if he did, he thought his mother's death would become real. The payoff takes place when Chris accidentally runs over Georgina – he could have just escaped after hitting her. But his guilty conscience for not doing anything when his mother died plays as a setup, and the act of going back to get Georgina is a payoff, where he redeems himself.
- When Chris encounters Logan at the party, he realizes that he looks familiar and snaps a photo of him to share with Rod. When the flash goes off, Andre, the original owner of the body, regains consciousness for a brief second and

attacks Chris, telling him to get out. This encounter is the setup and the payoff occurs when Chris is losing the fight against Walter at the end of the film. Chris reaches for his phone and snaps a photo, causing the flash to go off. Walter regains consciousness for a few seconds, freeing Chris, shooting at Rose, and killing himself.

- At the beginning of the film, Rose confesses that she has never been in an interracial relationship. This lie plays as a setup to a payoff when Chris discovers a shoe box full of pictures of Rose with a different black man in each photo. Chris realizes that Rose has been lying to him.

- Missy hypnotizing Chris without his consent is a setup, and Missy using hypnosis on him during the climax is the payoff. Chris wants to go home, but when Armitage's family won't let him, Chris fights Jeremy, and Missy sends Chris to the "sunken place" by hypnotizing him.

- Rod, Chris's best friend and a T.S.A. agent, is skeptical about Chris visiting Rose's parents. Rod thinks it is a bad idea for a black person to visit his white girlfriend's parents for the weekend. What started out as a joke becomes a reality, and Chris's life is threatened. The writer sets up Rod as a supporting character to be used as comic relief for the story and has a subplot to help Chris at the end of the story. Rod's persistence in finding out what has happened to Chris pays off when he saves him in the end. This is an example of a subplot that has a setup and payoff, but also shows how the subplot's payoff helps the main plot.

LADY BIRD
(Comedy/Drama), 2017

Written and directed by Greta Gerwig

I. THEME AND PREMISE

Theme

Family and home are a reminder of who we are and where we are from. The film's theme could be described as follows: "The value of the moment is realized after it's left behind." Writer and director Greta Gerwig reveals this theme by showing us the contrast between Christine's senior year and Christine's arrival as a college freshman. Growing up and getting ready for adulthood is not easy, but her family helps her get through it, and Christine realizes their value after she leaves home. Gerwig reveals her theme for the film in an interview: "I started to write the movie with the intention to make something about what home means and what family means and how it doesn't really come into focus until you're leaving them."

Premise

The premise is about a teenage girl in high school and her growing pains, which come at a high price. Throughout her senior year in high school, Christine has an identity issue. She wants to go to college on the East Coast. She gives herself a new name, "Lady Bird." She is a misfit – a confused and spontaneous but honest teenage girl. The screenplay captures family issues, especially the relationship between a mother and daughter, the stressful college application process, feeling out of place, exploring new friendships, experiencing social class dynamics, and falling in and out of love.

DOI: 10.4324/9781003138853-15

II. CHARACTER STUDY

Characters

Protagonist: Christine, aka Lady Bird
Antagonist: Marion
Supporting characters: Julie, Larry, Danny, Kyle, Jenna, and Miguel

Backstory

One of the main opposing forces of the protagonist's objective is explained through a backstory. Marion explains why Christine goes to a private Catholic school. Her brother, Miguel, went to Sacramento High School, a public school, and he saw someone get knifed in front of him. Furthermore, Marion explains that her brother graduated from U.C. Berkley, and he works as a cashier at a supermarket. It seems she has lost faith in higher education, and justifies her actions by opposing Lady Bird's decision to go to school on the East Coast.

Another backstory worth mentioning is Marion's past. In one heated argument, Lady Bird asks her mom if she ever did anything imperfect as a kid and wished that her mom wasn't angry about it, and Marion answers that her mother was an abusive alcoholic. Marion is letting the audience into her past, and, in doing so, we get to know and process why Marion is the way she is. She has a great loving heart, but the way she communicates comes out mean and blunt at times.

Protagonist's Introduction

When Christine is introduced, she is lying next to her mother. They are in the exact same position, but facing each other. Later, Christine checks herself in the mirror and asks, "Do you think I look like I'm from Sacramento?" Marion responds, "You are from Sacramento." If you read through the subtext of her first line, Christine is self-conscious about where she is from. The introduction continues as they drive back from visiting nearby colleges. They get into a heated argument about where she should go to college and out of frustration, Christine jumps out of a moving car. By performing this action, Christine exposes her characteristics and traits as an impulsive and rebellious kid.

Psychological, Physical, and Social Attributes

Lady Bird is a curious teenager who pushes the boundaries of her existence. Psychologically, she is naive, impulsive, insensitive, self-centered, and stubborn. She is preoccupied with wanting to "live through something." She believes the only way to make her life matter is to live somewhere that is full of culture. Physically, Lady Bird is a teenager who is a senior in high school, at an age where she wants to explore relationships and sexuality. Socially, she attempts to be who she is not and becomes friends with rich kids. Lady Bird learns a lesson about the values of true friendship as she reunites with Julie, her best friend.

Protagonist's Worldview

The grass is always greener on the other side of the fence. Lady Bird's point of view of the world is very naive and optimistic. She wants to break out of the insular community of Sacramento and gain a different life experience.

Antagonist's Worldview

Marion believes she wants what is best for her family. Sometimes that means going against what your children want.

Protagonist's Life and Personas

Christine writes "Lady Bird" next to her name on a school bulletin board. This action says a lot about her character: she wants to create a new persona by changing her identity from Christine to Lady Bird. Her persona at her Catholic private school is rebellious, indifferent, impulsive, and spontaneous. She interrupts a school assembly and insults the presenter while she is discussing sensitive abortion topics. Lady Bird plays a prank on her high school principal, taping a "Just Married to Jesus" sign on the back of her car. She lies about her grades to the math teacher when his grade book goes missing.

Lady Bird's persona at home is different – confrontational, and selfish. Lady Bird constantly fights with her brother and his girlfriend, whether it is at the breakfast table or the supermarket; they don't seem to get along. With Marion, her mom, the fighting is even worse. Beyond her college application issues, the two of them are continually butting heads about everything. Marion argues that Christine is selfish in wanting to attend college on the East Coast, as the family is facing financial difficulties.

Lady Bird has a different persona when she is with her best friend Julie. She is honest, friendly, and full of camaraderie. Lady Bird can be herself with Julie. She opens up about her family and boy problems. Her persona with the cool kids from school, Jenna and Kyle, is awkward, superficial, and dishonest. Lady Bird lies about her social status to Jenna in order to get to Kyle. She tries to belong with them, but she is not happy with herself, and she learns that they are not her real friends.

When she arrives in New York, her persona is of someone who has matured. She presents herself differently, as she is more calm and down to earth. She has a moment of realization when she walks alone one Sunday morning and voluntarily attends Catholic mass. As the choir sings, she reflects on where she came from. After the service, she calls home, leaving a message to her mom and saying, "I love you." Her persona changes again as she goes from being Lady Bird to Christine.

Protagonist's Objectives

Christine wants to go to college on the East Coast. As Christine and Marion drive back from visiting colleges, Christine talks about how she wants to go to college on the East Coast: "I want to go where culture is like New York, or Connecticut or New Hampshire where the writers live in the woods." Immediately, Christine is confronted with her mother's opposition.

Antagonist's Objectives

Marion wants her daughter to go to a state school, where college tuition is cheaper. She doesn't see the value of her daughter going away to college, and she puts up a strong resistance.

Protagonist's Conflicts

Lady Bird's biggest conflict is with her mom, Marion. Love is not the issue. The issue is with the conflict of interest. They both want different things. Christine goes behind her mother's back and submits college applications to schools on the East Coast, and she asks her father, Larry, to fill out the financial aid application form. When Marion finds that she has been waitlisted for an East Coast school, she gives Christine the silent treatment. But in the end, Marion gives in, and Christine gets on the plane to New York.

Protagonist's Transformation

At the beginning of the screenplay, Christine is going through adolescence. But when she arrives in New York at the end of the story, she changes. Perhaps being alone in an unfamiliar city helps her reflect back on what she had back in Sacramento. She appreciates what she has left behind. The action that shows her transformation is calling home. She leaves a message saying how much she loves where she came from and how much she loves her mom.

```
                    CHRISTINE
          Hi Mom and Dad, it's me. Christine.
          It's the name you gave me. It's a
          good one. Dad, this is more for Mom
          - Hey Mom: did you feel emotional
          the first time that you drove in
          Sacramento? I did and I wanted to
          tell you, but we weren't really
          talking when it happened. All
          those bends I've known my whole
          life, and stores, and the whole
```

```
thing. But I wanted to tell you. I
love you. Thank you, I'm . . . thank
you.
```

III. STORY ELEMENTS

Protagonist

The protagonist is Christine McPherson, aka Lady Bird. She is a high school senior from Sacramento, California.

Inciting Incident

The inciting incident takes place during the opening scenes. The incident which triggers the protagonist's objective is the drive back from visiting colleges. Christine has been thinking about where she wants to go to school. She says, "I don't want to go to school in this state anyway, I hate California. I want to go to the East Coast." "I wish I could live through something . . . I want to go where culture is, like New York, or Connecticut or New Hampshire, where writers live in the woods." Marion objects and tells her to go to City College in Sacramento.

Protagonist's Objective

Christine has several minor objectives in addition to the main objective of wanting to attend college on the East Coast. She has objectives in every aspect of her life. At school, she wants to get through her senior year. She runs for class president as Lady Bird. Knowing she is not going to win, she auditions for her high school musical. Her family/personal life objective is to convince Marion to let her go to the college of her choice, but first, she has to be accepted. Her personal life objective is to explore a different group of friends. And her private life objective is to explore her sexuality.

Main Tension

Can she go to school on the East Coast?

Action

She has to survive her senior year. She fills out the college application and asks her dad to fill out the financial aid application for the school she is applying to on the East Coast. To achieve her private life objective, she starts to go out with Danny, but he breaks her heart when she accidentally sees him kissing another boy. She gets over Danny as she discovers an interest in Kyle.

In order to get to Kyle, her second love interest, she quits her relationship with her best friend, Julie, and hangs out with Jenna and her friends. Ultimately, she realizes the value of true friendship and goes back to being friends with Julie. When Marion finds out Christine was waitlisted for an East Coast school, she gives her the silent treatment, but Christine tries her best to remedy the situation by apologizing for going behind her back. She pleads forgiveness.

Main Conflict

The central conflict in the story is between Christine and Marion. Christine knows what's best for her, but Marion also knows what would be best for her daughter's future. What each of them wants is completely different. They both have valid reasons for wanting what they want, and the main conflict arises from that.

Crisis

The crisis takes place, crossing the halfway point of the screenplay. Lady Bird has a fight with her best friend, Julie, when she becomes friends with Jenna and Kyle. Lady Bird insults a presenter during a school assembly and gets suspended. She gets in trouble at home for getting suspended, and Marion is furious. Jenna discovers that Lady Bird lied about her house being in the "Fab Forties" neighborhood where the rich people live. Lady Bird loses her virginity to Kyle, thinking that he did too, but she gets upset and hurt when she finds out it wasn't his first time. The crisis takes Lady Bird to the lowest emotional point of the story. However, all of her troubles fade away when she makes the waitlist at an East Coast school.

Climax

Two major events make up the climax of the film. The story deals with her school life and family life, and the climax is presented through two significant events: prom night and graduation day. On prom night, Lady Bird looks pretty in her dress. She has a moment with Larry before leaving for the dance. Kyle, Jenna, and her boyfriend pick up Lady Bird on their way, but Kyle decides to ditch the prom and hang out with his friends. Instead, Lady Bird asks Kyle to drop her off at her best friend's place. Lady Bird and Julie go to prom together, and she appreciates Julie's true friendship.

During graduation day, her family is out celebrating at a Mexican restaurant. Danny stops her and asks if she's heard about being waitlisted. Before she has a chance to cover it up, Larry gives it away with his expression. Marion discovers that she has applied to East Coast schools. Hurt and upset, Marion does not speak to Lady Bird.

Answer to the Main Tension

Yes, she gets accepted to a university on the East Coast. She goes to school in New York City.

Resolution

Via a montage, the resolution is revealed as the writer ties up the loose ends. Larry and Lady Bird go to a bank to figure out how to secure a loan for her college tuition. Lady Bird packs her room and paints over the scribbles on the pink walls, closing an era of her life. Marion writes a departing letter to her daughter. Larry gives Christine a mobile phone and asks her to only use it during an emergency. The montage ends with Marion and Larry driving Lady Bird to the airport.

Christine arrives in New York City. She stops calling herself Lady Bird and goes back to Christine. After a night of partying, she goes to the hospital for alcohol poisoning and attends church the following day. Spending the weekend alone in a new environment makes her feel something about home and where she is from, helping her with the character transformation. Christine calls her mother and father and leaves a message, finally understanding the value of having a home, appreciating where she comes from, and feeling grateful for all her mother has done for her.

IV. STRUCTURE

Three-Act Structure

The screenplay has a clear structure, but it is hiding behind the dramatic elements of the story. The writer presents multiple objectives for the protagonist: wanting to go to the university of her choice and having a relationship. The first act sets up the story with Lady Bird and Marion driving back from visiting colleges, and as Christine starts her senior year in high school. The first act introduces her school life and her family life. Lady Bird has a best friend, Julie. She has a brother, Miguel, who works at the grocery store as a cashier. Her mom works at a hospital and they live in a modest home with one bathroom. As her father drives her to school, she asks him a favor. She asks him to help her with her financial aid application for an East Coast school without letting her mom know. Lady Bird has a crush on Denny, whom she met at the fall musical audition, and they start to hang out together. The first act ends after the homecoming dance, where Lady Bird and Denny have their first kiss, but she gets in trouble with Marion for sneaking into the house late at night and not cleaning her room.

As the second act begins, she takes action in both her private life, at school, and in her personal life. She speaks to her guidance counselor about her college applications and she starts a relationship with Denny. The second act ends with two events taking place back to back: prom night, where she reconnects with her best friends, and the graduation day, where Marion finds out about Lady Bird applying to East Coast schools and getting waitlisted at one of them.

The third act begins as Lady Bird spends her last summer before going to college. She works two jobs: as a cashier at the grocery store and as a barista at a coffee shop. She passes her driver's license test, turns 18, and finally receives an acceptance letter at the school where she was waitlisted. The third act ends with Lady Bird going to New York City and displaying her character transformation.

V. SETTING

The *geographic location* plays a dramatic element in the story instead of being a backdrop for the characters. The film's premise deals with the protagonist's leaving her hometown and arriving in New York City. The protagonist, Christine, realizes the value of the moment after she leaves her family behind. She finally realizes the precious moments she had back in Sacramento with her family when alone and miles from home. The story *takes place during* the years 2002 and 2003. As for the *sociocultural setting*, the film takes place after the catastrophic events of 9/11. The screenplay makes several references to the event, like when Lady Bird and Julie are at the supermarket talking about her desire to go to New York, and Julie worries about terrorism. The attack not only had a social impact but a severe consequence on the economy. Many corporations were financially struggling during this time, and in the film, Larry gets laid off. Throughout the screenplay, whenever Lady Bird is in the living room alone, the TV is on and on the news, the anchors comment on the Iraq war, which was taking place during this time period. The *world of the story* takes place within Lady Bird's working-class family home in Sacramento and her private Catholic High School as she gets through her senior year.

VI. TECHNIQUES AND TOOLS

Events/Occurrences

- *College tour:* The screenplay begins with Lady Bird and Marion coming back from college visits.
- *Drama Club audition:* As school starts, Lady Bird signs up for the fall musical audition, where she sees Denny first.
- *The homecoming dance:* Lady Bird dances with Denny and after they have their first kiss.
- *Thanksgiving day has three separate events:* Denny picking up Lady Bird and meeting her family. Lady Bird goes to Denny's grandmother's house for Thanksgiving dinner. Later that evening, Lady Bird and her friends go to see a band, and she sees Kyle for the first time.
- *Fall semester musical opening night:* After a successful show, Lady Bird and her friends go to a dinner to celebrate, and Lady Bird accidentally sees Denny kissing another boy.

- *Christmas Day:* The McPhersons gather to open presents in the morning.
- *House party:* Lady Bird goes to a party to be with Kyle.
- *School assembly:* During an anti-abortion presentation, Lady Bird insults the presenter and gets suspended from school.
- *Favorite Sunday activity:* Lady Bird and Marion go to open houses, seeing other people's homes.
- *Prom night:* Lady Bird ditches her new friends and goes back to being best friends with Julie.
- *Graduation Day:* Marion finds out about Lady Bird getting waitlisted.
- *The airport:* Lady Bird gets dropped off at the airport.
- *The college party:* Lady Bird introduces herself as Christine.
- *Sunday Mass:* After recovering from alcohol poisoning, she attends the service where she reflects on where she is from.

Dramatic Irony

Lady Bird applying to East Coast schools behind Marion's back is a dramatic irony in the screenplay. The audience knows more than Marion all throughout the second act, and when she finds out, we understand why she is upset with Lady Bird. The second dramatic irony occurs when Lady Bird lies about where she lives. The audience knows more than Jenna; they know it's a lie. Tension builds when Jenna calls Lady Bird, saying she is outside the house.

Reversal

Lady Bird's first relationship with Denny has a reversal: Denny turns out to be gay. Miguel cleans up his act and goes for an interview. The biggest reversal is Marion accepting Christine going to school on the East Coast.

Setup and Payoff

The main setup and payoff of the screenplay is how the writer sets up the main tension: Will Lady Bird get to go to an East Coast school? The answer to this question is the payoff: Yes, Lady Bird goes to school in New York City. The second noticeable setup and payoff is the lie she makes up telling Jenna that the blue house in the Fab Forties neighborhood is her house. At first, she lies to fit in with the rich kids, but the lie reveals itself when Jenna visits the house unannounced and discovers the truth. Another example of a setup and payoff in *Lady Bird* is Marion writing a letter to Lady Bird, who is going away to college. There are crumpled sheets of paper lying all around the kitchen table and the floor as Marion tries to write the perfect letter. Larry, Marion's husband and Lady Bird's father, slips a folder into Lady Bird's luggage before she departs for New York City. When Lady Bird arrives at the dorm and unpacks, she notices the folder. In it, she finds all the different versions and drafts of the letters her mother wrote and crumpled up. Actions speak louder than words. The writer sets up the sequence by showing how much Marion loves her daughter, despite her being against her daughter going away to college. The screenwriter shows Marion's feelings through actions. Now, the payoff takes place when Lady Bird gets to see and is reassured by her mother's love for her, which she sees in Marion's attempts to write one perfect letter. The screenwriter used a character's intent of showing the love for her daughter as a setup and used Larry as a mediator who connects Marion's action to the payoff Lady Bird will have when she sees the letters. In the end, Lady Bird understands how much Marion loves her.

PARASITE
(Comedy/Drama/Thriller), 2019

Written by Bong Joon-ho and Han Jin-won

I. THEME AND PREMISE

Theme

It's hard for poor people to move up in the social class system. This theme is so specific that it resonated as a universal truth with the global audience. Because the film's premise mirrors the period's global socioeconomic setting, the ramification of social class differences shown in the film is felt in every culture worldwide. Everyone who watched *Parasite* or read the screenplay can empathize with the main characters as they struggle to escape poverty.

Premise

A destitute family struggles to make their ends meet until the son lands a tutoring job for a wealthy family after faking his credentials. Soon the entire family infiltrates the lavish household, hiding their identities as family members, pretending to be an art therapist, a driver, and a housemaid. However, an unexpected visit from the previous housemaid threatens to destroy it all by exposing the truth.

II. CHARACTER STUDY

Characters

Protagonist: Ki-woo
Supporting characters: The Kims: Ki-jung, Ki-tek, Chung-sook
The Parks: Dong-ik, Yeon-kyo, Da-hae, Da-song
Antagonists: Mun-kwang, Kun-sae

DOI: 10.4324/9781003138853-16

In an interview, the director, Bong Joon-ho, said that there are no true antagonists in *Parasite*, as every character has sympathetic and unsympathetic qualities, especially the Kims and the Parks.

Backstory

- None of the Kim family members have jobs. Their phones have been disconnected for nonpayment and they can't afford Wi-Fi.
- Through Ki-woo's conversation with his friend Min, the audience learns Ki-woo has made four attempts to pass the college exams. He calls himself a "loser."
- The Parks' mansion was built by a famous architect, with a secret bunker, which is not revealed until the midpoint of the screenplay. The previous housekeeper, Mun-kwang, has been hiding her husband for four years in the secret bunker, without the Parks ever finding out.

Protagonist's Introduction

Ki-woo is introduced sitting in the small living room of his family's semi-basement apartment. He has lost a free Wi-Fi signal on his phone and wanders around the small apartment, telling everyone in the house and introducing his family members, his sister Ki-jung, his father Ki-tek, and his mother Chung-sook. We learn that their phones have been disconnected and they can't afford to have a Wi-Fi connection through exposition. In the opening scenes, we are let into their financial struggles. Finally, Ki-woo finds a free Wi-Fi connection near the toilet in the bathroom.

Psychological, Physical, and Social Attributes

Ki-woo is a healthy 24-year-old man. He is a smooth talker, street smart, a problem-solver, and he doesn't let his emotions get in the way of achieving his wants. His attributes are first seen when a pizza shop owner comes to pick up the pizza boxes. She complains about how the boxes have been folded, and reduces his payment. Chung-sook argues over the payment deduction, and as the tension rises, Ki-woo jumps in and defuses the situation, turning a challenging situation into an opportunity. First, Ki-woo blames the part-time worker who didn't show up to do the job in the first place, and gets on her good side by sympathizing with how she had to go through all the troubles of hiring someone to do the job. Then Ki-woo says to fire him and hire a new employee. He continues by saying he is available for an interview tomorrow. This incident reveals Ki-woo's characteristics and traits. Furthermore, Ki-woo does not feel guilty lying about his credentials to land a job; he justifies it by saying he will attend the same college he used to forge the enrollment letter from the following year. And it's not just him: the entire family's state of mind is the same. They will let go of their ethics and morals to find a job, a sign of desperation to escape the current situation. Now, when the Kim family locks up

Mun-kwang and Kun-sae in the secret bunker after their real identity is revealed, Ki-woo feels responsible for the crisis, and he wants to take the matter into his own hands. When he comes back to the mansion, he brings a scholar rock with him, and takes it downstairs. His action, carrying the large rock, shows a clear intention: he doesn't want anyone else to find out about their secret identity. He wants to protect what he and his family have achieved by working for the Parks.

Protagonist's Worldview

Hiding one's true identity in order to advance in society is not only acceptable, but needed. Lying about oneself is fair, as long as you are trying to escape poverty.

Antagonist's Worldview

It's better to hide in a secret bunker than deal with reality. As Kun-sae is running away from the loan sharks, Mun-kwang hides in the secret bunker. Mun-kwang has a similar point of view of the world as the Kims. She lies about hiding her husband in the secret bunker, and she also believes hiding one's true identity is acceptable to acquire a job.

Protagonist's Life and Personas

Ki-woo displays two major personas in the screenplay. The first persona we encounter is when he is with his family members in his personal life. His persona at home is sincere, honest, respectful, and caring; he loves and respects his family, and he is the mastermind behind getting every one of his family members hired by the Parks. We encounter the second persona when he is with the Parks in his work/professional life. He acts sharp, smart, decisive, sympathetic, and charismatic.

Protagonist's Objectives

Ki-woo wants his family members to have a job and find financial stability. In his professional life, he wants to continue tutoring Da-hye. And in his private life, he wants to marry Da-hye and become the Parks' son-in-law.

Antagonist's Objectives

At first, Kun-sae wants to remain in the secret bunker, but after witnessing his wife die from a concussion, his objective is to avenge her and kill the Kims.

Protagonist's Conflicts

*   *Inner conflict:* Ki-woo wants to marry Da-hye when she becomes older. Also, an internal conflict is displayed at the end of the second act, when he contemplates the fate of the two people they have hiding in the secret bunker. This

inner conflict is manifested when he takes the scholar rock to the secret bunker on the day of Da-song's birthday party.

- *External conflict:* Character vs. environment – the Kims vs. their current financial situation. From the start of the film, the conflict involves their financial struggles. Character vs. character – Ki-woo's main objectives are jeopardized because Mun-kwang and Kun-sae want to reveal his secret identity.

Protagonist's Transformation

Ki-woo's emotional arc goes from being hopeful to hopeless. As we find him in the same spot as the beginning of the film, it shows he is back at the same place he started from, but what he went through has transformed him. The journey has changed him. Ki-woo is no longer the same person. He is not the same hopeful person he used to be.

III. STORY ELEMENTS

Protagonist

Ki-woo, a 24-year-old man who has failed to pass college exams four times, lives in a small semi-basement apartment with his parents and sister.

Inciting Incident

Ki-woo's friend, Min, visits, bringing a scholar rock as a gift. Min is a college student tutoring a high-school girl from a wealthy family, the Parks. Min is planning to study abroad and asks Ki-woo to take over his tutoring responsibility while he is gone. It is a great opportunity, but Ki-woo feels unqualified because he is not a college student. Min convinces Ki-woo, reassuring him that he knows the material because he has taken the college aptitude test on four separate occasions, and says that he is more than qualified to teach a sophomore in high school. Ki-woo would come highly recommended by Min. He just needs to forge an official letter of enrollment from a prestigious university.

Protagonist's Objective

Ki-woo wants the tutoring job. Later, he wants every family member to get a job as the Parks' servants.

Main Tension

Can Ki-woo successfully land the tutoring job and maintain the lie without getting caught?

Action

Ki-woo walks through the hills of a rich neighborhood and arrives at the Park residence – a mansion. Ki-woo meets Mrs. Park, Yeon-kyo, who asks to sit in on the first tutoring session so that she can determine if he is qualified for the job. Ki-woo nails the tutoring session and agrees to take the job. Ki-woo's hustle doesn't end there: he sees an opportunity to introduce his sister to Yeon-kyo as an art therapist/tutor for her son, who is suffering from a traumatic event. Ki-jung is introduced as Jessica; she becomes the therapist for the younger son. Then Ki-jung sees an opening to get the driver of the house in trouble. After that, he introduces her father, Ki-tek, and he becomes the new driver for the Parks. Now the three of them unite to get the housemaid, Mun-kwang, fired and Ki-woo's mom, Chung-sook, becomes the housemaid.

Main Conflict

The conflict arises with the return of the ex-housemaid, Mun-kwang, who comes to the Park residence when no one is home, except for the Kims, who are enjoying the Parks' luxury lifestyle while the owners are on a camping trip. But when Mun-kwang rings the doorbell, saying she left something in the basement, Chung-sook lets her in. Mun-kwang has been hiding her husband, Kun-sae, from loan sharks in the Parks' secret underground bunker for the past four years. Mun-kwang asks Chung-sook to care for her husband, but she refuses. Having the upper hand, Chung-sook threatens to call the police, but when the three other family members who were eavesdropping accidentally reveal themselves, the roles reverse. Mun-kwang realizes that four of them are together when Ki-woo calls Ki-tae "Dad." Immediately she takes out her phone, films all four of them, and threatens to send the clip to Yeon-kyo. Ultimately, Mun-kwang is another lower-class person hiding her true identity. When she discovers the scheme the Kims are pulling, Mun-kwang wants revenge. She wants to take back her job and throw the Kims under the bus. Mun-kwang's persona changes drastically when she gets the upper hand, she is not the same polite and sophisticated housemaid. She turns into a mean, cruel, and nasty person who is determined to take revenge on the Kims.

Crisis

As the Kims regain control of the situation, Chung-sook is forced to answer the house phone and discovers that the Parks are unexpectedly returning from the camping trip. The Kims rapidly clean up the mess and also hide Mun-kwang and Kun-sae from the Parks. As Ki-tek tries to tie up Mun-kwang, she tries to run away, but before Yeon-kyo has a chance to see her, Chung-sook kicks her back down the stairs. She hits her head and falls unconscious. Ki-tek brings Mun-kwang inside the bunker and locks them up. As the three of them make an attempt to run away from the mansion, they are forced to hide under a large coffee table in the living room as Mr. and Mrs. Park watch their son sleeping in a tent on the front lawn. The crisis doesn't end there; as they make their escape with the help of their mother, Chung-sook, they walk back to the apartment to find that it has been flooded and they have lost all of their belongings.

Climax

The dramatic tension reaches its peak in the story at Da-song's birthday party. All hell breaks loose on the front lawn of the house. The morning after the rainstorm, Yeon-kyo decides to throw a surprise party for Da-song. She calls Ki-tek to come and help her drive to the supermarket and invites Ki-jung and Ki-woo to the party.

As the guests are gathering, Ki-woo plans to take care of the matter. His objective is not clear, but seeing him carry the scholar rock to the secret bunker reveals his intentions. Once in the bunker, he is attacked by Kun-sae; as he tries to escape, Kun-sae smacks Ki-woo's head with the scholar rock, which Ki-woo has been carrying around. Meanwhile, Ki-tek and Dong-ik hide behind the bushes to surprise Da-song while pretending to be Native Americans, but tension builds up as Ki-tek crosses the line, mocking Dong-ik. Dong-ik, offended, puts Ki-tek in his place, reminding him that he is just a servant. As everyone gathers around while Ki-jung is bringing out the birthday cake, Kun-sae comes out with a kitchen knife and stabs Ki-jung in the chest. Da-song passes out seeing Kun-sae. Ki-tek runs to Ki-jung, and Chung-sook is attacked by Kun-sae, and defends herself at first, but then stabs him and kills Kun-sae. Dong-ik screams at Ki-tek to drive the car and then asks to throw the car keys instead, but Ki-tek is busy attending to his daughter, who is bleeding to death, but manages to throw the car keys. Dong-ik can't stand the smell coming from Kun-sae. He makes a face, and Ki-tek, raging, picks up a knife and stabs Dong-ik in the chest. At the end of the climax, we see that Ki-woo and Chung-sook survive, Ki-jung, Kun-sae, and Dong-ik die, and Ki-tek commits murder and disappears.

Answer to the Main Tension

Ki-woo gets the tutoring job and more. He helps his family members land roles as servants for the Parks, but a tragic event takes everything away from him and he is back to where he started at the beginning of the film.

Resolution

Ki-woo is back where he started at the beginning of the film, sitting in the apartment, but now without Ki-tae, Ki-jun, and without any hope to move up the social ladder. After the tragic incident, Ki-woo recovers from his wounds. Ki-woo and his mom are put on trial for their crimes but avoid serving time and walk away with probation. From time to time, Ki-woo goes to a mountain with a view of the mansion, as he knows where his father might be hiding. One evening, he sees the entrance ceiling light blinking in different internals. Ki-woo thinks it's Morse code and writes down the code to discover that it is Ki-tek's letter to his son, Ki-woo. Confirming the whereabouts of his father, he dreams of making a lot of money and buying the mansion one day, which he knows is an impossible task.

IV. STRUCTURE

Three-Act Structure

The first act sets up the story by introducing the main characters and their financial struggles. They fold boxes for a local pizza joint as a part-time gig, which says a lot about their money situation. The first act ends with an event: Ki-woo goes for a tutoring interview. Ki-woo comes highly recommended by Min and lies about attending a prestigious university in Seoul. Both Yeon-kyo and her daughter Da-hye are impressed with Ki-woo's knowledge and teaching approach that he gets hired immediately. This event serves as a plot turning point, as it alters Ki-woo's life trajectory.

The second act starts with Ki-jung being introduced to Yeon-kyo. As Da-hye's younger brother, Da-song, is suffering from a traumatic experience, and Yeon-kyo has been looking for an art therapist, Ki-woo pretends to know someone who can help and introduces them. The first half of the second act is about the Kims becoming the Parks' servants and Ki-woo secretly developing a relationship with the high-school teenager he is tutoring. He dreams of becoming the son-in-law someday. As the story approaches the midpoint of the second act, the tone of the film changes from a family drama to a suspense thriller with the return of Mun-kwang, the previous housemaid. When the housemaid discovers the Kims' scam, she threatens to tell Yeon-kyo, her boss. To take control of the situation, Ki-woo and his family use force to apprehend the housekeeper and her husband, and in an accident, Mun-kwang injures her head. The second act ends with an occurrence, as Ki-woo, Ki-jung, and Ki-tek make their way back to the apartment and find their apartment flooded. They are miserable; they reach the lowest point of their emotional state at the end of second act.

As the third act begins, Yeon-kyo is planning a spontaneous birthday party for Da-song. Ki-jung and Ki-woo are invited. Ki-tek comes to work on his day off to drive Yeon-kyo to shops and the supermarket. Ki-woo feels responsible and wants to take the matter into his own hands, and takes the scholar rock downstairs to the secret bunker, only to be ambushed by Kun-sae. During the climax, Ki-woo gets hurt, his sister is killed, and his father kills Dong-ik and hides in the secret bunker. The third act ends with Ki-woo and his mother back in the apartment. Ki-woo tried to move up the social ladder, but he failed. The screenwriter has shaped the plot to resonate with the theme of the film.

V. SETTING

The *geographic location* of the story takes place in Seoul, Korea. The *time period* of the film is set in the same era as when the film was released, 2019. *Parasite* is a satire *set in a world* examining social class differences by displaying the lifestyle contrast between the destitute Kim and the wealthy Park families. The *sociocultural setting* is an extremely stratified society with social class immobility.

VI. TECHNIQUES AND TOOLS

Events/Occurrences

- *The visit:* Ki-woo's friend, Min, pays him a visit at his house. He brings Ki-woo a scholar rock as a present, and he asks Ki-woo to take over his tutoring duties when he leaves to study abroad.
- *The interview:* Ki-woo goes for an interview and meets Yeon-kyo, Da-hye, Da-song, and Mun-kwang.
- *The introduction:* Ki-woo brings Ki-jung to meet Yeon-kyo.
- *The camping trip:* The Parks decide to go on a camping trip to celebrate Da-song's birthday.
- *The unannounced visit:* Mun-kwang comes to the mansion to take care of unfinished business.
- *The rainstorm:* The Parks return from the camping trip, and Kim's apartment is flooded.
- *The birthday party:* Da-song's birthday party is where the climax of the film takes place.

Dramatic Irony

- Ki-woo and his family lie about their credentials and family relationships, but nobody else knows except the audience.
- Ki-woo, Ki-jung, and Ki-tek hide under the large coffee table, while Dong-ik and Yeon-kyo are watching over their son, Da-song, who is camping out on the front lawn. Ki-tek is extremely self-conscious of his smell, and the way Dong-ik talks about the smell causes Ki-tek to fly into a rage.
- Dong-ik and Yeon-kyo do not know Mun-kwang has been hiding her husband in the secret bunker.
- Ki-woo discovers where his dad is hiding, but no one else knows.

Reversal

The biggest reversal takes place at the center of the story. As Mun-kwang returns to the mansion, we discover she has been hiding her husband in a secret bunker. The story takes a turn in a new direction. At first, Chung-sook has the upper hand knowing that Mun-kwang has been hiding her husband behind the Parks' back, but when Mun-kwang learns the four of them are a family, she gets the upper hand in the situation, because she has a video clip as proof. Furthermore, after this reversal, the plot not only twists in a new direction, but the genre of the screenplay also changes. It goes from being a family drama to a suspense thriller.

Setup and Payoff

- *The scholar rock:* The rock is introduced when Min brings it as a present. This is the setup. The payoff takes place when Kun-sae hits Ki-woo's head with the rock.
- *The hot sauce:* When the Kims plan to get Mun-kwang fired, they use hot sauce from the local pizza joint and apply it on the used tissue Mun-kwang threw away to mimic blood. This is the setup. The payoff: Convinced that Mun-kwang suffers from tuberculosis, Yeon-kyo fires the housemaid to protect her family.
- *The security camera:* The setup takes place when Mun-kwang cuts the wire to the security camera as she visits on a rainy night, so no one will know she was there. The payoff takes place when Ki-tek uses the parking garage to get back in the house; Ki-tek can vanish as the wire of the security camera hasn't been fixed.
- *The morse code:* Kun-sae uses Morse code to express his gratitude toward Dong-ik by blinking the ceiling light on and off. The payoff to this setup occurs when Ki-tek uses the same method to communicate with his son at the end of the film.

REFERENCES

Aristotle. (1961). *Aristotle's Poetics*. Hill and Wang Publishing.

Bong Joon-ho, and Han Jin-won. (Screenwriters). (2019). *Parasite* [Screenplay]. Barunson E&A.

Cameron, James. (2021). *Pursuing and Developing the Idea*. James Cameron's Masterclass [Video]. *masterclass.com*.

Campbell, Joseph. (2018). Joseph Campbell and The Power of Myth with Bill Moyers [Documentary]. Kino Lorber.

Chazelle, Damien (Screenwriter). (2014). *Whiplash* [Screenplay]. Bold Films, Blumhouse Productions, Right of Way Films.

Chazelle, Damien. (2020). How I Wrote Whiplash (Writing Advice from Damien Chazelle). *Behind the Curtain* [Video]. https://youtu.be/Xa_deyk8yMQ. Mar 6, 2020.

Crowe, Cameron. (1999). *Conversations with Wilder*. Knopf, Borzoi Book, Radom House, Inc.

Egri, Lajos. (2004). *The Art of Dramatic Writing* (First Touchstone Edition). Simon & Schuster.

Gerwig, Greta. (2017). *Greta Gerwig on Directorial Debut 'Lady Bird'* [Video]. https://variety.com/video/lady-bird-greta-gerwig-toronto-sacramento/. Sept 2017.

Gerwig, Greta (Screenwriter). (2017). *Lady Bird* [Screenplay]. IAC Films, Scott Rudin Productions, Management 360.

Lemmon, Jack. (2020). 'The Apartment': An Undervalued American Classic. By Grahm Fuller. *New York Times*.

Lucas, George. (1999). Of Myth and Men. By Bill Moyers. *Time Magazine*.

McKee, Robert. (1997). *Story* (First Edition). ReganBooks, HarperCollins Publishers.

Nolan, Christopher. (2008). *The Dark Knight Christopher Nolan Interview* [Video]. https://youtu.be/yp94gmtVTfs. Aug 13, 2008.

Nolan, Christopher. (2019). How I Wrote the Dark Knight. *Behind the Curtain* [Video]. https://youtu.be/yqlhU6hE14A. Aug 31, 2019.

Nolan, Christopher, Nolan, Jonathan, and Goyer, David. (2008). *The Dark Knight* [Screenplay]. Warner Bros. Pictures. DC Comics. Syncopy.

Nolan, Jonathan. (2008). David Goyer and Jonathan Nolan Interview – The Dark Knight. By Steve Weintraub. *collider.com*. July 20, 2008.

Peele, Jordan. (2017). *GET OUT keynote | 2017 Film Independent Forum* [Video]. Curator: Elvis Mitchell. https://youtu.be/YnpDiuE8HJU Film Independent. Oct 23, 2017.

Peele, Jordan (Screenwriter). (2018). *Get Out* [Screenplay]. Blumhouse Productions, QC Entertainment, Monkeypaw Productions.

Ramis, Harold. (1990). *The Making of Groundhog Day – Harold Ramis* [Video]. https://youtu.be/2d7kkecft4w. Aug 19, 2018.

Scott, A. O. (2008). 'The Apartment' | Critics' Picks | The New York Times [Video]. *New York Times*.

Vogler, Christopher. (2007). *A Writer's Journey, Mythic Structure for Writers* (Third Edition). Michael Wiese Productions.

Whedon, Joss, Stanton, Andrew, Cohen, Joel, and Sokolow, Alec. (Screenwriters). (1995). *Toy Story* [Screenplay]. Walt Disney Pictures, Pixar Animation Studios.

Wilder, Billy, and Diamond, I. A. L. (Screenwriters). (1959). *The Apartment* [Screenplay]. The Mirisch Company.

Winding Refn, Nicolas. (2016). *Character Piece: Driver (Ryan Gosling) In Drive (2011)*. By Erin Free. FILMINK. May 24, 2016.

INDEX

Taylor & Francis Group
an **informa** business

Taylor & Francis eBooks

www.taylorfrancis.com

A single destination for eBooks from Taylor & Francis
with increased functionality and an improved user
experience to meet the needs of our customers.

90,000+ eBooks of award-winning academic content in
Humanities, Social Science, Science, Technology, Engineering,
and Medical written by a global network of editors and authors.

TAYLOR & FRANCIS EBOOKS OFFERS:

A streamlined
experience for
our library
customers

A single point
of discovery
for all of our
eBook content

Improved
search and
discovery of
content at both
book and
chapter level

REQUEST A FREE TRIAL
support@taylorfrancis.com

 Routledge
Taylor & Francis Group

 CRC Press
Taylor & Francis Group